Born-Digital Archives

Thorsten Ries • Gábor Palko
Editors

Born-Digital Archives

Previously published in *International Journal of Digital Humanities* "Special Issue: Born-Digital Archives" Volume 1, issue 1, April 2019

 Springer

Editors
Thorsten Ries
Department of Germanic Studies
University of Texas
Austin, USA

Gábor Palko
Centre for Digital Humanities
Eötvös Loránd University
Budapest, Hungary

Spinoff from journal: "International Journal of Digital Humanities" Volume 1, issue 1, April 2019

ISBN 978-3-031-19943-1

This Springer imprint is published by the registered company Springer Nature Switzerland AG
The registered company address is: Gewerbestrasse 11, 6330 Cham, Switzerland

Contents

The original version of this book has been revised: the affiliation of the editor "Thorsten Ries" has been
updated. A correction to this book can be found at https://doi.org/10.1007/978-3-031-19941-7_10.

International Journal of Digital Humanities (2019) 1:1–11
https://doi.org/10.1007/s42803-019-00011-x

Born-digital archives

Thorsten Ries[1,2] · Gábor Palkó[3]

Published online: 25 March 2019
© Springer Nature Switzerland AG 2019, Corrected Publication 2023

The first special issue of *International Journal of Digital Humanities* (*IJDH*) is about born-digital archives, their preservation and research perspectives involving born-digital primary records in the humanities. This is not only a result of the collaboration between the journal's editor-in-chief, Gábor Palkó, Co-Director of the Centre for Digital Humanities at the Eötvös University, who is interested in the practice and theory of digital archives, and the editor of this volume, Thorsten Ries, who conducts research on born-digital *dossiers génétiques* with digital forensic methods at Ghent University. It is also meant to be a programmatic call to intensify cross-sectoral collaboration between galleries, libraries, archives, and museums (GLAM institutions), digital preservation projects, and humanities research working with digital primary sources.

The born-digital historical record of the present age poses great challenges for archival science, librarianship, museology, and information science on the one hand, and to humanities research on the other, next to offering exciting opportunities. Personal digital archives, legal, governmental, institutional, scientific, public, and non-governmental organisations' documentation records or datasets, public repositories of digital publications, web archives, and social media archives are incredibly rich, diverse and multi-faceted treasure troves for historians, political scientists, sociologists, philologists, literary scholars, art historians, digital humanists, and researchers from other humanities disciplines. The effort of long-term preservation, curator- and custo-dianship for these records and the development of setups, applications and application programming interfaces (API) to make them available for research has been subject of multiple large, successful international projects in archival science, librarianship, and information science. Landmark projects such as the archiving of the digital collections of Salman Rushdie at Emory University Library (Rockmore 2014; Waugh and Russey

Chapter 1 was originally published as Ries, T. & Palkó, G. International Journal of Digital Humanities (2019) 1: 1–11. https://doi.org/10.1007/s42803-019-00011-x.

The original version of this chapter has been revised: the affiliation of the editor "Thorsten Ries" has been updated. A correction to this chapter can be found at https://doi.org/10.1007/978-3-031-19941-7_10.

✉ Thorsten Ries
Thorsten.Ries@ugent.be; T.Ries@sussex.ac.uk

✉ Gábor Palkó
palko.gabor@btk.elte.hu

[1] Ghent University, Ghent, Belgium

[2] University of Texas, Austin, USA

[3] Eötvös Loránd University, Budapest, Hungary

Roke 2017); Hanif Kureishi at The British Library (Foss 2017), Friedrich Kittler at the German Literature Archive Marbach / Neckar (Enge and Kramski 2014), Franz Josef Czernin at the Austrian National Library (Catalogue ÖNB, accessed 2018) and the Thomas Kling Archive at Stiftung Insel Hombroich (Ries 2017, 2018), to name but a few, as well as national (e.g. UK, Germany, the Netherlands, Belgium, etc.) and international repositories and web archives (Internet Archive, etc.) with sophisticated frontends such as RESAW (REsearch Infrastructure for the Study of Archived Web materials), SHINE UK Web Archive and Wayback Machine, are just some of the most visible results of this broad development of born-digital archiving. Memory institutions, international archival, and information science projects are very active on addressing fundamental issues of born-digital archiving such as developing workflows for identification, selection, triage and bibliographic documentation. Management of the sheer data volumes and curatorship that caters for the fragility and obsolescence of legacy hardware, software and formats of complex, context-dependent digital records are ongoing challenges. Key research and development areas in this interdisciplinary sector are the development of preservation formats and workflows that ensure authenticity, fixity, physical as well as logical stability and accessibility by forensic imaging, virtualisation, emulation, migration and the development of environments, tools and API's for secure, controlled access to the archive for researchers. Currently, archival and information science, memory institutions, and archiving projects are working towards interoperable standards and making standardised workflows, protocols, expert resources, tools and infrastructure for born-digital curation available to archives, libraries, memory institutions, and projects of all sizes and all levels. The early beginnings of born-digital archiving practice and applications of digital forensic methodology in libraries and archives are mostly associated with the names of individual archivists, librarians, archival and information scientists, and humanists such as Susan Thomas, Kirschenbaum (2008, 2013, 2016a, b); Kirschenbaumet al. (2009, 2010); Jeremy Leighton John (2012); Duranti (2009); Duranti and Endicott-Popovsky (2010) and Doug Reside (2011a, b, 2017). Since then, we have seen an enormous growth of these efforts in archival research, development and professional practice, which today are orchestrated by large, national and international, often high-level projects such as InterPARES and InterPARES Trust (International Research on Permanent Authentic Records in Electronic Systems, Canada, Europe, international, since 1994, 4th phase), Digital Presevation Coalition, DPC (Europe, UK, international, 2002-today), PArA-DigM (Personal Archives Accessible in Digital Media, Europe, UK, 2005–2007), CASPAR (Cultural, Artistic and Scientific knowledge for Preservation, Access and Retrieval) and Digital Preservation Europe, DPE (Europe, 2006–2009), PLANetS (Preservation and Long-term Access through NETworked Services, Europe, 2006–2010), nestor (Kompetenznetzwerk Langzeitarchivierung, Germany, 2003–2006, 2006–2009, since 2009 self-sustained), PREMIS (Preservation Metadata: Implementation Strategies, USA, since 2003), the CLIR and OCLC research initiatives (Council on Library and Information Resources, Online Computer Library Center, Incorporated, USA, international, 2010: CLIR report, 2013 „Demystifying Born Digital"), VIMM (Virtual Multimodal Museum, Europe, Cyprus, 2016–2019) and the Computational Archival Science working group (international, since 2016). National repositories for born-digital publications, research infrastructures, and web archives are mostly hosted and run by the national library system of individual countries, and complemented by supranational humanities research infrastructures such as DARIAH (Digital Research Infrastructure for the Arts and Humanities) and CLARIN (Common Language Resources and Technology Infrastructure) in the European context. On a meso-level, however, there seems to be less institutions and projects that are enabling born-digital preservation, curation, and research at the level of smaller archives and individual researchers. We would like to highlight PACKED (Centre of Expertise in Digital Heritage, Belgium, since 2003), the DCC (Digital Curation Centre, UK, 2004-today), the BitCurator project (USA, 2011–2014, now BitCurator NLP) and BitCurator Access (USA, 2014–2016). It is encouraging to see that, at least every now and then, memory institutions reach out to humanities research in order to collaboratively identify in which digital formats, with which metadata and by which access tools born-digital records might be most useful for researchers and encourage them to find out about the possibilities. Excellent examples are the hands-on exhibition of Salman Rushdie's emulated computer at Emory Libraries (Rockmore 2014), the pilot of born-digital reading room at the British Library featuring materials from the Hanif Kureishi Archive (Foss 2017), the workshop on born-digital archives access at Wellcome Collection (Sloyan 2018), the inclusion of both humanities researchers and representatives of memory institutions responsible for web-archiving in the RESAW network (Winters 2018a), and the Personal Digital Archiving conference series (e.g. PDA conferences 2017 at Stanford University Libraries, 2018 at Houston, TX). This interdisciplinary and intersectoral collaboration between archival and humanities research, methodological development and practice is of crucial importance and the humanities certainly need to take Matthew Kirschenbaum's imperative to heart:

> Digital archivists need digital humanities researchers and subject experts to use born-digital collections. Nothing is more important. If humanities researchers don't demand access to born-digital materials then it will be harder to get those materials processed in a timely fashion, and we know that with the born-digital every day counts. (Kirschenbaum 2013, 38)

Despite the fact that Kirschenbaum rather stated the obvious when he defined that „the concept of a primary record can no longer be assumed to be coterminous with that of a physical object" and that „electronic texts, files, feeds and transmissions of all sorts are also indisputably primary records" relevant to historical research (Kirschenbaum 2016b, 25:27), humanities researchers still seem to be rather reluctant when it comes to include born-digital primary sources into their research. There is probably no simple answer to the question why this is the case. If we look at personal digital archives, legal and ethical considerations concerning the protection of privacy and personal rights of the data subjects and of third parties as well as copyright are probably the most important reasons for the hesitation of humanities researchers (Carroll et al. 2011; Baker 2018). Jane Winters argues that "web archives, and other kinds of born-digital data, do bring the possibility of, and perhaps even necessitate, a radical reframing of humanities research – through their scale, their heterogeneity, their complexity, their fragility", which might not be sufficiently accessible with "the tools and methods available to us at present" (Winters 2018b). Further concerns about born-digital archives, especially web-archives, might have to do with inherent biases and misrepresentations introduced through a focus on "significant and/or traumatic events, [...]

personal interest and enthusiasm or a serendipitous partnership" that comes with individual archiving efforts, triggered by events or specific research interests (Winters 2018b). Born-digital primary sources (and archives), according to Winters, are different from analogue ones in many ways, and she further makes the point that historians still need to embrace the fact "that a digit[al] manuscript is an object in its own right, with its own context of production" (Winters 2018a). For this delayed development among historians, she identifies disciplinary and sectoral boundaries as reasons, next to the methodological issues:

> One explanation is that while digital history has embraced a range of historical sub-disciplines, and borrowed readily from subjects like archaeology and histor-ical geography, it has largely failed to take account of developments in two crucial areas: library, archive and information studies; and digital preservation. Libraries and archives have necessarily been at the forefront of web archives research and practice. [...] (Winters 2018b)

This diagnose is indeed consequential. The gap between the progress in born-digital preservation development and archival science research, on the one hand, and (digital) humanities research on the other, needs to be closed, first and foremost in order to enable GLAM institutions, institutional networks and infrastructures to develop their born-digital collections in meaningful ways, improve preservation formats, curation workflows, repositories, services, and access for researchers. This can only be achieved by cross-sectoral and interdisciplinary collaboration to support active research on born-digital collections. This is precisely what this first special issue of *International Journal of Digital Humanities* seeks to encourage. The necessary collaboration will benefit from the new European General Data Protection Regulation (GDPR) guidelines, as these regulations provide an excellent basis for GLAM institutions and researchers to establish trust relationships with archive depositors and creators. This will, moreover, encourage them to enable research by having their materials preserved, archived, and made available to research in a secure, controlled, and authentic way with security procedures that empowers them as data subjects.

Kirschenbaum and Winters urge those in the field of humanities to embrace the born-digital historical record as an object and primary source in its own right – a claim which, of course, has precursors in media history and theory, historical bibliography, textual scholarship, and digital humanities (see Dahlström 2000; Manovich 2001; Gitelman 2006). This implies the critical appraisal of the born-digital primary record's specific historical materiality, along the lines of philological and forensic disciplines such as diplomatics, palaeography, philology, and analytical bibliography. Since Kirschenbaum's *Mechanisms. New Media and the Forensic Imagination* (2008) and Duranti's introduction of the concept of digital diplomatics (Duranti 2009); Duranti and Endicott-Popovsky (2010), digital forensic methods and tools, especially bitstream-preserving imaging (also known as forensic imaging), became a standard practice in memory institutions for the preservation of digital storage media and born-digital records. Kirschenbaum's seminal definition of formal and forensic digital materiality (2008, 10–11, see also Ries 2018, 389–401) – a selective focus on one dichotomic dimension in the spectrum of digital materiality (for an overview, see Drucker 2013) – conceptually enabled an analytical perspective on the materiality of the physical characteristics of storage media and the bitstream of the historical born-digital record that reveals its digital history, embedded as latent forensic artefacts, recoverable data, and traces of processing and user interaction. While his work on digital materiality is certainly indebted to New Bibliography (Lebrave 2011) and oriented towards a relative physical stability of the forensic record, his more recent theoretical considerations of the born-digital archive seem to rather reflect issues of the instability, context-dependency, authenticity, and intangibility of the born-digital historical record as a logical digital object within formal materiality (Kirschenbaum 2013, 2016b).

> But this also means that this data is fundamentally unstable in the sense that they rest upon the foundations of other data, what is quite literally in the trade known as metadata, in order to be legible under the appropriate computational regiments, which I have previously termed as formal materiality in my own work. (Kirschenbaum 2016b, 30:05)

> In the terms I put forth in *Mechanisms*, each access engenders a new logical entity that is forensically individuated at the level of its physical representation on some storage medium. Access is thus duplication, duplication is preservation, and preservation is creation — and recreation. That is the catechism of the .txtual condition, [...]. (Kirschenbaum 2013, 16)

As questions of stability, authenticity, and technological context-dependency (on different concepts of authenticity relating to context, see Rogers 2015, 100) and materiality of the born-digital historical record become even more complex for preservation and research tasks, the role of archival custodian- and curatorship, digital signing (Blanchette 2012), digital forensic methodology, and context-preservation of complete operating systems by emulation or virtualisation and even computer hardware (Kirschenbaum et al. 2009) becomes even more prominent. In the light of inevitable ageing and obsolescence of hard- and software, bitrot, fading network contexts, and online services going offline, memory institutions already today have to decide according to which standards and criteria to select relevant materials. They have to decide which aspects of digital objects and their contexts are relevant to future research and have to be preserved in order to achieve an authentically preserved record, and what would be acceptable loss. Is it just the text or the content of a document that has to be preserved, metadata in the document or in the surrounding operating system, contextual material in file folders, the materiality of the complete operating system or file server – as „dead" system in a forensic, fixed, bit-precise image or emulated at runtime –, or is the hardware or network context an important aspect to be preserved? Or is the experience of contemporary interaction a main factor that needs documentation? Some of the contributions to this special issue of *IJDH* revolve around these key questions of born-digital archives.

The archival and digital forensic perspective sheds light on the specific historicity of the born-digital record. Digital historicity does not only become apparent when one interacts with still functional legacy hard- and software in computing musea, experiencing the look and feel of historic operating systems and applications, the today unusual feel of thick cables, old port connectors and adapters, motherboards, controllers and storage media. The forensic materiality of the born-digital record, preserved in the form of forensic images and other forensic formats, bears a highly specific signature of historical computing that can best be understood from the vantage point of Jean-Francois Blanchette's *A Material History of Bits* (2011). He remarkably takes the perspective of a historian who analyses historical hard- and software architectures, such as the processing and networking stack, principles such as layering and modularity of operating systems and applications, read as historical documents of design decisions taken by hard- and software engineers, programmers, and tech companies in their pursuit to overcome the physical constraints of computing by architecture abstraction and error-correction mechanisms to maintain an 'illusion of immateriality' (Kirschenbaum 2008, p. 135). Blanchette stresses that maintaining the illusion of immateriality of resources, and hiding their physical limitations and characteristics to programmers and users is in itself a resource-intensive, critical and error-prone task that is mostly implemented at the cost of technical 'efficiency trade-offs'.

> This purported independence from matter would have two distinct and important consequences: (a) digital information can be reproduced and distributed at negligible cost and high speed, and thus, is immune to the economics and logistics of analogue media; (b) digital information can be accessed, used, or reproduced without the noise, corruption, and degradation that necessarily results from the handling of material carriers of information. [...] Yet, this abstraction from the material can never fully succeed. Rather, it stands in dialectical tension with the evolution of these material resources and with the efficiency trade-offs their abstraction requires. (Blanchette 2011, p. 1042)

Blanchette especially names the efficiency trade-offs implied by modularity, the efficiency cost of necessary garbage collection and error correction at runtime as 'design trade-offs inherent in abstracting from physical resources are rarely acknowledged in the computing literature' (Blanchette 2011, p. 1047). While some might want to nuance Blanchette's argument and note that modularity as a foundational principle of system architecture, code organisation, and programming language implementation is a necessity to ensure maintainability, manageability and extensibility of almost any larger system rather than be regarded as a performance penalty (which it can be), most will agree that overcoming the quirks of physical materiality is a resource-intensive task:

> The digital abstraction can be maintained in spite of this "noise" because, as Kirschenbaum notes, through error-correction codes, buffering, and other techniques, computers can self-efface the static—scratches on a record, smudges on paper—that typically signals the materiality of media: [...] These mechanisms, formally described in information theory, are used throughout networked computing systems: the impact of media irregularities on hard drive platters can be mitigated through the use of error-correction codes; the unpredictability of network bandwidth can be mitigated through the use of buffering, ensuring smooth delivery of latency-sensitive content [...]. It is this ability to ceaselessly clean up after its own noise that so powerfully enables computers to seemingly sever their dependency on physical processes that underlie processing, storage, and connectivity. Yet the physical characteristics of a resource (be it computation, storage, or networking) cannot simply be transcended, and noise can only be

conquered at the expense of other resources. [...] error-correcting codes, widely used to protect against transmission interference, result in both data expansion (and thus, reduced capacity) and increased processing load. [...] Once again, then, independence from the material can only be obtained at the costs of certain trade-offs. (Blanchette 2011, p. 1047)

Blanchette's reasoning could serve as a foundation for a historical theory of digital forensics, an explanatory framework for many digital forensic phenomena, and the specific historicity of forensic digital materiality. Many phenomena that digital forensic tools and methods analyse are ultimately rooted in the mitigation of material constraints of hard- and software. Deleted data can be recovered because effective deletion through overwriting is a very resource-expensive task that would slow down a computer, which is why effective deletion does not take place by default. Often deleted data and documents "survive" on a system because of bugs, file system corruption, and system crashes: in CHKDSK error correction or hibernation files created by the operating system, in temporary and auto-recovery files not deleted because of system crashes. Temporary files are created on hard drives especially when a runtime environment runs out of physical RAM and has to swap memory with the storage medium. On some operating systems, automatic system snapshots are being created (e.g. VSS shadow copy partitions) in order to mitigate the risk of data loss through system instability. Files and file fragments are preserved in the so-called "drive slack" of data clusters because modern storage media are organised in blocks, which speeds up the process of data lookup and the navigation of large storage spaces on storage media with physical moving parts, such as conventional hard drives: it is the physical block size on the storage medium that determines where exactly a file is cut off. Fastsave artefacts in Microsoft Word documents and in temporary files are a result of a saving mechanism that was implemented to mitigate the relatively slow operation of early hard drives, at the cost of deleted text passages still present in documents and temporary files (Ries 2017, 2018). This incomplete list names just a few of the effects, mechanisms and design decisions that digital forensics is about and which are based on the computing-historical perspective that Blanchette describes. The digital forensic record, in turn, is deeply informed by designs that are specific for different types of hardware, versions of operating systems and application software, giving it a highly specific historicity that is accessible and readable through the forensic traces of digital processing. The latent digital forensic features of the born-digital historical record are not only of interest for philologists who search for hidden draft versions of a text. They are also relevant for historians and archivists who have to determine whether a historical record is authentic or might have been manipulated. Furthermore, they are relevant to the historian who investigates the history of the digitisation of society using original archived computing systems.

When we speak about the born-digital record, there is another aspect to be kept in mind, an aspect that is not in the foreground in this volume, but hopefully will be scrutinized in more detail during further issues of *IJDH*. As Blanchette rightly emphasizes, the historicity of born-digital phenomena is rooted in the material constraints of hard- and software, it is embedded in an infrastructure context without which it cannot be understood. The infrastructure of the digital archive, which serves as an interface between the researcher and their subject of research, requires attention in itself, regardless of the fact that the research is based on born-digital or digitised materials. Michel de Certeau has pointed out in his seminal work *The Writing of History* (De Certeau 1988; Palkó 2019) that the computer, as an archive, forms a new apparatus for research and as such will fundamentally change the way historical documents will be formed. The materiality of the archive as medium of knowledge formation is one of the main research questions media archaeology focuses on (Ernst 2011; Parikka 2012). Parikka sheds light on the interdependence of problems current archiving practices face in a born-digital culture, and on the theoretical challenges of understanding how a digital archive as an apparatus forms our documents of the past and present.

> the theoretical problems of recent media archaeologies of technical media and software along with a rethinking of the archive, go hand in hand with the practical challenges faced by cultural heritage institutions and professionals: how do you archive processes and culture which is based on both technical processes (software and networks) and social ones (participation and collaboration, as in massive online role-playing platforms as cultural forms). (Parikka 2012, 115)

The analyses of the institutional archiving practices have always been complicated for their medial and material mechanisms tend to stay in the shadow (Groys 2000; Palkó 2017). However, the analyses of the apparatus of the digital archive, which includes born-digital, processual, network- or environment-based material, is even more complicated. Although a lot has been done in the last decade to provide a stable digital object by forensic imaging on the level of forensic materiality, the actual documents extracted from a forensic image depend highly on the technical infrastructure (e. g. the chosen software and workflow), and requires technical skills that are normally not part of a humanities scholar's qualification. The same is true for the growing importance and complexity of searching the digital medium. As both digitized and born-digital records are available in a quantity impossible to fathom through the methodology of close reading, records relevant for a research question will mostly be gathered by using query services. Digital archives normally radically limit the possibility to use custom search tools and query languages, they only provide predefined and simplified options.

A lot has been done by national institutions and international projects both on technical, institutional, and discursive level to augment the traditionally analogue field of scientifically relevant material to the born-digital. Trusted formats, standards, methodologies, and services are available for GLAM institutions and researchers as well, but it remains an open question how the complexity of handling born-digital primary records and the thus established digital archives will be manageable for the humanists of the twenty-first century.

The current special issue of *International Journal of Digital Humanities* features articles by international researchers from the libraries and archives sector, as well as from the (digital) humanities that address born-digital archives on several levels, ranging from the digital forensic perspective on individual records (Archival Methodology: Digital Forensics), via personal digital archives and born-digital cultural heritage archives (Digital Culture and Literature Archives), web archives (Web Archives), to born-digital archiving in large digital infrastructures (Born-Digital Archives and Infrastructures).

Corinne Rogers (University of British Columbia, Vancouver, Canada) strikes the connection between digital forensics and born-digital archival science and practice with a historical introduction to how digital forensics became a viable tool for digital curatorship.

Bénédicte Vauthier (Bern University, Switzerland), after her studies on Robert Juan-Cantavella's born-digital dossier génétique of his novel *El Dorado* (Vauthier 2014, 2016), traces the inherent connection between Anglo-American textual scholarship and analytical bibliographyon the one hand and the introduction of digital forensic methodology to archival science on the other, in an effort to find an explanation why European textual scholarship and philology seems to lag behind in this field. Vauthier also presents the results of her survey among Spanish-speaking writers about their digital self-archiving practice and their willingness to deposit their digital archives at memory institutions and make them available for research. Nicholas Schiller and Dene Grigar (Washington State University, Vancouver, Canada) provide an insight into their work at the *Electronic Literature Lab* (ELL) at Washington State University Vancouver on the process of archiving electronic literature, specifically about documenting the interactive experience with Sarah Smith's *King of Space* in the 'traversal' format. Schiller and Grigar's discussion and example show some of the important challenges of electronic literature archiving and the solutions practiced at ELL. Libi Striegl and Lori Emerson (University of Colorado Boulder, USA) describe their archival and 'anarchival' experience- and practice-based approach to research and research creation at the Media Archaeology Lab (MAL) at the University of Colorado at Boulder. As an example, they document the project on mesh-networked *One Laptop Per Child* XO laptops at MAL. The *One Laptop Per Child* initiative with its tailored technological ecosystem is an important educational inclusion project worth documenting, its use of mesh networks and hardware design introduced an innovative approach to local networking, network capacity sharing and solutions for operation under technologically difficult circumstances and infrastructure.

In the web archives section of the current issue, Trevor Owens, editor of Owens 2013a, b, and Grace H. Thomas (Library of Congress, USA) trace the history and functional changes of the Spacer GIF and the resulting challenges for web archiving. Eveline Vlassenroot (Ghent University, Belgium), Sally Chambers (Ghent University, Belgium), Emmanuel Di Pretoro (Haute École Bruxelles-Brabant, Brussels, Belgium), Friedel Geeraert (Royal Library and State Archives of Belgium, Brussels, Belgium), Gerald Haesendonck (Ghent University, Belgium), Alejandra Michel (Namur University, Belgium) and Peter Mechant (Ghent University, Belgium) discuss national and international web archives as a data resource for digital scholars in Europe.

In the *Born-Digital Archives and Infrastructures* section, Tibor Kálmán (GWDG Göttingen, Germany), Matej Ďurčo (Austrian Academy of the Sciences, Austria), Frank Fischer (Higher School of Economics, Moscow, Russia), Nicolas Larrousse (Huma-Num, Paris, France), Claudio Leone (State and University Library Göttingen, Germany), Karlheinz Mörth (Austrian Academy of the Sciences, Austria) and Carsten Thiel (State and University Library Göttingen, Germany) map the challenges, approaches and solutions of born-digital archiving and access, especially for born-digital research datasets, learning materials, services and software in the context of the European DARIAH research infrastructure, and beyond.

The special issue concludes with Peter Mechant's (Ghent University, Belgium) review of *Web 25. Histories from the first 25 years of the world wide web*, edited by Niels Brügger in 2017.

References

Baker, J. (2018). *Outlook: Email archives, 1990–2007*, guest lecture at Ghent University, Belgium, 8 May 2018.

Blanchette, J.-F. (2011). A material history of bits. *Journal of the American Society for Information Science and Technology, 62*(6), 1042–1057.

Blanchette, J.-F. (2012). *Burdens of proof. Cryptographic culture and evidence law in the age of electronic documents.* Cambridge: MIT Press.

Carroll, L., Farr, E., Hornsby, P., & Ranker, B. (2011). A comprehensive approach to born-digital archives. *Archivaria, 72*, 61–92.

Catalogue ÖNB (2018). Catalogue entry at Austrian National Library , ÖNB. https://www.onb.ac.at/bibliothek/sammlungen/literatur/bestaende/personen/czernin-franz-josef-geb-1952/. Accessed 11 July 2018.

Dahlström, M. (2000). Drowning by versions. *Human IT 4*, http://etjanst.hb.se/bhs/ith/4-00/md.htm. Accessed 11 July 2018

De Certeau, M. (1988). *The writing of history*, (trans: Conley, T.). New York: Columbia UP.

Drucker, J. (2013). Performative materiality and theoretical approaches to interface. *Digital Humanities Quarterly, 7*(1). https://www.digitalhumanities.org/dhq/vol/7/1/000143/000143.html. Accessed 11 July 2018.

Duranti, L. (2009). From digital diplomatics to digital records forensics. *Archivaria, 68*, 39–66.

Duranti, L., & Endicott-Popovsky, B. (2010). Digital records forensics. a new science and academic program for forensic readiness. In *ADFSL Conference on Digital Forensics, Security and Law*. http://arqtleufes.pbworks.com/w/file/fetch/94919918/Duranti.pdf. Accessed 11 July 2018.

Enge, J., & Kramski, H. W. (2014). "Arme Nachlassverwalter ...". Herausforderungen, Erkenntnisse und Lösungsansätze bei der Aufbereitung komplexer digitaler Datensammlungen. Filthaut, J. (Ed.), *Von der Übernahme zur Benutzung. Aktuelle Entwicklungen in der digitalen Archivierung. 18. Tagung des Arbeitskreises Archivierung von Unterlagen aus digitalen Systemen on 11–12 March 2014 in Weimar*, (pp. 53–62) Weimar: Thüringisches Hauptstaatsarchiv.

Ernst, W. (2011). Media archaeography method and machine versus history and narrative of media In: Huhtamo, E. and Parikka, J. (Eds.), *Media archaeology. Approaches, applications, and implications* (pp 239–255). Los Angeles: University of California Press.

Foss, R. (2017). The British Library: *Learning from users of personal digital archives at The British Library. Research paper at conference Personal Digital Archiving* 2017, 29-31 Mar 2017, Stanford Libraries.

Gitelman, L. (2006). *Always already new. Media, history, and the data of culture.* Cambridge: MIT Press.

Groys, B. (2000). *Unter Verdacht. Eine Phänomenologie der Medien.* Hanser.

John, J. L. (2012). *Digital forensics and preservation. DPC technology watch report 12–03 November 2012.* Digital Preservation Coalition. https://doi.org/10.7207/twr12-03. Accessed 11 July 2018.

Kirschenbaum, M. (2008). *Mechanisms. New media and the forensic imagination.* Cambridge: MIT. University Press.

Kirschenbaum, M. (2013). The .txtual condition: digital humanities, born-digital archives, and the future literary. *Digital Humanities Quarterly, 7*(1), http://www.digitalhumanities.org/dhq/vol/7/1/000151/000151.html. Accessed 11 July 2018.

Kirschenbaum, M. (2016a). *Track changes. A literary history of word processing.* Cambridge: Harvard University Press.

Kirschenbaum, M. (2016b): The transmissions of the archive. Literary remainders in the late age of print. Kirschenbaum, M. (Ed.), *Bitstreams. The Future of Digital Literary Heritage.* Lecture Series at KISLAK Center for Special Collections, Rare Books and Manuscripts, Penn Libraries. 14 March 2016. https://www.youtube/6TuA4dkRegQ. Accessed 11 July 2018.

Kirschenbaum, M., Farr, E.L., Kraus, K., et al. (2009). Digital materiality. Preserving Access to Computers as Complete Environments. In: *iPress 2009. 6th International Conference on Preservation of Digital Objects.* 5. October 2009. University of California. California Digital Library. http://www.escholarship.org/uc/cdl_ipres09. Accessed 11 July 2018.

Kirschenbaum, M., Ovenden, R., Redwine, G., et al. (Eds.) (2010). *Digital forensics and born-digital content in cultural heritage collections.* Washington, D.C.: Council on library and information resources, Washington, D.C. Dec. 2010. http://www.clir.org/pubs/reports/reports/pub149/pub149.pdf. Accessed 11 July 2018.

Lebrave, J.-L. (2011). Computer forensics: la critique génétique et l'écriture numérique. *Genesis, 33*, 137–147.

Manovich, L. (2001). *The language of new media*. Cambridge: MIT Press.

Owens, T. (Ed.) (2013a). *Preserving.exe: Toward a national strategy for software preservation*. National Digital Information Infrastructure and Preservation Program at the Library of Congress, Washington, D.C. http://www.digitalpreservation.gov/multimedia/documents/PreservingEXE_report_final101813.pdf. Accessed 11 July 2018.

Owens, T. (2013b). *Historic iPhones: Personal digital media devices in the collection*. 15 November 2013. http://www.trevorowens.org/2013/11/historic-iphones-personal-digi-tal-media-devices-in-the-collection/. Accessed 11 July 2018.

Palkó, G. (2017). Media archaeology of institutional archives? *Studia UBB Digitalia,* 7(62), 75–82. https://doi.org/10.24193/subbdigitalia.2017.1.05. Accessed 11 July 2018.

Palkó, G. (2019). Sites of digita l humanities. About virtual research environments. In Kelemen, P. & Pethes, N. (Eds.). *Philology in the Making. Analog/Digital Cultures of Scholarly Writing and Reading* (pp. 221-230). Bielefeld: Transcript.

Parikka, J. (2012). *What is media archaeology*. Cambridge: Polity.

Reside, D. (2011a). "Last modified January 1996". The digital history of RENT. *Theatre Survey,* 52(2), 335–340.

Reside, D. (2011b, April 22). "No day but today". A look at Jonathan Larson's Word Files [Blog post]. http://www.nypl.org/blog/2011/04/22/no-day-today-look-jonathan-larsons-word-files. Accessed 11 July 2018.

Reside, D. (2017). West side story: The journey to Lincoln center theater. In L. MacDonald & W. A. Everett (Eds.), *The palgrave handbook of musical theatre producers* (pp. 359–367). New York: Palgrave Macmillan.

Ries, T. (2017). Philology and the digital writing process. *Cahier voor Literatuurwetenschap,* 9, 129–158.

Ries, T. (2018). The rationale of the born-digital dossier génétique: Digital forensics and the writing process: With examples from the Thomas Kling archive. *Digital Scholarship in the Humanities,* 33(2), 391–424.

Rockmore, D. (2014). The digital life of Salman Rushdie. *The New Yorker* published 29 July 2014. http://www.newyorker.com/tech/elements/digital-life-salman-rushdie. Accessed 11 July 2018.

Rogers, C. (2015). Authenticity of digital records. A Survey of Professional Practice. *Canadian Journal of Information and Library Science,* 39(2), 97–113.

Sloyan, V. (2018). *Overview of a born-digital archives access workshop held at Wellcome collection*. Findings of a workshop held on 24th November 2017. https://doi.org/10.6084/m9.figshare.6087194.v1. Accessed 1 March 2019.

Vauthier, B. (2014). Tanteos, calas y pesquisas en el dossier genético digital de El Dorado de Robert Juan Cantavella. In M. Kunz & S. Gómez-Rodríguez (Eds.), *Nueva narrativa española* (pp. 311–345). Barcelona: Linkgua.

Vauthier, B. (2016). Genetic criticism put to the test by digital technology: Sounding out the (mainly) digital genetic file of El Dorado by Robert Juan-Cantavella. *Variants,* 12-13, 163–186.

Waugh, D. & Russey Roke, E. (2017). *Second-generation digital archives: What we learned from the Salman Rushdie project*. Research paper at conference Personal Digital Archiving 2017, 29–31 Mar 2017, Stanford Libraries.

Winters, J. (2018a). *Humanities and the born digital: Moving from a difficult past to a promising future?* Keynote at DHBenelux 2018, Amsterdam. 7 June.

Winters, J. (2018b). Web archives and (digital) history: a troubled past and a promising future? In N. Brügger & I. Milligan (Eds.), *Sage Handbook of Web History* (pp. 593–606). Newcastle: Sage.

International Journal of Digital Humanities (2019) 1:13–28
https://doi.org/10.1007/s42803-019-00002-y

From time theft to time stamps: mapping the development of digital forensics from law enforcement to archival authority

Corinne Rogers[1]

Published online: 4 March 2019
© Springer Nature Switzerland AG 2019

Abstract

The field of digital forensics seems at first glance quite separate from archival work and digital preservation. However, professionals in both fields are trusted to attest to the identity and integrity of digital documents and traces – they are regarded as experts in the acquisition, interpretation, description and presentation of that material. Archival science and digital forensics evolved out of practice and grew into established professional disciplines by developing theoretical foundations, which then returned to inform and standardize that practice. They have their roots in legal requirements and law enforcement. A significant challenge to both fields, therefore, is the identification of records (archival focus) and evidence (digital forensics focus) in digital systems, establishing their contexts, provenance, relationships, and meaning. This paper traces the development of digital forensics from practice to theory and presents the parallels with archival science.

Keywords Archival science · Digital forensics · Digital records forensics · Digital evidence

1 Introduction

The field of digital forensics seems at first glance quite separate from archival science and digital preservation, but these disciplines have overlapping histories and legacies deriving from similar goals, common challenges, and shared theoretical perspectives (Rogers and John 2013). In the 1980s forensic investigation of computer crime was largely unknown – indeed, some questioned whether computer crime existed. At the same time, archivists were beginning to discuss the characteristics and implications for practice of machine-readable records. Today, crime involving digital evidence is the norm and digital forensics is a growth industry in legal investigations. Archives and

---

Chapter 2 was originally published as Rogers, C. International Journal of Digital Humanities (2019) 1: 13–28. https://doi.org/10.1007/s42803-019-00002-y.

✉ Corinne Rogers
  cmrogers@mail.ubc.ca

[1] School of Library, Archival and Information Studies, University of British Columbia, Vancouver, Canada

records are increasingly born digital, and archivists need new tools to access digital sources, and assist in processing archival material. Elizabeth Diamond foreshadowed these developments when she wrote in 1994: "[i] f the historian is the lawyer in the court of history, then the archivist is the forensic scientist" (Diamond 1994: 140).

Both fields are concerned with discovering, understanding, describing, and presenting or making accessible digital material. Digital forensics was developed to assist law enforcement in investigations of crimes using computers in order to bring digital evidence to trial and is concerned with the authenticity, reliability, and accuracy of digital material. Archival science traces its roots to administration and law, and studies the relationships between records, the persons, procedures, actions, and means through which they are created. Archivists support accountability and trustworthiness of records by establishing their identity and assessing their integrity, reliability, and accuracy through analysis of records and record aggregations. But digital records require the mediation of technology to read and understand them, and so present the archivist with new layers of abstraction for analysis. In recent years, archivists have adopted and adapted digital forensics tools in service of accountability and preservation of societal memory (c.f. Kirschenbaum et al. 2010; Lee 2012), and digital forensics practitioners have noted similarities between their work and records' management (c.f. Irons 2006).

Much of the published material about digital forensics focuses on the techniques and tools of practice, and is highly technical, falling within the realm of computer science and mathematics. The purpose of digital forensics is predominantly in service of legal evidence, admissible in court, incident response and security. But throughout the development of the discipline, there has been a small but steadily growing body of literature that calls for digital forensics research to be situated within a broader social and theoretical framework (Palmer 2001; Mocas 2004; Irons 2006; Duranti 2009; Duranti and Endicott-Popovsky 2010).

While the tools and techniques of digital forensics are necessarily technical, the conceptual underpinnings of the discipline can be examined through the lens of archival science, diplomatics, and law. The following review of predominantly non-technical literature endeavors to understand the genesis and evolution of digital forensics as law enforcement practice and academic discipline in order to explore parallels with archival science.

This paper traces the chronological development of digital forensics from its evolution in the 1980s to the present through the issues that have shaped it. These issues include the evolving challenges presented by society's increasing reliance on computer technology, a collaborative approach by legal personnel, law enforcement, and IT specialists in identifying and solving these challenges, the spread of digital forensic practice from law enforcement to other domains, specifically archival practice.

A note about terminology: early practitioners referred to the practice of computer forensics. As digital devices became ubiquitous and were not necessarily traditional computers, the term "digital" began to replace "computer" (c.f. Whitcomb 2002). However, there is little consistency even today. While the tendency may be to prefer-ence "digital", the term computer forensics is still in use.

2 The legal context

Digital forensics and archival science both have roots in law. The nature of archives and the responsibilities for their care and custody are discussed in the Justinian Code of ancient Rome, and in the literature of the jurists of the eleventh century (Duranti 1996). Archival research focuses on establishing the evidentiary capacity of records and documents. According to Menne-Haritz, '(e)vidence means patterns of processes, aims and mandates, procedures and results, as they can be examined. It consists of signs, of signals, not primarily of words. ... All those are nonverbal signs that must be interpreted in context to disclose their meaning. To one who understands them, they will tell how processes worked and who was responsible for which decision' (1994, 537).

Digital forensics developed in response to the needs of law enforcement to investigate computer crime. It has been defined as the use of scientifically derived and proven methods toward the preservation, collection, validation, identification, analysis, interpretation, documentation, and presentation of digital evidence derived from digital sources for the purpose of facilitation or furthering the reconstruction of events found to be criminal, or helping to anticipate unauthorized actions shown to be disruptive to planned operations (Palmer 2001).

While admissibility requirements for traditional documentary evidence have a long-established history and are well understood, digital evidence has raised a host of problems that the judicial system, regardless of jurisdiction, was (and in some cases may still be) ill equipped to handle. The inadequacies and inconsistencies of the law of evidence and rules of court to deal with digital media despite the passage of new laws to address it, the explosive increase in quantity of potential evidence to be examined, lack of understanding of the nature of digital media and its differences from traditional media all contributed to the need for a scientific and theoretical base for digital forensics.

The legal context has been approached in the digital forensics discourse in one of two ways. First, those concerned with the development of the discipline have sought, through standards, principles and guidelines, a scientific basis for practice. Second, several practitioners have advocated for the development of open source tools which, by nature of the availability of their source code, would support the forensic expert witness in asserting their reliability (Carrier 2003b; Kenneally 2001).

While it is not within the scope of this paper to address the legal context in full, it is worth citing a few milestones. In 1993 the ruling in *Daubert v. Merrell Dow Pharmaceuticals*, 509 U.S. 579 changed the law with respect to the admissibility of scientific evidence and expert testimony. *Daubert* required that scientific evidence be based on theory and technique that has been reliably tested, subject to peer review, with known or potential error rates, and generally accepted as a standard in its particular scientific community. These requirements were expanded in *Kumho Tire v. Carmichael* (1999) to include technology expertise. Because digital evidence is extracted from digital media, its reliability and integrity depends in part on the means of its extraction, which must be conducted and accounted for according to scientific principles. These two cases have, therefore, had a profound impact on the development of the digital forensics discipline (Marsico 2005).

3 A brief history of digital forensics: looking back to look forward

At the end of the 2010s, three short historical retrospectives captured past development and predicted future directions of digital forensics (Charters 2009; Pollitt 2010; Garfinkel 2010). These articles are important first-hand accounts of the evolution of the discipline and predictions for future growth reflecting the perspectives of the intelligence community, law enforcement and academic researchers. Each author has been and continues to be influential in shaping the field. Each has approached the task from his particular point of view, and yet there are similarities. All accounts track the changes in computer technology, which have driven the course of digital forensics, and arrive at complementary yet distinct conclusions about future directions.

Ian Charters' background is in IT security and information assurance spanning more than 20 years in the United States' Intelligence Community. He describes the development of computer forensics in terms of stages of evolution – the Ad Hoc Phase, the Structured Phase, and the Enterprise Phase. He suggests that these phases are cyclical, repeating as developments in technology offer new opportunities for criminality and introduce new challenges for investigators. Charters explains the development of digital forensics through the development of policy, procedure, and forensic tools. He characterizes the Ad Hoc Phase by shortcomings in investigative structure, goals, policies and procedures, and lack of accuracy of forensic tools. The resulting confusion of the Ad Hoc phase gives way to the imposition of structure expressed in policy-based programs, defined and coordinated procedures closely aligned with the policy, and a requirement for – and development of – more forensically sound tools – the Structured Phase. The Enterprise Phase is characterized by real-time collection, tailored field tools and forensics-as-a-service, built seamlessly into the technological infrastructure. The future, he predicts, will be aimed at greater automation and interoperability, proactive collection and analysis, and increased focus on standards in software architectures and reporting.

Mark Pollitt begins his paper *A History of Digital Forensics* with an apology. His is not, he claims, a fully-informed, objective and unbiased account of the rise of digital forensics, but his personal story – the journey of a digital forensic investigator (Pollitt 2010). One may argue, of course, that there is no such thing as an objective and unbiased account. No matter one's intention to present "the facts and nothing but the facts," every narrator chooses what to include and what to ignore in the telling of a story, and in so doing shapes that story through the material she choses. Pollitt's personal account is nevertheless a particularly clear summary of the development of the field, outlining the salient characteristics of the practice and the profession. He presents the history of computer forensics through the notion of epochs, beginning with pre-history, and then adopting a lifecycle model, moving from infancy through childhood and adolescence, with maturity still to come. Within that framework, he defines the discipline through the elements of people, targets, tools, organizations, and the community as a whole. Pollitt, a former military officer with over twenty years' service experience as a Special Agent of the Federal Bureau of Investigation, approaches the history from the perspective of law enforcement. His experience spans the epochs he describes, and his influence is evident in the development of standards, and the recognition of digital forensics as a forensic discipline by the American Society of Crime Laboratory Directors/Laboratory Accreditation Board.

Simson Garfinkel is an academic practitioner who has developed computer forensics tools, conducted computer-related research and authored books and articles published in the academic and popular press. In *Digital forensics research: The next 10 years* (2010), he suggests a research agenda that will carry digital forensics into the next phase of development, and sets the stage by summarizing the characteristics of past phases. He argues that 2010 marks the approaching end of a "Golden Age" of computer forensics, characterized by relative stability of operating systems and file formats, examinations largely confined to a single computer system, removable storage devices, and reasonably good and easy-to-use tools coupled with rapid growth of research and increasing professionalism. An impending crisis looms, brought on by advances and fundamental changes in the computer industry – specifically increased storage capacity, proliferation and diversification of devices, operating systems and file formats, pervasive encryption, use of the cloud for remote processing and storage, and increasing legal challenges to search and seizure that limit the scope of investigations. Current forensics tools are challenged to meet these needs for law enforcement because they focus on finding specific pieces of evidence for presentation in court. However, this evidence-oriented model – what Garfinkel calls the 'visibility, filter, and report model', is well suited to archival processing needs, if not all law enforcement needs. Garfinkel has contributed to the development of forensics tools for archivists through his participation in the BitCurator project that supports digital forensics practices in libraries, archives, and museums (Lee 2012).

4 A view from the field – the 1980s and 1990s

Clifford Stoll's book, *The Cuckoo's Egg: Tracking a Spy Through the Maze of Computer Espionage*, is an early account of finding a computer hacker and bringing him to court (Stoll 1989). An astronomer supporting the computer systems at a California research laboratory in the mid-1980s, Stoll stumbled upon a hacker when he investigated a 75-cent discrepancy in the accounting charges for computer use time in his lab. This led him on an intercontinental cyber chase that lasted over a year through the networks that linked research and military computers in Europe and the United States. Law enforcement and military personnel alike were slow to take interest; because there was no financial or other damage, they could not determine if a crime was being committed. Nor, until they could locate the hacker's point of origin, could they agree on jurisdictional responsibility. This story highlights the characteristics of intentional computer misuse and response in the late 1980s: uncertainty about what constituted a crime using computers; the practice of a lone investigator working on his own, often with little support; and use of tools adapted or created by the investigator for a specific incident.

As early as 1984, some law enforcement agencies had begun to develop programs to examine computer evidence. The Computer Analysis and Response Team (CART), developed by the FBI, was duplicated in law enforcement agencies in North America and Europe (Noblett et al. 2000; Whitcomb 2002). However, while some progressive investigators delved into the new frontier of digital evidence, there was also reluctance, as Stoll's experience illustrates. The Inspection Service Lab of the US Postal Service expressed dismay when first confronted in the late 1980s with a request for an examination of a computer – "What should we do with this?", they asked. They questioned how they could secure and preserve digital evidence, how they could collect it without changing it, what practices would withstand the scrutiny of the court, and what examination protocols they should follow. However within ten years the Postal Inspection Unit had not only established a Computer Forensic Unit, but considered changing the name to Digital Evidence Unit to reflect the growing variety of digital sources of evidence.

The first published use of the term "computer forensics" in the academic literature appeared in an article entitled *A forensic methodology for countering computer crime* (Collier and Spaul 1992). The authors proposed the term 'computer forensics' as a label for 'existing but very limited activities amongst the police and consultancy firms' (204) and advocated for its inclusion in the realm of traditional forensic sciences. They identified the skills required of a computer forensic expert to be multi-disciplinary, including investigative capacity, legal knowledge (including the law of evidence, rules of hearsay and admissibility), courtroom presentation skills as well as knowledge of computers.

The bulk of published material begins in the mid-1990s, originating from international gatherings of law enforcement. Some of these, like the FBI international conferences on computer evidence, were symposia devoted to computer crime (Noblett et al. 2000). Others were long-established gatherings that began to include sessions on computer forensics, such as INTERPOL's International Forensic Science Symposia (Internet / Home - INTERPOL n.d.).

Mark Pollitt's frequent reports and presentations to international law enforcement in the 1990s give a clear picture of the state of development of the discipline. Through observation and experience, Pollitt developed one of the first high-level models of the computer forensic process, reflecting the common principles that guide the conduct of an examination. His "three-tiered approach" consists of principles, methodologies (practices), and procedures. With this three-tiered model he formulates a basis for standards development. Moving from the general to the specific, he identifies universal principles: that evidence should not be altered; that examination results should be accurate; and that the results are verifiable and repeatable (Pollitt 1995a, b). This model was further developed in a later article (Noblett et al. 2000) and has been the foundation of many subsequent models.

Digital evidence was recognized as a principle type of evidence at INTERPOL's International Forensic Science Symposium in 1998 (Pollitt 2001) and each subsequent conference has received a report on the status of digital evidence collection and analysis, as well as areas of growth and challenge. The reports outline the growth of community through working groups, professional organizations, and scientific bodies (DiClemente et al. 2004); challenges and concerns such as increased workload, and need for accreditation and certification balanced by professional maturity and methodology; and the increasing complexity of computer crime with its parallel demands on computer forensics, and the spread beyond its original stakeholders (Reedy et al. 2007). In 2010 a sobering picture was presented of a 'coming digital forensic crisis' caused by rapidly increasing storage capacity, data volume on networks, an expanding variety of computing devices, growing case loads, and limited resources (Garfinkel 2010, S66:).

5 Definitions, standards, and the building of community

Early in the evolution of digital forensics practice, the need for standards to guide and regulate the discipline and increase the acceptance of digital material offered as evidence in court became an important subject of discussion. Standards were recognized as instruments that ensured quality and served as a guarantee of reliable results, dictated a minimum acceptable level of performance, ensured proper training of examiners, and limited liability for the actions of both examiner and examining organization (Pollitt 1995a). However, some questioned the ability to develop standards for digital forensics because of the variety and pace of change of technology. The challenge was to build in sufficient flexibility to balance meaningful standards with rapid change and individual investigative approaches. Digital forensics working groups sought to develop universal principles that could be applied irrespective of the media under investigation.

In 1998 the US Federal Crime Laboratory Directors group established the Scientific Working Group on Digital Evidence (SWGDE), with a mandate to explore digital evidence as a forensic discipline (Pollitt 2003). Shortly after it was formed, the SWGDE proposed draft definitions and, on the principle that digital evidence must be 'collected, preserved, examined, or transferred in a manner safeguarding the accuracy and reliability of the evidence', a draft standard was presented to the International Hi-Tech Crime and Forensics Conference in October 1999 (SWGDE and IOCE 2000). The draft defined digital evidence as information of probative value stored or transmitted in digital form, and identified that its acquisition begins when information and/or physical items are collected or stored for examination purposes. The process of collecting evidence should be conducted according to the rules of evidence in the relevant jurisdiction. Data objects are defined as information of potential probative value that are associated with physical items, and may occur in different formats without altering the original information. The draft standard also distinguished original digital evidence from duplicates or copies. Original digital evidence is defined as the physical items and data objects associated with such items at the time of acquisition or seizure. Duplicate digital evidence is an accurate digital reproduction of all data objects contained on an original physical item, while a copy is an accurate reproduction of information contained on an original physical item, independent of the original physical item.

Other organizations were also pursuing the development of standards and best practices. In the United Kingdom, the Association of Chief Police Officers (ACPO) drafted good practice guidelines for search, seizure and examination of digital evidence. The original four principles of digital forensics examination still stand today, in the fifth edition of their guidelines (Association of Chief Police Officers (ACPO) 2012). They require that no action taken by law enforcement agencies or their agents should change data held on a computer or storage media which may subsequently be relied upon in court; that in exceptional circumstances, a competent person may need to access original data held on a computer or on storage media and must be able to give evidence explaining the relevance and the implications of their actions; that an audit trail or other record of all processes applied to computer based electronic evidence should be created and preserved, and an independent third party should be able to examine those processes and achieve the same result; and that the person in charge of the investigation (the case officer) has overall responsibility for ensuring that the law and these principles are adhered to. Standards and practice guidelines continue to be updated as the field matures.

With standards and principles drafted for forensic investigations related to law enforcement, the discipline was ready to explore a more theoretical focus and build a multi-disciplinary community. In 2001 the first Digital Forensics Research Workshop (DFRWS) was convened in Utica, New York. The conference represented the nucleus of a multi-disciplinary digital forensics community that included law enforcement, military and civilian partners; participants included academics and digital forensic practitioners, with keynote speakers from law enforcement, military operations, infrastructure protection, industry, academia and government. These domains each employed a difference paradigm for forensic analysis—prosecution (law enforcement), security and continuity of operations (military), and availability and security of service (business and industry) (Palmer 2001). The report from that conference provides an important benchmark of the profession—a synchronic snapshot of digital forensic science at that moment, and a blueprint for future research. It provides a base from which much of the subsequent literature derives.

Participants agreed that to be considered a discipline, digital forensics must be characterized by a combination of theory, abstractions and models, elements of practice, a corpus of literature and professional practice, and confidence and trust in results. They also agreed that these areas had not all yet been adequately addressed. The keynote speakers expressed strong concern for development of the profession that goes well beyond the solely technical aspects. This "full-spectrum" approach does not rest on technology alone, but draws on the procedural, social and legal realms to create a holistic body of knowledge that both informs and supports the primary objectives of forensic analysis and leads to an integration of "forensic hooks" into live computer and network systems and away from the "current band aid approach that produces point solution tools." Lack of standardization of analytical procedures, protocols and terminology; issues of accuracy, efficiency and retention of extracted material; the conflict between individual privacy rights and data collection requirements were all identified as holding back the development of the profession.

Participants agreed that future research should build on collaboration. Important foci included work to define terms and develop taxonomies and ontologies that would make communications more effective and research more applicable, increasing opportunities for training and certification, and continuing to work on standards and standardized procedures, among many more specific goals.

6 Towards a theory of digital forensics

Theory develops through contemplation of practice intended to uncover general or abstract concepts, which are modeled and tested, and eventually transcend the specific, returning to inform and guide practice. In relation to disciplined knowledge creation, theory 'denotes systematic ideas to explain or account for observed facts or phenomena' (Eastwood 1994, 123). Digital forensics is practiced in an investigative context, regardless of the domain of the investigation. The roots for the development of a theory of digital forensics, then, may be found in the early practice guidelines and principles developed by law enforcement and technical working groups (Mocas 2004).

The call for development of a theory of digital forensics was first broadly articulated in the DFRWS report (Palmer 2001; Carrier and Spafford 2004). The framework proposed by the DFRWS modeled a typical investigation: identification, preservation, collection, examination, analysis, presentation and decision (Palmer 2001). Models have been proposed that elaborate on the stages of investigation, outline incident response, frame the process through a particular lens, or define the discipline through abstracted concepts (c.f. Pollitt 1995a; Noblett et al. 2000; Palmer 2001; Reith et al. 2002; Carrier 2003a; Carrier and Spafford 2004; Ciardhuáin 2004; Beebe and Clark 2005; Ieong 2006; Selamat et al. 2008; Blackwell 2011). They share similarities as they present more or less detailed abstractions of investigative steps.

There is no consensus about the maturity of the models that have been proposed, or a universally accepted theory. Perhaps there can never be, as process models are subjective, and must be evaluated with respect to scalability for future technologies and applicability to different types of investigations (Carrier and Spafford 2004). They are descriptive in nature, presenting in greater or lesser detail the elements of an investigation in linear detail as it unfolds.

Proposed theoretical foundations begin to enter the literature with the search for functional requirements that a process model must meet. Carrier and Spafford propose five requirements: that the model be practical and follow the steps of an investigation, that it be technology-neutral, but allow enough specificity to support technology requirements for each phase, that it be based on existing theory for physical crime investigations, and that it must apply across domains to law enforcement investigations, corporate investigations and incident response.

They approach the development of a model from a particular perspective—that the computer or system under investigation is analogous to a physical crime scene. This offers a way of organizing the steps of the process into five categories: readiness phases; deployment phases; physical crime scene investigative phases; digital crime scene investigative phases; and review phase. This model contributes to developing knowledge in several ways. Its foundation in the theory of physical crime scene investigation is intended to enhance credibility in the eyes of the court. Considering the digital environment as a crime scene rather than simply an object of physical evidence supports a richer and more holistic analysis, and identifies interaction between the physical and digital investigation. The model is abstract enough to be generalized to any investigative situation (Carrier and Spafford 2003, 2004).

6.1 Digital forensics concept models and functional requirements

Descriptive process models, however, are necessarily limited in their ability to suggest a theory of digital forensics that identifies concepts and functional requirements of the discipline. The goal is to develop a conceptual model that is based on more than "investigative experiences and biases" (Carrier and Spafford 2006). A model that succeeds in this will conceptualize the requirements for "forensic soundness," and support the development of procedural methods and tools (Casey 2007).

Rather than propose a model for the forensic process, Sarah Mocas defined a set of organizing principles for the development and evaluation of digital forensics research (2004). She identified five abstractions, or properties, through which the researcher can frame questions, model behaviors and evaluate procedures. Integrity, authentication, reproducibility, non-interference, and minimization also define what properties are necessary and/or sufficient for evidence to be viable in a specific investigative context. These properties are considered within that context, including reasons for the investigation, constraints on its scope, and a set of potential and desired outcomes that provides the framework for the model. The Reasons-Constraints-Outcome framework and the necessary/sufficient digital forensics properties, she claims, can be adapted to any domain.

Michael Andrew has proposed further theoretical considerations (2007). He outlines the overall forensic process as Acquisition-Preservation-Analysis, and focuses in particular on formalizing the analysis phase. Starting with basic system concepts (that the whole is more than the sum of its parts, the whole determines the nature of the parts, the parts cannot be understood if considered in isolation from the whole, and the parts are dynamically interrelated or interdependent), he argues in favour of analysis in context, rather than isolating information items. Starting with two principles of well designed systems – the principle of consistent results (a well designed system will produce consistent results from any given action unless corrupted by an outside force) and the principle of static storage (data at rest will remain at rest unless accessed for a directed purpose), he poses five requirements (stated as laws): association (data must be correctly associated with the processes that created it and the source that initiated the process), context data can only be interpreted correctly in context, internal and external), access (it must be demonstrated that the individual had access to the device at the time the data was created), intent (it must be demonstrated that the data was created as the result of an intentional action taken by the user), validation (the integrity, authenticity, and accuracy of the data must be validated before it can be presented as evidence in support of conclusions and opinions). The parallels with archival science are clear, and discussed below.

6.2 Interdisciplinarity

Legal theory, computer security and information assurance, and computer science (systems architecture and computer history models) have all driven the development of digital forensics. Several writers, however, look beyond digital forensics' traditional partners to find similarities and mutual affordances in other disciplines: information theory (Hama and Pollitt 1996), records management (Irons 2006), archival diplomatics (Duranti 2009; Cohen 2015), and archival science (Kirschenbaum et al. 2010; Duranti and Endicott-Popovsky 2010; John 2012; Dietrich and Adelstein 2015).

Alistair Irons made explicit the parallels and complementarity of digital forensics and records management in his analysis of the principles of computer forensics in the context of record characteristics of authenticity, reliability, integrity and usability. 'Computer forensics', states Irons, 'should be based around the characteristics of good records, levels and nature of access and an indication of the completeness of the records'. (Irons 2006, 107) Likewise, computer forensics techniques can help the records manager monitor the integrity, authenticity, reliability and completeness of records. Irons also proposed that computer forensics could benefit through the application of theoretical models of the record.

In *Digital Forensics and Born Digital Content in Cultural Heritage Collections,* Michael Kirschenbaum, Richard Ovenden, and Gabriela Redwine examine the relevance of digital forensics for archivists, curators, and others working in the field of cultural heritage. One purpose of the report was to promote interdisciplinarity between fields increasingly recognized as having converging interests (2010).

The Digital Records Forensics Project, conducted at the University of British Columbia from 2009 to 2011 and funded by the Social Sciences and Humanities Research Council of Canada studied the challenges presented by digital technology to the records management, archival and legal professions, including the identification of records among all the digital objects produced by complex digital systems, and the determination of their authenticity when they are removed and stored outside of their originating systems. The interdisciplinarity explored by the project is represented in Fig. 1 (Rogers 2010).

One of the research objectives of the DRF project was to develop the theoretical and methodological content of a new discipline, called Digital Records Forensics, resulting from an integration of archival diplomatics,[1] digital forensics, and the law of evidence (Duranti 2009; Rogers 2013). The project also led to a new proposed academic curriculum that weaves the complementary knowledge from archival science and digital diplomatics with digital forensics and information assurance (Duranti and Endicott-Popovsky 2010). A course entitled Digital Diplomatics and Digital Records Forensics (ARST 556H) taught in the Master of Archival Science program at UBC addresses the convergence of digital forensics and archival science for the purpose of furthering digital archival work.

7 Digital forensics and archival diplomatics – pulling it all together

Archival science and digital forensics are, first and foremost, applied sciences. Both evolved out of practice and grew into established professional disciplines by developing theoretical foundations, which then returned to inform and standardize practice. They have roots in law and legal practice, and professionals in both fields are trusted to attest to the identity and integrity of the materials for which they are responsible – they are regarded as experts in the acquisition, interpretation, description and presentation of that material. A significant challenge to both fields, therefore, is the identification of records (archival focus) and evidence (digital forensics focus) in digital systems, establishing their contexts, provenance, relationships, and meaning.

The digital archivist is concerned with identifying records among all the digital objects present in digital media, and assessing their reliability, authenticity, and accuracy. When an archivist acquires records contained in a digital storage device for appraisal and accessioning (ingest) into a repository, it is critical that she be able to identify the records on the device, analyze them to ascertain their provenance, assess their authenticity and accuracy, establish whether there are issues regarding intellectual property or copyright, privileged communication, or personal information that will be subject to redaction, data privacy protection, or access restrictions. The digital forensics investigator is similarly concerned with identifying digital objects that may serve as

---

[1] Diplomatics is a discipline first developed in the seventeenth century to assess the authenticity of documents, taught in faculties of law and archival science in Europe, and subsequently applied to modern office documents and digital records (Duranti and Thibodeau, 2006).

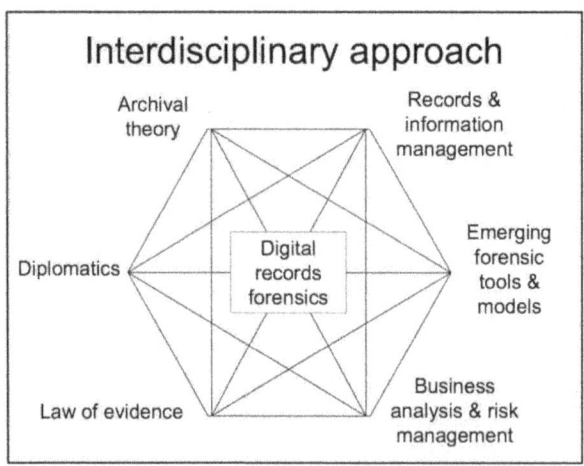

Fig. 1 Interdisciplinary approach

evidence of criminal or other activity, and analyzing those objects for their evidentiary capacity, that is, their attribution, integrity, and verifiability. Privileged information must also be identified and protected from unauthorized disclosure (Rogers 2013).

Archivists and digital forensics practitioners share the challenges of appraising and analyzing large volumes of digital material. The core archival functions are appraisal and acquisition, arrangement and description, retention and preservation, management and administration, reference and access (Duranti and Giovanni 2015). The ability to preserve digital records that are authentic and reliable over time and across technological change also depends on the circumstances of records creation and record keeping, thereby extending the archival functions across the entire life of the records. This compares with the functions of digital forensics practice: identification, preservation, collection, examination, analysis, presentation and decision (Palmer 2001). At the root of each is investigative research into the material in question – namely the story revealed by analyzing the digital objects and traces of activities, and the relationships of those objects and traces to the actors and actions that gave rise to them.

The archival first principle is *respect des fonds*, essentially equivalent to the principle of provenance and the principle of original order. These principles demand that the records of one creator are maintained separately from another creator, and that a creator's records are kept in the same order in which they were created and used. When they are respected and articulated through archival description, the authenticity of the record aggregations is protected (MacNeil 1995, 2005; Millar 2006). A presumption of authenticity derives from the context of creation and chain of custody, and the processes of establishing intellectual, administrative, and usually, physical control – appraisal, accessioning and archival arrangement. Description is the primary means of illuminating provenancial and contextual relationships that are at the heart of the principles.

Archival description is the expression of the essence of the archivist's accountability, which confers authority, and in court, affords the status of expert witness. Records offered in evidence must be authenticated, and the archivist who is responsible for the records has that authority. By exerting intellectual control over the records through archival description, the archivist becomes accountable for the records and can speak with authority to their identity and integrity—to their trustworthiness. The archivist is recognized as a trusted custodian and confers trustworthiness on the records by virtue of his or her accountability.

The digital forensics practitioner, confronted with a digital crime scene, may be compared with the archivist, who, when processing a new acquisition by the archives, must approach the task of arrangement and then description of these records, which have been removed intellectually and physically from their creator, that is from their functional, documentary and technological context, and placed in the context of the investigation. We have seen that accountability is intertwined with responsibility, authority, and trust (Millar 2006). Just as the archivist acquires the status of trusted custodian through accountability for the records, digital forensics practitioners are called upon as expert witnesses to account for and report their investigative process.

Digital forensics practitioners act as expert witnesses because of their accountability to the investigative process. They are bound, however, by a different set of demands than archivists: theirs is scientific testimony given to justify their tools and techniques in identifying and authenticating digital evidence. Scientific testimony may be tested for credibility in a *Daubert* hearing.

Digital objects are examined not as documentary residue of business activity, but as latent trace evidence of digital processes. They are bound not by business rules and procedures, but by 'the physics of digital information', which governs 'the artificial digital world of bits and machines that operate on them' (Cohen 2011). It is the physics of digital information that is the scientific grounding of the digital forensics practitioner.

The authority conferred upon these professionals has different roots deriving from the particular ontological view of the evidence they seek to authenticate. However, despite the different vantage points of the archival and digital forensic analysis of digital evidence, the goals are the same: to identify and authenticate digital evidence. To that end, the examiners from either profession must establish, document, and be prepared to justify, or account for, the identity, integrity, and context of the evidence and their role in discovering and describing it. As Cohen has shown, there can be a crosswalk drawn between the concepts of diplomatics and the elements of forensic examination (Cohen 2011).

Records are considered trustworthy if they can be shown to be authentic (by establishing their identity and assessing their integrity), reliability, and accuracy. In the digital environment, archivists benefit from also incorporating concepts from digital forensics: concepts of authentication, reproducibility, non-interference, and minimization (Mocas 2004), and laws of association, context, access, intent, and validation (Andrew 2007).

References

Andrew, M. (2007). Defining a process model for forensic analysis of digital devices and storage media. In Northwest security institute and pacific northwest national laboratory (Eds.), *SADFE 2007: Second International Workshop on Systematic Approaches to Digital Forensic Engineering: Proceedings: 10–12 April* 2007, *Seattle, Washington, USA*, 16–30. Los Alamitos, Calif: IEEE Computer Society.

Association of Chief Police Officers (ACPO). (2012). *Good practice guide for computer-based electronic evidence, v. 5.* Retrieved from https://www.7safe.com/about-7Safe/downloads/acpo-guidelines.

Beebe, N., & Clark, J. G. (2005). A hierarchical, objectives-based framework for the digital investigations process. *Digital Investigation, 2*(2), 147–167.

Blackwell, C. (2011). A framework for investigating questioning in incident analysis and response. In G. Peterson & S. Shenoi (Eds.), *Advances in digital forensics VII* (pp. 23–34). IFIP AICT 361. IFIP International Federation for Information Processing.

Carrier, B. (2003a). Defining digital forensic examination and analysis tools using abstraction layers. *International Journal of Digital Evidence, 1*(4), 1–12.

Carrier, B. (2003b). Open source digital forensics tools: The Legal Argument. www.digital-evidence. org/papers/opensrc_legal.pdf.

Carrier, B., & Spafford, E. (2003). Getting physical with the digital investigation process. *International Journal of Digital Evidence, 2*(2), 1–20.

Carrier, B., & Spafford, E. (2004). An event-based digital forensics investigative framework. Presented at DFRWS 2004, Baltimore, MD. http://www.digital-evidence.org/papers/dfrws_event.pdf. Accessed 6 Jan 2017.

Carrier, B., & Spafford E.H. (2006). Categories of digital investigation analysis techniques based on the computer history model. *Digital Investigation, 3*, (Supp 1), 121–130.

Casey, E. (2007). What does 'forensically sound' really mean? *Digital Investigation, 4*(2), 49–50.

Charters, I. (2009). The evolution of digital forensics: Civilizing the cyber frontier. http://www. guerilla-ciso.com/wp-content/uploads/2009/01/the-evolution-of-digital-forensics-ian-charters.pdf. Accessed 21 April, 2018.

Ciardhuáin, S. (2004). An extended model of cybercrime investigations. *International Journal of Digital Evidence, 3*(1), 1–22.

Cohen, F. (2011). Digital forensic evidence examination. 3rd ed. Livermore, CA: Fred Cohen & Associates.

Cohen, F. (2015). Digital Diplomatics and forensics: Going forward on a global basis. *Records Management Journal, 25*(1), 21–44. https://doi.org/10.1108/RMJ-03-2014-0016.

Collier, P. A., & Spaul, B. J. (1992). A forensic methodology for countering computer crime. *Artificial Intelligence Review, 6*, 203–215.

Diamond, E. (1994). The archivist as forensic scientist—seeing ourselves in a different way. *Archivaria, 38*, 139–154.

DiClemente, A., Horvath, M., & Pollitt, M. (2004). Digital evidence-a review: 2001–2004. *Proceedings of the 14th International Forensic Science Symposium*, 412–549. Lyon, France. https://pdfs.semanticscholar. org/6d39/4c44dc354e90986ed14c56cbf13e66905a7d.pdf. Accessed 21 April, 2018.

Dietrich, D., & Adelstein, F. (2015). Archival science, digital forensics, and new media art. *Digital Investigation, 14*, 137–145. https://doi.org/10.1016/j.diin.2015.05.004.

Duranti, L. (1996). *Archival science. Encyclopedia of Library and Information Science* (pp. 1–19). New York, Basel, Hong Kong: Marcel Dekker.

Duranti, L. (2009). From digital Diplomatics to digital records forensics. *Archivaria, 68*, 39–66.

Duranti, L., & Endicott-Popovsky, B. (2010). Digital records forensics: A new science and academic program for forensic readiness. *Journal of Digital Forensics, Security and Law, 5*(2), 1–12.

Duranti, L., & Giovanni, M. (2015). The archival method: Rediscovering a research tradition. In A. Gilliland, S. McKemmish, & A. Lau (Eds.), *Research in the archival multiverse* (pp. 75–95). Melbourne: Monash Publishing.

Duranti, L., & Thibodeau, K. (2006). The concept of record in interactive, experiential and dynamic environments: The view of InterPARES. *Archival Science, 6*(1), 13–68.

Eastwood, T. (1994). What is archival theory and why is it important? *Archivaria, 37*, 122–130.

Garfinkel, S. (2010). Digital forensics research: The next 10 years. *Digital Investigation, 7*, 64–73. https://doi.org/10.1016/j.diin.2010.05.009.

Hama, G., & Pollitt, M. (1996, August). Data reduction - refining the sieve. Presented at *International Conference on Computer Evidence*. Melbourne, Australia: IOCE. www.digitalevidencepro. com/Resources/Sieve1.pdf. Accessed 21 April, 2018.

Ieong, R. (2006). FORZA – Digital forensics investigation framework that incorporate legal issues. *Digital Investigation, 3*(1), 29–36.

Internet / Home - INTERPOL. (n.d.). Accessed March 1, 2018. https://www.interpol.int/.

Irons, A. (2006). Computer forensics and records management – compatible disciplines. *Records Management Journal, 16*(2), 102–112. https://doi.org/10.1108/09565690610677463.

John, J. (2012). Digital forensics and preservation. Digital preservation coalition. http://www.dpconline. org/component/docman/doc_download/810-dpctw12-03pdf. Accessed 21 April, 2018.

Kenneally, E. (2001). Gatekeeping out of the box: Open source software as a mechanism to assess reliability for digital evidence. *Virginia Journal of Law and Technology, 13*, www.vjolt.net/vol6/issue3/v6i3-a13-Kenneally.html.

Kirschenbaum, M., Ovenden, R., & Redwine, G. (2010). *Digital forensics in born digital cultural heritage collections.* Washington, D.C.: Council on Library and Information resources.

Lee, C. (2012). Archival application of digital forensics methods for authenticity, description and access provision. *Comma, 2012*(2), 133–140. https://doi.org/10.3828/comma.2012.2.14.

MacNeil, H. (1995). Metadata strategies and archival description: Comparing apples to oranges. *Archivaria, 39*, 22–31.

MacNeil, H. (2005). Picking our text: Description, authenticity, and the archivist as editor. *The American Archivist, 68*(2), 264–278.

Marsico, C. (2005). Computer evidence v. Daubert: The coming conflict. Purdue University. https://www.cerias.purdue.edu/apps/reports_and_papers/view/2819/.

Menne-Haritz, A. (1994). Appraisal or documentation: Can we appraise archives by selecting content? *The American Archivist, 57*(3), 528–542.

Millar, L. (2006). An obligation of trust: Speculations on accountability and description. *The American Archivist, 69*(1), 60–78.

Mocas, S. (2004). Building theoretical underpinnings for digital forensics research. *Digital Investigation, 1*(1), 61–68.

Noblett, M. G., Pollitt, M., & Presley, L. A. (2000). Recovering and examining computer forensic evidence. *Forensic Science Communications, 2*(4) http://www.ncjrs.gov/App/publications/abstract.aspx?ID=186015. Accessed 16 Feb 2019.

Palmer, G. (2001). A road map for digital forensic research. DFRWS Technical Report. http://www.dfrws.org/2001/dfrws-rm-final.pdf.

Pollitt, M. (1995a). Principles, practices, and procedures: An approach to standards in computer forensics. Presented at *Second International Conference on Computer Evidence.* Baltimore, Maryland: IOCE. www.digitalevidencepro.com/Resources/Principles.pdf. Accessed May 17, 2018.

Pollitt, M. (1995b). Computer forensics: An approach to evidence in cyberspace. In Wakid, S. and Davis, J., Eds. *Proceedings of the 18th International Systems Security Conference*, (pp. 487–91). Baltimore, Maryland: NIST. https://csrc.nist.gov/CSRC/media/Publications/conference-paper/1995/10/10/proceedings-of-the-18th-nissc-1995/documents/1995-18th-NISSC-proceedings-vol-1.pdf. Accessed 21 April 21, 2018.

Pollitt, M. (2001). Report on digital evidence. Lyon, France. http://citeseerx.ist.psu.edu/viewdoc/download?doi=10.1.1.304.8748&rep=rep1&type=pdf. Access 21 April, 2018.

Pollitt, M. (2003). Who Is SWGDE and what is the history? https://www.swgde.org/pdf/2003-01-22%20SWGDE%20History.pdf. Accessed 21 April, 2018.

Pollitt, M. (2010). A history of digital forensics. *IFIP Advances in Information and Communication Technology, 337*, 3–15. https://doi.org/10.1007/978-3-642-15506-2_1.

Reedy, P. Diplock, B., & Dunlop, M. (2007). Digital evidence-a review: 2004–2007. *Fifteenth International Forensic Science Symposium* (pp. 414-36). Lyon, France.

Reith, M., Carr, C., & Gunsch, G. (2002). An examination of digital forensic models. *International Journal of Digital Evidence 1*(3). https://utica.edu/academic/institutes/ecii/publications/articles/A04A40DC-A6F6-F2C1-98F94F16AF57232D.pdf. Accessed 21 April, 2018.

Rogers, C. (2010, June). *Digital records forensics: Preliminary findings. Presented at the Association of Canadian Archivists.* Canada: Halifax.

Rogers, C. (2013). Digital records forensics: Integrating archival science into a general model of the digital forensics process. *Proceedings of the Second International Workshop on Cyberpatterns: Unifying Design Patterns with Security, Attack and Forensic Patterns*, C. Blackwell (Ed.), 4–21. Oxford, UK: Oxford Brookes University.

Rogers, C., & John, J. (2013). Shared perspectives, common challenges: A history of Digital Forensics & Ancestral Computing for digital heritage. In *In The Memory of the World in the Digital Age: Digitization and Preservation (pp. 314–36). Vancouver, BC: UNESCO* http://iibi.unam.mx/archivistica/UNESCO%202013%20MOW%20vancouver%20declaration.pdf. Accessed 21 April, 2018.

Selamat, S., Yusof, R., & Sahib, S. (2008). Mapping process of digital forensic investigation framework. *IJCSNS International Journal of Computer Science and Network Security, 8*(10), 163–169.

Stoll, C. (1989). The cuckoo's egg: Tracking a spy through the maze of computer espionage. Doubleday. http://bayrampasamakina.com/tr/pdf_stoll_4_1.pdf. Accessed 21 April, 2018.

SWGDE, & IOCE. (2000). Digital evidence: Standards and principles. *Forensic Science Communications* *2*(2). http://www.fbi.gov/about-us/lab/forensic-science-communications/fsc/april2000/swgde.htm/. Accessed 21 April, 2018.

Whitcomb, C. (2002). An historical perspective of digital evidence: A forensic Scientist's view. *International Journal of Digital Evidence 1*(1). http://www.utica.edu/academic/institutes/ecii/publications/articles/9C4 E695B-0B78-1059-3432402909E27BB4.pdf. Accessed 21 April, 2018.

International Journal of Digital Humanities (2019) 1:29–46
https://doi.org/10.1007/s42803-019-00003-x

RESEARCH ARTICLE

The .txtual condition, .txtual criticism and .txtual scholarly editing in Spanish philology

Bénédicte Vauthier[1]

Published online: 5 March 2019
© Springer Nature Switzerland AG 2019

Abstract

The impact of New Technologies on writing proccess is not new at all. This digital revolution first resulted in the appearance of new text formats and the development of an ad hoc literary theory. In Angloamerican area, this revolution made philologists and patrimonial institutions reflect on the necessity of developing formats of study, edition and perennial conservation of these new formats of digital texts. What is the reason for such a delay in these disciplines that can be observed in Europe? Why can we say that *digital forensics* and *media archaeology* (Kirschenbaum) are not trasnational disciplines? In this paper, I assess the impact in Europe and in Angloamerican area of *.Txtual condition*. Moreover, I make a contrast between these conclusions and the answers given by three emblematic writers of the 'new Spanish narrative' to a survey about ways of managing and preserving digital files.

Keywords Spanish .txtual condition · .txtual criticism · .txtual editing · New comparative filology · Spanish filology

1 The .txtual condition and .txtual criticism in Spanish philology

A little more than ten years ago, in June 2007, around forty representatives of contemporary book culture—among them, authors, critics, journalists, publishers and booksellers—gathered in Seville at the initiative of a prestigious Spanish publishing house, Seix Barral, and the José Manual Lara Foundation. The aim of the three-day summit and its round-tables was to exchange ideas about and survey into the achievements, objectives and innovations of a

Chapter 3 was originally published as Vauthier, B. International Journal of Digital Humanities (2019) 1: 29–46. https://doi.org/10.1007/s42803-019-00003-x.

Dedicated to Thorsten Ries for his interest in my work.

Also dedicated to Agustín Fernández Mallo, Robert Juan-Cantavella and Vicente Luis Mora, without whose generous support this study would not have the same relevance.

✉ Bénédicte Vauthier
    benedicte.vauthier@rom.unibe.ch

[1]   Institut für spanische Sprache und Literaturen, Universität Bern (Schweiz), Bern, Switzerland

group of writers who were born between the early 1960s and mid-1970s and began publishing their work in the early years of this millennium.

Although, for many of these writers, the meeting in Seville was not strictly speaking a debut—and neither were they members of the so-called "Nocilla generation", which, nonetheless, became synonymous for the group after the event[1]—it was a fortunate choice of timing to bring together such a heterogenous group of authors. By biological age, they could belong to different generations, but this meeting proved to be the foundational act of the "New Spanish Narrative."[2]

While a reader of their works will notice many compositional, stylistic and thematic differences between these authors, there are two features many of their works have in common and which have received scholarly attention in the form of doctoral theses (Calles Hidalgo 2011; Barker 2011; Pantel 2012; del Pozo Ortea 2012; Saum-Pascual 2012): hypertextuality, on the one hand, and inter-, multi- or transmediality on the other. As is widely known, both concepts have been usually linked to the impact that new media has had on literary production and creative writing and this has most prominently been reflected in the pioneering and internationally well-known studies by Bolter, Landow, Ryan, Douglas, etc.

Compared to the most influential works in the Anglo-American area (Michael Joyce's *afternoon, a story*, Stuart Moulthrop's *Victory Garden*) Spanish electronic literature has received less scholarly attention so far (Pérez 2015), especially in Spain. This might be understandable in some cases with respect to limited innovative aesthetic quality and the ephemeral character of the digital works in question. As a matter of fact, several works of Spanish electronic literature which have been collected, preserved and presented in a section of the institutional online portal Virtual Library Miguel de Cervantes are not available online anymore.[3]

There is a risk that some of the "expanded literature" texts—or *exonovels*, to use the neologism one of the New Spanish Narrative's most famous representatives coined (Fernández Mallo 2012: 67)—will sooner or later be confronted with digital obsolescence. The second part of this article discusses this problem, but will also address another issue. I will look beyond contemporary literary studies, focused on the interpretation of singular authorised texts published under their author's name, which often fail to recognise the multitude of reprints,[4] and instead turn to questions of the (digital)

---

[1] The label "Nocilla generation" refers to the title of a novel by Agustín Fernández Mallo called *Nocilla Dream*. Nuria Azancot reused part of the title in an article published just a few weeks after the meeting (07.07.2007). Other labels used - related to monographs, anthologies or compilations - are "afterpop", "mutant", "last generation Spanish narrative", "pangeic", "postmodern", "New Spanish Narrative", "post-humanist narrative".

[2] According to the literature, the number of writers that would be part of the group varies from six to twenty. Among them, it is common to find Lolita Bosch, Javier Calvo, Harkaitz Cano, Jorge Carrión, Diego Doncel, Domenico Chiappe, Álvaro Colomer, Juan Francisco Ferre, Javier Fernández, Agustín Fernández Mallo, Eloy Fernández Porta, Salvador Gutiérrez Solís, Robert Juan-Cantavella, Milo Krmpotic, Gabi Martinez, Javier Moreno, Vicente Luis Mora, Sofia Rhei, Isaac Rosa, Mario Cuenca Sandaval, Germán Sierra, Manuel Vilas, etc.

[3] Literatura Electrónica Hispánica 2018 Fundación Biblioteca Virtual Miguel de Cervantes (Ed.): Biblioteca Virtual Miguel de Cervantes. URL: http://www.cervantesvirtual.com/bib/portal/literaturaelectronica/obras. html (accessed 06/27/18).

[4] An exception is the three volumes: *Nocilla Dream* (2006), *Nocilla Experience* (2008) and *Nocilla Lab* (2009) that form a trilogy, republished under the common title *Proyecto Nocilla* (2013).

writing process, scholarly editions (of born-digital material) and (born-digital) archives.[5] In this area, the landscape of European research, especially for Spanish studies,
seems to offer less encouraging prospects.

It is clear that European research in Digital Humanities lags behind its counterpart in
the Anglo-American world for reasons that are not easy to overcome. Matthew
Kirschenbaum's concept of the ".txtual condition" in the digital age does indeed apply
to many European writers—Spanish in particular—and I will refer to three of them in
the second part of my study: "In the specific domain of the literary, a writer working
today will not and cannot be studied in the future in the same way as writers of the past,
because the basic material evidence of their authorial activity—manuscripts and drafts,
working notes, correspondence, journals—is, like all textual production, increasingly
migrating to the electronic realm" (Kirschenbaum 2013: par. 4). However, very little, if
any, scholarly attention has been paid since to this change that will affect *in crescendo*
four branches of literary studies—analytical bibliography, philology, scholarly editing
and interpretive studies—when it comes to the literary production of the twenty-first
century. It is useless to bemoan the situation. It is much more interesting to try to
understand the causes and to examine the difficulties, or perhaps the resistances, that
will have to be overcome in Europe in order to create the digital humanities community
that Kirschenbaum has called for.

2 Digital forensics: a transnational discipline?

In the context of Anglo-American academia and research, authors, textual scholars,
editors and, above all, cultural and memory institutions work hand in hand to meet the
".txtual Condition" (Kirschenbaum 2013: par 38). Regarding European countries where
English is not the official, but rather a second language, the delay of GLAM institutions
(galleries, libraries, archives, and museums), the lack of digital edition projects that are
comparable to the pioneering work in the Anglo-American area[6] and the scarce
curiosity of researchers for the impact of the digital transformation on literary ways
of writing that Kirschenbaum exhibits in *Track Changes* (2016) cannot be properly
explained unless we make explicit how an apparently transnational discipline—the
adaptation of *computer forensics* methods in archival science and philology—is rooted
in the specific philological tradition of Anglo-American analytical bibliography and
textual criticism. This is probably the key reason for the success of this approach.

> Media archaeology [...] offers one set of critical tools for coming to terms with
> the .txtual condition. Another, of course, is to be found in the methods and
> theoretical explorations of textual scholarship, the discipline from which McGann
> launched his ongoing program to revitalize literary studies by restoring to it a

---

[5] *Text* in the broad sense of the word, that is, as defined by Donald McKenzie: "I define 'texts' to include
verbal, visual, oral, and numeric data, in the form of maps, prints, and music, of archives of recorded sound, of
films, videos, and any computer-stored information, everything in fact from epigraphy to the latest forms of
discography" (1999: 13).

[6] In *Mechanisms*, Kirschenbaum cites, as a representative sample button, *The Electronic Beowulf*, *The
Canterbury Tales Project*, *The William Blake Archive* and *The Rossetti Archive* (2008: 16 note 26).

sense of its roots in philological and documentary forms of inquiry. As I've argued at length elsewhere, the field that offers to most immediate analog to bibliography and textual criticism in the electronic sphere is computer forensics, which deals in authenticating, stabilizing, and recovering digital data. […] Digital forensics is the point of practice at which media archaeology and digital humanities intersect (Kirschenbaum 2013: par. 31).

The double philological root to which Kirschenbaum refers is undoubtedly at the center of the success and fruitful development of this research paradigm within the digital humanities in his field of research. However, it might be more straightforward to say that the analogue precursor of the adaptation of *computer forensics* as a tool in born-digital philology was McKenzie's "*heterodox bibliography* or *sociology of texts*" and McGann's "*New Textualism or Modern Textual Criticism*". The reference to Jerome McGann, who is given the honor of having revitalised literary studies, may be seen as proof of this assertion.

In textual criticism and scholarly editing of *modern* English literature texts—the stress on "modern" is essential here—the names Donald McKenzie, "heterodox" bibliographer (Darnton 2003: 43) and book historian, and Jerome McGann, American critic and philologist of modern texts, are often mentioned together and may seem synonymous with the paradigm shift that took place in literary disciplines during the mid-1980s (Greetham 2013: 37, Sutherland 2013: 57; Shillingsburg 1996: 24). McGann's and McKenzie's books *A Critique of Modern Textual Criticism* (McGann 1983, 1st ed., 1991, 2nd ed.) and *Bibliography and the Sociology of Texts* (McKenzie 1986, 1st ed., 1999, 2nd ed., the result of the *Panizzi Lectures,* McKenzie 1985), published within a narrow time frame, have contributed to this misconception. The fact that the two authors sought to distance themselves almost at the same time—though they did it regarding different corpus and interests—from the "Greg-Bowers-Tanselle theory", which at the time was the predominant paradigm in the field of textual criticism and scholarly editing of premodern texts (Lernout 1996), may also have contributed to the shakeup of the discipline.[7]

A survey into the academic reception of the two scholars not only in the Anglo-American sphere, but also in European research, reveals, however, that things are not simple at all, and neither their names nor their proposals are interchangeable. McKenzie is an undisputed authority on Anglo-American bibliographical research. However, it is the name and the work of Jerome McGann that has become the most emblematic reference among the representatives of *New Textualism*. His book *A Critique of Modern Textual Criticism* became part of the school's "canon" (Greetham in Shillingsburg 1996: vii). The earlier *The Textual Condition* (1991) is one of the most frequently cited works among researchers interested modern scholarly editing, such as *Scholarly Editing in the Computer Age* (Shillingsburg 1996), *The Fluid Text. A Theory of Revision and Editing for Book and Screen* (Bryant 2002) and the *.txtual Condition* (Kirschenbaum 2013), to mention just three important works by McGann's followers.

---

[7] In his assessment of Anglo American textual criticism, Lernout (1996) suggests that McGann calls into question Greg's "base text" theory and the concept of "authorial aim" later introduced by Bowers in the context of his philological study on manuscripts and modern texts. McKenzie, however, tries to widen the field of analytical bibliography with his new definition of "text" and his reflection on the production and spreading of printing history.

In the part of Europe where English is not a lingua franca, however—particularly in Romance-speaking Europe (e.g. France, Italy, Spain)—with the exception of English literature studies, the work of McGann is hardly known, while "the second McKenzie" (Willison 2002: 204) enjoys international reputation throughout Europe, although more among book historians than among modern philologists. The French book historian Roger Chartier is the one who mainly disseminated McKenzie's work and ideas in the European context.[8] The absence of a modern philology in France and Spain at the time allowed Chartier to leave out the dominant bibliographical facet in the New Zealander's work by skipping the outset of his reflection to highlight the second key idea[9] underlying McKenzie's *Panizzi Lectures*: the *material* and *social* dimensions of *text*, which led to his own *history of books, reading and readers*. In this way, Chartier did away with the strong link between librarianship and bibliography, between archives and editing, in McKenzie's work and diluted his very early concerns about the emergence of new technologies that were substantially affecting the understanding of text and its circulation (Vauthier 2018a, b).

> These lectures were conceived and prepared, not as a text destined for print, but as lectures occasions. The challenge, as I saw it, was to sketch an extended role for bibliography at a time when traditional book forms must share with many new media their prime function of recording and transmitting texts.

could we read in the preface to the first edition of his book (1986: IX). In its second edition, following a review of McGann's (1988) response and, thanks to Chartier's work, the unexpected international reception of the book in Europe (McKenzie 1986: 23; 1999: 6); he resumes:

> The familiar historical processes by which, over the centuries, texts have changed their form and content have now accelerated to a degree which makes the definition and location of textual authority barely possible in the old style. Professional librarians, under pressure from irresistible technological and social changes, are redefining their discipline in order to describe, house, and access

---

[8] McKenzie's book, *Bibliography and sociology of texts*, was translated to French in 1991, to Italian in 1998 and to Spanish in 2005. In all three cases, translations were accompanied by a substantial prologue by Chartier, who has channeled the author's reception, very particularly in France and then in Spain, in the somewhat exclusive direction of the history of the book (Vauthier 2018a).

[9] These three ideas are: 1. "an extended role for bibliography", as it is shown in the first lines of the preface that follows. In the second paragraph, McKenzie specifies: "there were *two other considerations* which it seemed timely to voice" (1986, ix, italics are mine).

2. The acknowledgment of historical bibliography as a discipline in itself: "Historical bibliography (as distinct from descriptive and analytical bibliography and stemmatics) has gained acceptance as a field of study" and

3. The essential instability of the text and the impossibility of fixing it for good: "Definitive editions have come to seen an impossible ideal" and "each version has some claim to be edited in its own right" (1986, 2).

These three ideas clearly show McKenzie's wide oversight, as bibliographer and book historian. Chartier is a book historian, not a philologist, and consequently only refers to the first and second idea.

sounds, static and moving images with or without word, and a flow of computer-stored information (1991: 1).

These two dimensions—the impact of new technologies and the necessary renovation of the traditional *bibliography*—explain the honored place that Donald McKenzie now occupies among Anglo-American scholars of modern text, particularly in the works of McGann and Kirschenbaum.[10] Although in *The .txual Condition* (2013: par. 7, 31 and 41) and in *Mechanisms* (2008: 9) Kirschenbaum admits his debt to McGann, in the opening pages of his collective report *Digital Forensics and Born-Digital Content in Cultural Heritage Collections*, he asserts very clearly that the necessary connections and interactions between the world of archives and digital forensics stem from McKenzie's work, particularly from his early attention to new technologies:

> We maintain that such parallels are not coincidental, but rather evidence of something fundamental about the study of the material past, in whatever medium or form. As early as 1985, D. F. McKenzie, in his *Panizzi lectures*, explicitly placed *electronic content* within the purview of bibliography and textual criticism, saying, 'I define *texts* to include verbal, visual, oral, and numeric data, in the form of maps, prints, and music, of archives of recorded sound, of films, videos, and any computer-stored information, everything in fact from epigraphy to the latest forms of discography (1999, 13) (Kirschenbaum et al. 2010: 5).

In the same way, McGann's recent popularity among modern philologists may be a consequence of the fact that he knew how to minimize his first book's precedence to McKenzie's *Panizzi Lectures*, which would be published two years later, and, consequently, could make McKenzie 'the Hero of Our Own Time', that is, the Hero of Scholarly Edition.

> D. F. McKenzie became The Hero of Our Own Time not because he discovered the sociology of the text – we've known about that for a long time. He became The Hero because he knew that *the idea* of the social text *had to be realized as a scholarly edition*.
> Such an edition would be addressing and answering some key – basically philological – questions. Could one develop a model for editing books and material objects rather than just the linguistic phenomena we call texts? To pose that question, as McKenzie did, was to lay *open the true dimensions of what he was after*: a model for editing texts in their contexts (McGann 2013: 281-282, italics are mine).

After having clarified the intrinsic alignment between the adaption of *digital forensics* as a philological and archival scientific method, on the one hand, and the traditions of theory and practice of modern scholarly editing, textual criticism and analytical

---

[10] It is very interesting to note that in the section "The History of the Book" of his review of "Textual Scholarship", Marcus does not mention McKenzie, but only Chartier and Darnton. Instead, he mentions McKenzie along with McGann in the section "Textual Scholarship in Present" (2010).

bibliography in the Anglo-American academia and research, on the other, I turn the scope of this survey back to Europe.

Unlike the Anglo-American context, where authors, textual scholars, publishers and, above all, cultural and memory institutions work hand in hand to meet the ".txtual Condition", the European cultural and research landscape features neither such a clear, nor such an unanimously shared strategy among the involved parties.[11] Moreover, there is no such thing as a standardized "continental" or "European theory of scholarly editing", nor are there language-specific models for scholarly editions (Lernout 2002, 2013; Vauthier 2018a, b). Even TEI encoding and TEI-based editions still face difficulties in establishing a standard model for digital scholarly editions (Marcus 2009: 93–94), which may complicate the long-term preservation of editions.

Last and above all, the idealistic understanding of the modern text that prevails among European philologists and an individualist or romantic concept of *authorship* have been the main factors which impeded studies focused on the materiality of the textual media, on the graphic dimension of prints and books, and on non-authorised or posthumous[12] versions of texts (Vauthier 2017; Vauthier 2018a, b). An article penned by Rüdiger Nutt-Kofoth illustrates this point, which allows me to further detail and expand my above claims regarding the lack of scholarly reception of McGann's work in Europe. In *Editionsphilologie als Mediengeschichte* (*Scholarly Editing as Media History*, Nutt-Kofoth 2006)—the simplicity of the title should be noted as meaningful—a German literary scholar and specialist for scholarly editions invites his colleagues to stop focusing solely on the "linguistic" dimension of the text and instead turn to the concept of "bibliographical orientation"[13] by Peter Shillingsburg (2006: 19), the representative of the *New Anglo-American Textualism*, which, in recent years, has made large efforts to build bridges between the scholars of German and English literature.[14] It is too early to see whether his colleagues will follow this invitation,[15] although it may

---

[11] Kirschenbaum's article illustrates how the invaluable legacy of an author, editor and educator like Deena Larsen, a pioneer of electronic writing, to an institution (the MITH) is not a result of chance, but of friendship that unites the writer to the center and its researchers. That is to say, the same scenario as the one at the origin of the legacy or the sale of working manuscripts of contemporary writers to memory institutions is repeated: Louis Aragon at the *Institut des Textes et Manuscrits Modernes* in Paris, Miguel Ángel Asturias at the Bibliothèque Nationale de France, Friedrich Dürrenmatt in Switzerland. In all three cases, the legacy was made with the explicit desire for exploration and evaluation using latest editing techniques.

[12] The geneticists—members of both French and German schools—have put a lot of emphasis on the materiality and the graphic substance of the drafts, of the *avant-texte*, a characteristic that they have not granted to the text completely (Lebrave, 2009; Mahrer 2017 Reuss 2005). In the same way, even among those who declare to be interested in the process, the death of the author remains an insurmountable frontier (Lebrave, 2009, Mahrer 2017) or remains clearly on the side of the history of reception (Reuss 2005). And that is what the Anglo-Americans question with the idea of "versioning" (Reiman 1987), "fluid text" (Bryant 2002), etc.

[13] "Based in the bibliographical studies of D. F. McKenzie, this orientation enlarges the definition of text to include all aspects of the physical forms upon which the linguistic text is written. This approach does not admit to any parts of the text or of the physical medium to be considered non significant and therefore emendable. [...] all aspects of the physical object that is the book that bear clues to its origins and destinations and social and literary pretentions [...] are text to the bibliographic orientation" (Shillingsburg 1996: 23–24). Two recent books of Italian philology (Cadioli 2012, Italia 2013) also draw attention to the importance of the works of McGann and even more of Peter Shillingsburg.

[14] Like the German editor of *Ulysses*, Hans Walter Gabler, did at his time and like it is still done by Belgian Anglists Geert Lernout and Dirk van Hulle (Lernout 2013: 74–75).

[15] That invitation is the same that Margarita Santos Zas and I made to edit Valle-Inclán (2017).

  Springer

seem unlikely that it will be possible to put an end to the debate about the issue of textual versions that opposes the scholars of German and English literature— an issue that hinges on questions of materiality on the one hand and "authorial intentionality" on the other (Shillingsburg 1996: 99–100).[16] More instructive may be Patrick Sahle's work (2013) on the typology of digital scholarly editions and on the definition of the term "text",[17] in which the historian reflects upon its polysemy and, instead of one definition, proposes a dynamic wheel of terminological perspectives on the term "*text*". In this way, he intends to overcome static definitions that construe "text" in antagonistic terms.

After this overview, in which some light was shed on the specificity of modern textual criticism and scholarly editing of modern texts both in European traditions and in the Anglo-American research context, it is necessary to return to memory institutions and to the urgent issue of the long-term preservation and curatorship of writers' private digital archives.

3 'I unpack my digital library and show you my digital desktop'

In their studies of librarianship and digital curatorship, Becker (2014) and Weisbrod (2015) highlighted the challenges and deficits that research and memory institutions— they take libraries and literary archives in Germany, Austria and Switzerland as an example—need to address in terms of long-term preservation, curatorship and scholarly appreciation of born-digital heritage and digital culture in comparison to memory institutions, archives and research in European countries where English is not the main language spoken. Both books seek to understand how writers write, how they organise their working process, and how they organise and preserve their documents in the digital era. Yet, the question arises: to what extent authors have an interest in and are willing to receive support from memory institutions to ensure long-term preservation of their literary and personal digital archives. Additionally, Dirk Weisbrod complemented the empirical part of his doctoral thesis with in-depth expert interviews with archivists and directors of memory institutions. Both authors in their conclusions put emphasis on the need for archivists to establish contact between memory institutions and likely donors or depositors of private digital archives as early as possible in order to make writers aware of the need and possibilities in place to preserve their published or ongoing work, for instance, in an institutional archive cloud (Weisbrod 2015: 416–453, here 423). In the course of his argument, Weisbrod forges the neologism 'präkustodiale Intervention' (*pre-custodial intervention*), which refers to the intervention of archivists with possible donors or depositors as a preliminary measure to ensure long-term preservation of and access to their archives. This conclusion is very much in line with the institutional collaboration with writers advocated for by Kirschenbaum.

From the more modest academic perspective of a scholar of contemporary Spanish literature, who is not directly connected to particular memory institutions and who does

---

[16] In *From Gutenberg to Google*, Shillingsburg lists the main works of the polemics (2006: 173–174) and Vauthier analyzes some of the editorial implications of the two paradigms (2017 and 2018a).

[17] This polysemy is activated or reactivated, if we consider McKenzie, through the problems of coding. That is, from what new technologies make the editors see.

not feel inclined to acquire *digital forensic* skills anytime soon, I still find it important to scrutinize the implications of the digital media turn for the scholarly edition and interpretation of twenty-first century literature.

It was Jean-Louis Lebrave's research program[18] that guided my steps when examining the hybrid *dossier génétique* of Robert Juan-Cantavella's transmedial novel *El Dorado*, a born-digital novel (Vauthier 2014: 2016). This research program, proposed to the French *critique génétique* by one of its pioneers, put forward his scholarly attention for the changes that the arrival of personal computers on the authors' writing desks meant for their ways of working. Having studied the *dossier génétique* of *El Dorado*, it became very clear to me that the *critique génétique* and scholarly editions of twenty-first century literature will depend on the preservation state of the private digital archives and that these disciplines will have to focus on the question of digital versions and variants—and on the complexity of the problem of the *versions* (Lebrave 2011: 145). Consequently, I contacted three writers of the "New Spanish Narrative" to start a survey about their way of working in the digital age.[19]

Without being aware of it at the time—given that I formulated my questions based on my years-long practice as a scholarly editor of *avant-textes* and modern Spanish texts and not aimed at the interviewees' way of writing—I happened to collect data about their methods of organising their work on the computer and about how they ensured the preservation of their creative work at the same time.

Despite the relatively small sample of three writers, the data collected is relevant in the context of the methodological framework of qualitative survey (Heigham and Croker 2009). Qualitative surveys gather generic information, illustrate general trends, may seek answers to research questions that cannot be operationalised and addressed in quantitative surveys or questions where the personal relationship and the interaction between interviewee and researcher may play a key role. In short, my survey responds to the research question formulated by Becker in her conclusion: "It would be interesting to have a closer look at the youngest generation of writers with respect to their ways of writing" (2014: 70).

In the present case, the answers are interesting with respect to two dimensions. *Nocilla Dream* (2006) by Agustín Fernández Mallo (1967), *El Dorado* (2008) by Robert Juan-Cantavella (1976) and *Alba Cromm* (2010) by Vicente Luis Mora (1970) are among the most representative *inter- and transmedial* works of the New Spanish Narrative. All of them meet the definition of the *exonovel*, a neologism coined by Fernández Mallo.[20]

---

[18] "It would be a much greater matter of urgency to mobilize the energy for approaching two crucial questions for the future of genetic criticism. First, it is about really knowing how the writers appropriate the computer, and which are the effects of this appropriation on writing. The second concerns the way in which geneticists will be able to construct real scientific objects based on data of a new type stored on computer memories" (Lebrave 2010: 155).

[19] The mention of the personal relationship and friendship is necessary, since the access to author files must be approved by the authors and / or beneficiaries. In the case of digital archives, the question of trust placed in the researcher and the confidentiality of the documents to which they may have access is more crucial than ever. I sent the questionnaire "I unpack my digital library and show you my digital desktop" during the Christmas period of 2017 and the answers came between 26th December and 25th January, allowing me to request additional information.

[20] In addition, Agustín Fernández Mallo and Vicente Luis Mora also have articles and / or essays that focus on the impact of new technologies and they maintain blogs of literary criticism.

  Springer

A neologism, based notion of a exoskeleton, *exonovel* refers to "that which sustains to novel, providing internal solidity and protection, without which the novel itself is not possible" (Fernández Mallo 2012: 68). "The model that this Exonovel follows is that of a protective shell on the outside of the book's body, but it is dislocated." (2012: 69) The examples that the author provides between the two definitions refer to digital formats that the three authors use on a regular, varying basis: websites, blogs (either installed for the purpose of a specific writing project or their pre-existing blog), videostreams on YouTube or other platforms, Facebook accounts operated by the authors under their real names or avatars, etc.

With respect to the problem of digital obsolescence of electronic literature, which has already been briefly addressed, this calls for precautionary measures; it is time to be concerned about the impact that a partial or complete loss of the elements "without which, the novel itself is not possible" would have on our understanding of the *exonovels*. I will postpone dealing with the private digital archive, the submerged part of the iceberg— the digital files poised to possibly disappear—and first address the work's digital representation in the public sphere.

Although the *texts* seem to be independent from the "cinematic poetics of their provenance", what would happen if the readers of the *Nocilla* trilogy—*Dream* (2006), *Experience* (2008), *Lab* (2009)—had no longer access to the movie *Proyecto Nocilla*?[21] Accordingly, what would happen to our understanding of the work if Cantavella's *Punk Journalism* website—available on punkjournalism.com—that complements the novel *El Dorado*, the URL of which already no longer corresponds to the one mentioned on the back cover, ceased to exist? Even so, if the two *texts* are autonomous, the parodistic weblog will not stop laying open its deck of cards, revealing to its reader parts of the documentary (digital photos, cutouts of scanned texts, etc.) and critical material (articles of the fictive character published in the press) that the author's alter ego Trebor Escargot used to write his *road movie*, a remake of *Fear and Loathing in Las Vegas* (1998),[22] inspired by Hunter S. Thompson's homonymous 1971 novel (Vauthier 2014, 2016). Furthermore, how could we not think about the implications for our understanding of *Alba Cromm* (2010) if we know that the author's logbook "Alba Cromm y la vida de los Hombres" ("Alba Cromm and the Life of Man"), which Vicente Luis Mora wrote parallel to his novel and to which the novel refers, and also know that this logbook "is only accessible through the *Internet Archive* search engine" (Ilasca 2015: 3)?

These preliminary observations may be sufficient to illustrate why it is essential to understand how writers imagine the future of their work, which they develop, almost exclusively, in digital media. Despite the fact that all of the authors' answers to the various survey blocks are interesting and relevant with regard to the issue, I will not document them in full. It would be impossible for several practical reasons, mainly because some of them are very long and some contain confidential information. Even without having access to the authors' computers or, in this case, their files,[23] but having seen some of their

---

[21] The film is available in the writer's blog "El hombre que salió de la tarta": "Proyecto Nocilla, la película" http://fernandezmallo.megustaleer.com/proyecto-nocilla-la-pelicula/ (accessed 13/2/19).

[22] *El Dorado* is based on both Thompson's novel and the film directed by Terry Gilliam, which stars Jonny Depp as Raoul Duke.

[23] The work on *El Dorado* was realized through the examination of the material collected in a USB key that the author gave me in 2011, along with personal documents (DVD, press, logbook, etc.) kept in a backpack (Vauthier 2014, 2016).

screenshots, it is clear that "access to someone else's computer is like finding a key to their house, with the means to open up the cabinets and cupboards, look inside the desk drawers, peek at the family photos, see what's playing on the stereo or TV, even sift through what's been left behind in the trash" (Kirschenbaum 2013: par. 3). This is the natural and understandable reason for the cautious reluctance of the authors to deposit or donate their private digital archives—and surely one of the greatest challenges for the effort of building future born-digital archives and pre-custodial interventions.

To give an overview, three quarters of the questions asked were related to what Weisbrod describes as "ways of administrating and managing work on the computer" (2015: 391–394, 524–525), one quarter was about the "methods to ensure preservation of the archives" (2015: 383–390, 523–523). To be more precise, I was interested in the following topics:

- how do authors organize their digital work and when do they start organizing their materials;
- the metadata and criteria they use to organize their work (date (timestamps), file name, file type, extension, title, etc.) and their possible variations according to textual genre (narrative, essay, poetry, academic work, etc.);
- the time and naming schemes according to which they create and name versions, the timing and regularity when they do so;
- the possible metadiscursive component ("notes de régie") in their work and the way they use visual queues for marking up certain digital writing operations (color, strikethrough, bold, track changes, etc.);
- the way of documenting their work in the digital environment (type of used sources and consulted documents) and, if applicable, the way this "external" material is stored;
- the possibility of recycling documents, versions, own and/or "external" texts and the concrete way this is done (duplication of documents, copy and paste, etc.);
- the use of the operating system's virtual recycle bin;
- the preservation of digital files and hardware (self-archiving): what do they keep (own and/or external documents, draft versions, final versions etc.)? When does the author self-archive their born-digital materials? Where is the archive stored (cloud, hard disk, hard copy)?;
- their possible representation of a digital library of literary authors that would replace traditional, paper-based archives, and their willingness to deposit or donate their born-digital archives.

Due to my interest in the writing process, on the one hand, and in scholarly editing of both *avant-textes* and authorised texts, on the other, I was especially interested in the way the authors document their own working materials and even more in the management of possible versions of their work. Moreover, their answers to my questions regarding their willingness and interest to deposit or donate their digital files to archives and about their self-archiving practice seemed somewhat unexpected to me, if not alarming. In the following section, before commenting on them altogether and coming to a conclusion, I will reproduce the answers they gave to the first block of questions—documentation and version-management– and I will outline the answers to the second block—archive preservation.

4 "Version"

Staying within the methodological context of a philological study that does not utilise *digital forensics* (Ries 2010), during the interviews, I used the term "version" in the sense of "text" that slightly differs from another text, saved by the author before or after the first text. A comparison between both texts would show a variation, that is, would allow a researcher to reconstruct the writing process.[24]

I did not try to establish a new definition of the term "version" in the context of this study that would allow to include, in a strict sense, textual versions in automatically saved backup or temporary files (von Bülow 2003: 3). I also did not take into account the definition of the term version that Kirschenbaum refers to, for whom "versioning is a hallmark of electronic textual culture—as a thriving industry of content management systems, file comparison utilities, and so-called version control or concurrent versions systems, […]", that is, Concurrent Versions System (CVS) (2008: 197).

I will argue, however, that the issue of "textual identity" still needs to be at the center of scholarly interest. With this clarification, my question and the answers by the three authors are documented below.[25]

Bénédicte Vauthier: What is your criterion to be met in order for you to save a new version or to duplicate the document on which you are currently working? What do you do with previous "versions"? How do you name them? How often do you save what you wrote?

Agustín Fernández Mallo: I create a new file version if the novel is very advanced and it seems that I can open a path that will radically change things. I usually keep the name of the original file and simply add a number at the end. "[...] 2," "[...] 3", etc. Sometimes I specify the reason of the change in order to remember it: "[…]SUBSTITUTIONdistortion". I keep the previous versions, even if I consider them complete failures—you already know my opinion about garbage and about how it can be recycled. Years may pass until I am able to see that something I had discarded was waiting for its natural place somewhere else. (email on 10 January 2018).

Robert Juan-Cantavella: The criterion is not very scientific. I save a new version every time I think that I have made many changes to a document, just in case I may have to review later once more what I discarded. Sometimes a long time passes (months), sometimes very little (days), depending on the changes made. When I return to a version, I usually save a copy of the previous version when I start, because I do not have everything under control; I keep the copy just in case. Previous versions are saved in a dedicated folder. I usually name it "out" or "ant", although it can be a different name. (email on 14 January 2018).

Vicente Luis Mora: [...] When I spoke about versions, I was referring to the same base document with some changes; sometimes with many changes, sometimes with

---

[24] Technically it would have been perhaps more accurate to speak about the "state of a text", to distinguish this *rewriting,* typical of "avant-texte", from another possible *rewriting*, posterior to a first publication.

[25] I translated my questions and their answers to English for this documentation.

fewer. The base document, however, is always the same and therefore keeps the same creation date.[26] Each one of these digital copies that you have is a backup copy of the same document in progress, in continuous change: I enter the document and I add new things, correct or delete some of the old ones, so the document is not the "same" anymore when I finish. This is why I said it is a version, while you called it a "changed draft". When I create a digital copy, it is because I think that I have made enough changes in the original to save it separately, and the chronological order is not marked by the date of the file, but by [...] [the date of the backup]. [This latest file] [...] contains the most recent version of each of the [texts]. [...] As I sometimes change minor things here and there in the document that are difficult to remember, and I hate the "track changes" mechanism of [Microsoft] Word, this is the only solution for me not to get lost: by successively saving multiple backups of the same document while it transforms towards its final "gestalt". It is possible that between these copies there are only a few variants, but all of them together are the writing-polishing process of the novel, the demanding toil of writing, which [...] includes even the proofeading. (email 24 January 2018).

5 Preservation

With a nod to Walter Benjamin's essay "Ich packe meine Bibliothek aus" ("Unpacking My Library", 1931), which is echoed in the title of my questionnaire, I formulated the following two blocks of questions that refer to the preservation of digital files.

1. Where do you keep the digital files related to the writing process of your works? Hard disk, cloud, hardcopy? Do you also keep the external documents that you have consulted?
2. How do you imagine a future library/digital archive of authors (for example, *Residencia de estudiantes*)? Can you imagine depositing or donating the digital archive of your works to a public research library? Do you organize your folders with this in mind when you finish a work? Do you manipulate them? Are there any documents that you would like to delete? When you buy a new computer, do you keep the hard drive of the one you dispose of?

To the first question, the three authors declared that they save their material to one or several hard drives separately. They save their work with varying regularity and, in any case, when they move or migrate to a different computer. Two of them also use email as a save and backup tool and none of them seem to use the cloud. Agustín Fernández Mallo even declared that he does not trust it. In general, working on paper, either for proofreading or to keep hardcopies of their work, has rather a marginal role in their working process. They may use it merely for "more sentimental than practical reasons", as Fernández Mallo puts it, referring to the gallery proofs his publisher sends him. The

---

[26] On my initiative, the author returns to the response he had given me in the first place: "I do not usually make different versions' (26.12.2017), which contradicted the status of a digital file to which I was given access." Specifically he refers to the 28 "digital versions" of the novel *Alba Cromm* that he sent me in 2014 through a cloud. I gave up studying them because I did not find a satisfactory form of exploring the genetic dossier composed of versions which, in addition, as the author suggests, all have the same date of creation.

three writers seem to move only a few of their digital documents to the virtual trash bin, and never while they are still in the writing process. Some of these documents end up bloating folders named "discard", "keep" or "out", which leaves the writer the option to recover or reuse the text, immediately or later. Draft versions may also be found in these folders. They mostly move material to the trash folder that may have turned up in the phase of documentary research, excerpts, early notes and drafts and that is not regarded as useful any longer (downloads, photos, etc.) or which is considered "external" to their work. Agustín Fernández Mallo and Vicente Luis Mora said that they keep their old computers when buying a new one. Vicente Luis Mora said that once when he was abroad (in the USA), he disassembled a laptop "in order to puverise all its main components one by one with a hammer" as a measure of destroying his data. In addition to laptops, he also has a personal desktop computer which serves as a "method of general physical backup of everything."

The answers referring to their interest or willingness to deposit or donate their digital archive to a library that ensures their preservation cannot be easily summarized, nor do they show an unified tendency. Agustín Fernández Mallo said that he imagined "a library in which the digital and the analogue are perfectly intermeshed, what I call Postdigitalism: I organize the folders thinking about my personal organization and nothing else." Robert Juan-Cantavella imagines "a library that is accessible from computers. I do not know whether one would be required to enter a physical space (a building) to go and consult them. I would not donate the digital working documents of my books to a library or to any other type of institution. When I finish a work, I do not organize the materials thinking about any later external research consultation. There are usually no documents that I want to eliminate more than others." As for Vicente Luis Mora, he seemed to doubt that there will be such libraries "when I will be older", imagining, in addition, a careful process of selection of "writers who wish to be included in their archive". However, he expressed his concern about the idea that "textgenetic researchers like me" could dig into his computer and into the drafts of his works, with which, even when finished, he is usually not satisfied. Hence, he declares: "you may be able to understand my feelings about the materials I have put aside. I guess, I will make many things disappear that would interest you, although I will keep others because the love for the work that took place during the consecutive drafts does not allow me to get rid of them." Having documented these answers by the authors, I would like to conclude by returning to the question of born-digital and the scholarly edition.

6 .txtual editing

Anyone who knows anything about digital files and is familiar with the concerns of writers —and even more those of their relatives—about the idea that researchers will search through their drafts as they please, have access to private materials, potentially reveal well-guarded or forgotten secrets, will understand certain fears triggered by the idea of delivering not just previously selected drafts and prints, but also the key to their digital "home" to unknown philologists, who would use *forensic methods* in order to access those digital secrets.

Regardless whether out of fear, lack of confidence or interest, if the artists of the 20th and twenty-first century do not deposit or donate their digital archives to professional memory institutions or take curatorial measures in order to preserve them, an important resource for understanding the works of this era would be lost. They would end up only printed and published, making them appear curiously single or decontextualised if we think of the heterogeneous modern archives that may consist of drafts, notes, gallery proofs, prints, annotated books, correspondences, photos, etc.

The apparent reluctance towards the archives of the future on the side of those authors who turned to and embraced the new media and their technologies to the extent of even becoming strongholds of the worldview of a connected society seems somewhat puzzling.

If these authors did not give researchers access to the materials and traces of the creation of their works, geneticists and philologists would have to, like other critics, turn to texts published in book format in the future—e.g. in the form of works reedited and republished by the authors themselves. The majority of scholars, who do not seem to feel much curiosity for the unpublished, archived part of the work, usually accept this situation and base their work on the texts that circulate in the public realm. Without reiterating the interpretation problem posed by *transmedia* works here, it obvious that failing to apply curatorial measures would risk losing the published, and even more these works' unpublished parts and materials, rendering their historical record incomplete, historically inaccurate and potentially incomprehensible.

In cases where authors give philologists and textual geneticists access to the folders of one or more of their works, e.g. via a pen drive or their cloud account containing a complete record of unaltered documents that could belong to the constellation of the works, the challenge for the researcher with standard user skills will be to determine the possible or actual number of textual states or versions of the work exist. Even if we content ourselves with the versions saved voluntarily by the authors, we could see that they do not hesitate to duplicate the most complete version of the text in order to avoid regrets in case they have to "come back" to a previous one. Although this duplication is not merely mechanical, it is – from a *critique génétique* perspective—a fundamentally different process compared to the isolated revision and the revision by rewriting of a text in the analogue medium.

In addition to this challenge, there are two other problems to be addressed: first, as the authors do not see their desktop full of drafts, they tend to avoid disposing of their things, which raises the issue of textual garbage and recycling that some of them have inscribed at the center of their work—this is, for instance, the case with Fernández Mallo (2009: 105–119) and Mora (2007: 29–31, 184–188). The second difficulty is related to the size of the digital files of narrative works: the systematic analysis of these is impossible without the aid of text collation tools such as included in Juxta, MEDITE, CollateX, iTeal. I would like to highlight a conclusion drawn by Lebrave at the end of his review of the Kirschenbaum's and Ries' work: "It is very likely that genetic *forensics* has to renounce being a poetic of processes and instead will content itself with being a poetic of transitions between textual states" (2010: 145). I think this is accurate.

However, as I do not want to give in to pessimism (Lebrave 2010: 145), I hope that the unexpected multiplication of "versions" or "states" of a text with which a researcher is confronted when accessing a digital archive, will prove an invitation for them to address the question of "textual identity" under a new digital perspective. Faced with "different states of what we *can suppose to be the same text*, with all the epistemic difficulties posed by the problem of simultaneously identical and different texts" (Ganascia and Lebrave 2009: 74, [italics mine]), it is time to *stop supposing* and start investigating this theoretical issue. However, it is necessary to investigate it before launching a digital collation tool (Mahrer 2017: 36–37) or before making available for the reader or user all the versions of a text to be edited (Bryant 2002: 87). To argue that beyond their differences two texts that can be compared, which is to say textually aligned, must be considered *together* in a genetic perspective (Mahrer 2017: 36–37), or that "a version, like any text of a work, is effectively an approximation of the attempt to achieve the work" (Bryant 2002: 86) is equivalent to solving the problem that was to be elucidated "in favor of identity" (Reuss 1990: 5–10).

References

Azancot, N. (2007). La generación Nocilla y el Afterpop piden paso. *El mundo*, hemeroteca de *El Cultural*, 25.07. Retrieved from http://www.elcultural.es/version_papel/LETRAS/21006/La_generacion_Nocilla_y_el_afterpop_piden_paso (Accessed 2/13/19).

Barker, J. (2011). *No place like home: Virtual space, local places and Nocilla fictions* (Doctoral Dissertation, University of British Columbia).

Becker, S. (2014). *Born-digital-Materialien in literarischen Nachlässen. Auswertung einer quantitativen Erhebung*. Berliner Handreichungen zur Bibiliotheks- und Informationswissenschaft. Berlin. Staats- und Universitätsbibliothek. Retrieved from : https://edoc.hu-berlin.de/handle/18452/2749 (Accessed 2/13/19).

Bryant, J. (2002). *The fluid text: A theory of revision and editing for book and screen*. University of Michigan P.

Cadioli, A. (2012). *Le diverse pagine. Il testo letterario tra scrittore, editore, lettore*. Il Saggiatore.

Calles Hidalgo, J. (2011). *Literatura de las nuevas tecnologías. Aproximación estética al modelo literario español de principios de siglo (2001–2011)*. Salamanca: Ediciones Universidad Salamanca (Col. Vitor).

Darnton, R. (2003) The heresies of bibliography. *The New York Review of Books*, May 29, 43–45.

del Pozo Ortea, M. (2012). *Hacia un reencantamiento posthumanista: poesía, ciencia y nuevas tecnologías* (Doctoral Dissertation, Massasuchets).

Fernández Mallo, A. (2009). *Postpoesía. Hacia un nuevo paradigma*. Anagrama.

Fernández Mallo, A. (2012). Topological time in Proyecto Nocilla [Nocilla project] and Postpoesía [post-poetry] (and a brief comment on the exonovel). *Hybrid Storyspaces: Redefining the Critical Enterprise in Twenty-First Century Hispanic Literature, Hispanic Issues On Line, 9*, 57–75.

Ganascia, J. G., & Lebrave, J.-L. (2009). Trente ans de traitements informatiques des manuscrits de genèse. In O. Anokhina & S. Pétillon (Eds.), *Critique génétique: concepts, méthodes, outils* (pp. 68–82). Paris: IMEC.

Greetham, D. (1996). Foreword. In P. Shillingsburg (Ed.), *Scholarly editing in the computer age: Theory and practice* (pp. vii–xvi). Ann Arbor: University of Michigan P.

Greetham, D. (2013). A history of textual scholarship. In N. Fraistat & J. Flanders (Eds.), *The Cambridge companion to textual scholarship* (Cambridge Companions to Literature, pp. 16–41). Cambridge: Cambridge University Press. https://doi.org/10.1017/CCO9781139044073.002.

Heigham, J., & Croker, R. A. (2009). *Qualitative research in applied linguistics. A practical introduction*. London: Palgrave Macmillan.

Ilasca, R. (2015). ¿Sueñan los escritores con obras electrónicas? La experiencia transmedial en *Alba Cromm* de Vicente Luis Mora. *Texto digital, 11*(1), 209–225.

Italia, P. (2013). *Editing Novecento*, Salerno.

Kirschenbaum, M. G. (2008). *Mechanisms*. Cambridge: New Media and the Forensic Imagination.

Kirschenbaum, M. G. (2013). The .txtual condition: Digital humanities, born-digital archives, and the future literary. *Digital Humanities Quarterly, 7*(1), 1–43. Retrieved from: http://www.digitalhumanities.org/dhq/vol/7/1/000151/000151.html (Accessed 2/13/19).

Kirschenbaum, M. G., Ovenden, R. & Redwine, G. (2010). *Digital forensics and born-digital content in cultural heritage collections*. Washington D.C., Council on Library and Information Resources.

Lebrave, J.-L. (2009). Manuscrits de travail et linguistique de la production écrite. *Modèles linguistiques, 59*, 13–21.

Lebrave, J.-L. (2010). L'ordinateur, Olympe de l'écriture? *Genesis, 31*, 159–161.

Lebrave, J.-L. (2011). *Computer forensics*: la critique génétique et l'écriture numérique. *Genesis*, (33), 137–147.

Lernout, G. (1996). La critique textuelle anglo-américaine: une étude de cas. Genesis, 9, 45–65. A version of this article in English is available at URL: http://www.antwerpjamesjoycecenter.com/genesis.html (Accessed 7/15/18).

Lernout, G. (2002). Genetic criticism and philology. *Text, 14*, 53–75.

Lernout, G. (2013). Continental editorial theory. In N. Fraistat & J. Flanders (Eds.), *The Cambridge companion to textual scholarship* (pp. 61–78). Cambridge: Cambridge UP.

Literatura Electrónica Hispánica. (2018) Fundación Biblioteca Virtual Miguel de Cervantes (Ed.): Biblioteca Virtual Miguel de Cervantes. Retrieved from : http://www.cervantesvirtual.com/bib/portal/literat uraelectronica/obras.html (Accessed 7/15/18).

Mahrer, R. (2017). La plume après le plomb. Poétique de la réécriture des œuvres déjà publiées. *Genesis, 44*, 17–38.

Marcus, L. S. (2009). Textual scholarship. In *Women editing/editing women: Early modern women writers and the new textualism* (pp. 75–101). Newcastle upon Tyne: Cambridge Scholars Publishing.

McGann, J. (1983). *A critique of modern textual criticism.* Chicago: University of Chicago Press.

McGann, J. (1988). Theory of texts. *London Review of Books, 10*(4), 20–21.

McGann, J. (2013). Coda: Why digital textual scholarship matters; or, philology in a new key. In N. Fraistat & J. Flanders (Eds.), *The Cambridge companion to textual scholarship* (Cambridge Companions to Literature, pp. 274–288). Cambridge: Cambridge University Press. https://doi.org/10.1017/CCO9781139044073.014.

McKenzie, D. F. (1986). *Bibliography and the sociology of texts.* London: The British Library.

McKenzie, D. F. (1991). *La bibliographie et la sociologie des textes.* Paris: Cercle de la Libraire.

McKenzie, D. F. (1998). *Bibliografia e sociologia dei testi.* Milan: Sylvestre Bonnard.

McKenzie, D. F. (1999). *Bibliography and the sociology of texts.* Cambridge: Cambrigde UP.

McKenzie, D. F. (2005). *Bibliografia y sociología de los textos.* Madrid: Akal.

Mora, V. L. (2007). *Circular. Las afueras.* Córdoba: Berenice.

Nutt-Kofoth, R. (2006). Editionsphilologie als Mediengeschichte. *Editio, 20*, 1–23.

Pantel A. (2012). *Mutations contemporaines du roman espagnol. Agustín Fernández Mallo et Vicente Luis Mora* (Doctoral Dissertation, Montpellier).

Pérez, J. A. (2015). *Digital storytelling in Spanish: Narrative techniques and approaches* (Doctoral Dissertation, University of California, Santa Barbara).

Reiman, D. H. (1987). "Versioning": The presentation of multiple texts. In *Romantic texts and contexts* (pp. 167–180). Columbia: University of Missouri P.

Reuss, R. (1990). "Michael Kohlhaas und Michael Kohlhaas". Zwei deutsche Texte, eine Konjektur und das Stigma der Kunst. *Berliner Kleist-Blätter, 3*, 3–43.

Reuss, R. (2005). Text, Entwurf, Werk. *Text. Kritische Beiträge, 10*, 1–12.

Ries, T. (2010). "die geräte klüger als ihre besitzer": Philologische Durchblicke hinter die Schreibszene des Graphical User Interface. Überlegungen zur digitalen Quellenphilologie, mit einer textgenetischen Studie zu Michael Speiers ausfahrt st. Nazaire. *Editio, 24*, 149–199.

Sahle, P. (2013). *Digitale Editionsformen. Zum Umgang mit der Überlieferung unter den Bedingungen des Medienwandels.* 3 vols. Norderstedt, Schriften des Instituts für Dokumentologie und Editorik.

Saum-Pascual, A. (2012). *Mutatis Mutandi. Literatura española del nuevo siglo XXI* (Doctoral Dissertation, Riverside, University of California).

Shillingsburg, P. (1996). *Scholarly editing in the computer age: Theory and practice.* Ann Arbor: University of Michigan P.

Shillingsburg, P. (2006). *From Gutenberg to Google. Electronic representations of literary text.* Cambridge: Cambridge UP.

Sutherland, K. (2013). Anglo-American editorial theory. In N. Fraistat & J. Flanders (Eds.), *The Cambridge companion to textual scholarship* (Cambridge Companions to Literature, pp. 42–60). Cambridge: Cambridge University Press. https://doi.org/10.1017/CCO9781139044073.003.

Vauthier, B. (2014). Tanteos, calas y pesquisas en el dossier genético digital de *El Dorado* de Robert Juan Cantavella. In M. Kunz & S. Gómez Rodríguez (Eds.), *Nueva narrativa española* (pp. 311–345). Barcelona: Linkgua.

Vauthier, B. (2016). Genetic criticism put to the test by digital technology: Sounding out the (mainly) digital genetic file of *El Dorado* by Robert Juan-Cantavella. Variants, 12-13, 163–186. Retrieved from: http://journals.openedition.org/variants/353 (Accessed 24/07/18).

Vauthier, B. (2017). Éditer des états textuels variants. *Genesis*, (44), 39–55.

Vauthier, B. (2018a). Donald McKenzie: historiador del libro y filólogo. *Revista Hispánica Moderna* in press.

Vauthier, B. (2018b). *Critique génétique* y filologías del texto moderno. Nuevas perspectivas —sobre 'el texto'— a partir de Ramón del Valle-Inclán,. *Ínsula*, 861, pp. 11–15 in press.

Vauthier, B. & Santos Zas, M. (Eds.) (2017). *Un día de guerra (Visión estelar). La Media Noche. Visión estelar de un momento de guerra de Ramón del Valle-Inclán. Estudio y dossier genético.* Santiago de Compostela, Biblioteca de la Cátedra Valle-Inclán/Servizo de Publicacións da Universidade, 3 vols. + DVD.

von Bülow, U. (2003). "Rice übt Computer, die Laune wird immer guter!": Über das Erschließen digitaler Nachlässe. Paper delivered at KOOP-LITERA Österreich. Literaturhaus Mattersburg, 8–9 May 2003. Retrieved from : https://www.onb.ac.at/koop-litera/termine/kooplitera2003/Buelow_2003.pdf. (Accessed 2/13/19).

Weisbrod, D. (2015). *Die präkustodiale Intervention als Baustein der Langzeitarchivierung digitaler Schriftstellernachlässe* (Doctoral Dissertation, Berlin). Retrieved from http://nbn-resolving.de/urn:nbn:de:kobv:11-100233595 (Accessed 2/13/19).

Willison, I. (2002). Don McKenzie and the history of the book. In J. Thomson (Ed.), *Books and bibliography: Essays in commemoration of Don McKenzie* (pp. 202–210). Wellington: Victoria UP.

International Journal of Digital Humanities (2019) 1:47–57
https://doi.org/10.1007/s42803-019-00004-w

RESEARCH ARTICLE

Born digital preservation of e-lit: a live internet traversal of Sarah Smith's *King of Space*

Nicholas Schiller[1] · Dene Grigar[1]

Published online: 11 March 2019
© Springer Nature Switzerland AG 2019

Abstract

Sarah Smith's *King of Space*, published in 1991, is the first work of science fiction produced as electronic literature. Released on a 3.5-in. floppy disk and requiring a Macintosh computer running System Software 7.0-MacOS 9x, it is now inaccessible to scholars interested in early digital literary forms, particularly of science fiction by women authors. Because this work is interactive and involves animations, images, sound, and words, preserving it requires an approach that retains as much of these experiences as possible for future audiences. To accomplish this task, our lab—the Electronic Literature Lab at Washington State University, Vancouver—used the Path-finders methodology developed by Grigar and Stuart Moulthrop, adding to it Live Stream play-throughs on YouTube promoted through social media channels. This essay outlines our process and discusses the potential of this methodology for preserving other kinds of multimedia and interactive work.

Keywords Electronic literature · Digital preservation · Digital humanities research lab

1 Introduction

Born digital literature, or electronic literature or e-lit, is a broad and varied field of artistic works combining text with the affordances of computers. In *Electronic Literature: New Horizons for the Literary* N. Katherine Hayles explains that electronic literature involves writing that is created and consumed using computing devices (Hayles 2008). Early examples include hypertext novels like Michael Joyce's *afternoon: a story* (1990),

---

Chapter 4 was originally published as Schiller, N. & Grigar, D. International Journal of Digital Humanities (2019)
1: 47–57. https://doi.org/10.1007/s42803-019-00004-w.

✉ Nicholas Schiller
  schiller@wsu.edu

✉ Dene Grigar
  dgrigar@me.com

[1] Washington State University Vancouver, Vancouver, WA, USA

Stuart Moulthrop's *Victory Garden* (1991) oxford, and Shelley Jackson's *Patchwork Girl* (1995); animated poetry like Rob Kendall's *A Life Set for Two* (1994); database narratives like Judy Malloy's *Uncle Roger* (1986–8); and flash poetry like Ingrid Ankerson and Megan Sapnar's *Cruising* (2001), to name just a few examples.

E-lit is more than just digitized print text, and the early field anticipated that using computers to create and consume text would be fundamentally different than using paper and ink (Hayles 2002).

Since the debut of early experimental e-lit, our assumptions and expectations of how to interact with writing have adapted as the tools we use to write and read have changed. For example, concepts we take for granted now, such as blue underlined links in a text that take us to another heading or another document, were once considered controversial and disruptive.

King of Space, Sarah Smith's hypertext novel from 1991, is an excellent example of this sort of early e-lit. This work predates the introduction of the web browser and the current experience with text and media through the internet that we have accepted as standard.

Pre-web works like Smith's exist only in physical media, such as floppy disks and CD-ROMs, that are no longer readily available to scholars and critics. Even with access to the media, contemporary scholars would lack the necessary software tools, such as HyperCard and Storyspace, and the legacy hardware required for the works. Without access to the media and the computers, it is difficult to access the work in order to archive it; additionally, copyright issues, relating to proprietary software with which some of these works are produced deter efforts to migrate or emulate them. Thus, there is a need to facilitate the preservation of these works through documentation.

The Electronic Literature Lab (ELL) at Washington State University Vancouver,[1] established to facilitate advanced study of born-digital literature, is equipped to undertake documentation of these challenging early works of electronic literature. ELL maintains 61 legacy computers running a variety of operating systems, from the 1970s, 1980s, and 1990s that allow scholars to interact with early works of electronic literature using appropriate software and hardware environment, with which they were created and disseminated to readers. This strategy allows us to preserve works as it creates new discussions, descriptions, and criticism that are collected and archived.

In addition to the legacy computers, ELL also is the home to a collection of over 300 works of e-lit. These works currently reside in the removable storage media (floppy disks and CD-ROM disks), on which they were originally published. ELL also maintains a catalog of the hardware available in the lab and the hardware requirements of each work of e-lit in ELL's collection. This allows scholars using the lab to easily locate the appropriate machine to use to interact with the literature.

Maintaining a legacy hardware lab is a difficult undertaking. That is to say, because it would be prohibitively expensive and time-consuming to acquire the range of hardware necessary to make additional labs like ELL, we are seeking an alternate method of preservation that does not require scholars interested in these works to create their own labs or to travel to ELL. In addition, while there is currently some extremely interesting work being done in the field of cloud-based emulation, copyright restrictions hinder our ability to use emulation to make our collection of e-lit accessible by scholars not based in ELL. Thus, in order to best preserve access to the seminal works of e-lit

---

[1] See Electronic Literature Lab web site, http://dtc-wsuv.org/wp/ell/.

housed in ELL, we needed a middle-ground between running e-lit off of perishable removable media in the ELL's legacy computing lab and making the works available through cloud-based emulation.

We decided to experiment with expanding the Pathfinders methodology described by Stuart Moultrop and Dene Grigar in their book *Traversals* (Moultrop and Grigar 2015) to include a Live Stream play-through of the work on YouTube that is promoted through social media channels like Facebook and Twitter.

In this article, we will first outline the need and issues with digital preservation of e-lit in particular. In the second section of the article, we will describe the case and the method that we implemented, building on the Pathfinders method where we included live-video streaming and social media elements to the Traversal. We conclude with a reflection on the advantages and shortcomings of this approach and provide practical implications for implementing a similar strategy for practitioners.

2 The drive to preserve

The idea of saving early born digital literature for posterity takes us to the question: 'Why?' Why is it important to undertake the preservation of this work?

Sarah Smith's hypertext novel *King of Space*, published in 1991 by Eastgate Systems, Inc., serves as an excellent example of the kind of work in danger of being lost and in need of preservation. It is the first work of science fiction produced as electronic literature and one of the first produced by a woman writer. Like hypertext e-lit, it is interactive, but it also involves animations, images, and sound. Built on the proprietary software program, Hypergate, developed specifically for it by the owner of the company, it was released on a 3.5-in. floppy disk and required a Macintosh computer running System Software 7.0-MacOS 9x. Because of the outmoded hardware and software, it is now inaccessible to scholars. This loss is keenly felt, especially due to *King of Space*'s role as the first e-lit work of science fiction.

E-lit reflects a time in which print writers like Smith were making the leap to the electronic environment in order to experiment with form. Not having access to this historical moment would be losing an important trajectory from the print culture of the late twentieth-century to the digital of the early twenty-first. Abby Smith Rumsey speaks to this issue in her book, *When We Are No More* (2016) where she suggests that we preserve artifacts because we value them as a cultural experience and as part of our collective memory. They impart information we need (2016: 161–2).

Previous generations, who faced the 'expense of maintaining vast and redundant stores of physical artifacts' and the costs of 'collect[ing] them and invest[ing] in their long-term access', struggled with the question: What can we afford to save? Today, however, with 'filters gone and information travel[ing] at the speed of electrons, virtually free of friction', where anyone and everyone is able to publish and distribute their work, we struggle with the question: "What can we afford to lose?" (2016: 7). In effect, Rumsey says, '[w]e face critical decisions as a society and as individuals about how to rebuild memory systems and practices to suit an economy of information abundance' (2016: 13).

If we take into account the born digital storytelling taking place on social media, like the most recent "Lazy Cat" narrative posted on Facebook by a group called TXT

Stories (2017), literary games, or even Twine stories created by students in our classrooms, there is an increased production of e-lit and thus no way of determining exactly how much e-lit is being produced daily. Rumsey's view is that '[o]ur obligation to future generations is to ensure that they can decide for themselves what is valuable' (2016: 176). In that light, we should consider retaining as much as we can despite Hans Obrist's reminder that 'everything has a limited life span' (2007: 25).

While books long served as the main method of documenting memory and culture, Abigail De Kosnik argues in her book *Rogue Archives* that the new 'cultural dominant' is digital media. More specifically, De Kosnik says that 'memory-based making—facilitated by digital tools published on digital networks, and saved mostly in "rogue" digital archives—is the cultural dominant of the early twenty-first century' (2016, 5–6). Today preservation does not rely on a system controlled by trained experts; instead, it requires individuals working largely independently but increasingly together to keep cultural memory alive. De Kosnik points to endeavors undertaken by non-trained practitioners and changing methods and formats as ways 'memory has gone rogue' (2016: 1).

Rumsey's and De Kosnik's call for changing preservation practices ties into the work that Richard Rinehart and Jon Ippolito are doing with their Variable Media approach to preservation. This is a method that attends to the need of each individual work rather than imposing a blanket methodology across all works (Dekker 2013: 88–89). Like Rinehart and Ippolito express concerns about cultural heritage, arguing that 'social memory'—that is, the 'long-term memory of civilizations—is predicated on the preservation of cultural artefacts' (2013: 92). Engagement with cultural memory harkens us back to De Kosnik who says, "[engagement is]... not only what comes after the making and distribution of cultural texts, it also not often precedes that making, or occurs at every step through the process of making" but "has come loose from its fixed place in the production cycle." It can "be found anywhere" and in any form" (2013: 4).

This rogue approach runs counter to methodologies put into place for print culture and certainly lies at the core of the preservation work taking place in the ELL. Preserving the body of early electronic literature, as we are doing, preserves not just the works—but as important—the cultural moment that carries implications of the period of history from which they came and the vision of the future they shared. The mid-1980s when the personal computer was introduced to mid-1990s when the browser was introduced constitute a decade when literary artists began to make the leap from print to the electronic medium, using (or creating for themselves) authoring systems like HyperCard, Storyspace, Narrabase, Intermedia, and others for creative expression. They experimented with databases, hypertext, animation and video, games and puzzles to tell stories, make poetry, and break out of essay writing traditions. It was also a time of great optimism of the future and the role digital technologies were to play in that future, as seen, for example, in Howard Rheingold's promise of great "democratic participation and sense of community, argued in his book *The Virtual Community* (2000). 'To be human, indeed to be living', Francisco Varela and authors tell us, 'is always to be in a situation, a context, a world' (1991: 59). This serves as proof that we even were once alive, and more specifically that we were making literature with computers as they became readily available (1991: 69).

The emergence of born digital works of literature coincided with the mainstreaming of the internet and infancy of the World Wide Web, and so standards and processes for creation and publication have changed rapidly. The uniqueness of the forms meant that many of the early works were not collected by libraries, or if they were, are not made accessible to the public for fear of damage to the disks, as seen in Judy Malloy's database novel *Uncle Roger* (1986–88), held at the Museum of Modern Art's library.[2] Additionally, many works published on the early World Wide Web have gone dark and exist only as files owned by the author, such as with Patricia Monaghan's poem, "Examination", (n.d.)[3] or by collectors, such as Diana Slattery's multimedia narrative *The Glide Project*, a copy of which was donated to the Electronic Literature Organization's archives by N. Katherine Hayles this year (2001). For many, the underlying software and hardware dependencies have rendered the work inaccessible or incomplete, such as the case of Sasha West and Ernesto Lavandera's Flash poem "Zoology" (2009). Even those that have been collected are more often stored in analog collections, like Stephanie Strickland's hypertext poem *True North* (1999), held at the David M. Rubenstein Rare Book & Manuscript Library at Duke University. The floppy disks are understandably preserved in a specialized location, but separated from the author's papers that contextualize them. Scholars, who manage to discover a work like Strickland's, likely lack access to the hardware necessary to experience it when they do travel to the Rubenstein to see it. In all cases, these innovative works of electronic literature involve varying degrees of interactivity and multimedia that cannot be easily presented with the cataloging and archiving practices of the time in which they were created. So many of them are disappearing before scholars have a chance to document them or archivists are able to preserve them for long-term access.

3 Preserving e-lit

One of the significant issues in preserving access to e-lit is that both the software and hardware infrastructures where the works were created to run on are now outmoded or obsolete. In the future, there is hope that emulation, or reproducing the original hardware and software environment on contemporary computing platforms can capture some or even most of the interactive experience of navigating an e-lit work. Currently, however, navigating the works using well-maintained legacy computing equipment provides the best access to and experience with these literary works. That said, it is difficult to share this experience with scholars and readers who are not able to travel to the physical location of labs capable of viewing these works. Grigar and Moulthrop (2015) developed the Pathfinders methodology as a means to maintain the cultural experience afforded by the original environment and reach a broader audience than possible by the limited access to legacy hardware.

---

[2] MOMA Library Catalog reference for Judy Malloy's *Uncle Roger* may be found at: http://arcade.nyarc.org/record=b550258~S8

[3] "Examination" is the short animated poem for the web that Patricia Monagham created along with the many books she wrote and published. It is the only work of e-lit by her known to exist. After going off- and online periodically while the author herself maintained the interactive version, the work has remained offline after the author passed away in 2012.

Using the Pathfinders methodology to document these deteriorating works is a stop-gap measure. It is a rogue-archives technique to save what we can with the resources we have to hand. In a perfect world, scholars would have ready access to legacy computing labs. In a perfect world, scholars would also have access to digital copies of these works and emulation environments that allow them to be experienced on contemporary computing hardware. In the absence of access to legacy hardware and emulation, documenting the experience of navigating a work of electronic literature can succeed in keeping these works alive and accessible to contemporary scholars.

The Pathfinders methodology includes the production of a Traversal – filming a reader or readers interacting with an e-lit work and reading aloud through a single path through the nodes and connections of the text (Moulthrop and Grigar 2015). While capturing a single Traversal flattens the multiple paths of the narrative, or just shows one out of many possible paths through the text, obscuring all of the possible alternate choices, it does allow a single perspective into the work to be captured and shared electronically to the widest possible audience. Multiple Traversals, by both author and readers, provide better insights into the possibilities offered by the hypertextual structure.

In addition to capturing a single Traversal of a hypertext story or a work of e-lit, the Pathfinders methodology also includes interviews with the author to provide additional context and relevant background information to the work as well as include critical response to the works, photos of the physical artifact, and sound files (Grigar and Moulthrop 2017, Moulthrop and Grigar 2015). Together, these components provide insight, background, and conversation about these works that otherwise may be forgotten.

One shortcoming to the Traversal process is that it captures one reading among many possible readings of a work. Smith's hypertext novel contains 317 nodes and offers 25 different endings. The interface offers nine different choices to enter the narrative: 'All', 'text', 'is', 'a', 'game', 'history', 'Begin King of Space', 'Playing the Game', 'Story Background', and 'Hypertext Theory'. 'All', for example, provides a short narrative with three options to choose from, while "text" takes the reader to a puzzle. The other options offer their own entry points into the story. The Traversal can only capture one combination of choices and cannot reveal the rich complexity of hypertext. In the Pathfinders project, Grigar and Stuart offered three different readings for each of the four hypertext novels that they studied. But the problem still remains that there are exponentially more readings than what can be offered using this methodology. Despite this limitation, the Traversal does make it possible for digital scholars to experience these works in a meaningful way.

4 Methodology: live internet traversals

For our project, we asked ourselves: How can we expand on the existing success of the Pathfinders model to engage an even wider audience? In terms of providing access to a library of previously inaccessible texts, the existing methodology is successful. However, the availability of streaming media via YouTube and social media like Facebook and Twitter offer advantages that suggest ways to broaden that access and reach a larger audience. Thus, we decided to take advantage of these technologies to broadcast our Traversals live and implement a social and participatory aspect to our scholarship.

Capturing a Traversal live introduces a few new challenges. The role of the reader, the one who is navigating the work, has more of a performative aspect. Since the live broadcast removes the option of splicing together multiple takes in post-production, the reader's role requires more preparation and rehearsal. The video and audio mixing process requires more camera angles and microphone positions, as the live performance does not allow for the set to be taken down and re-arranged between reading, author interview, and audience Q & A portions of the Traversal.

Broadcasting our reading live also enables us to capture more participation in the process of generating the Traversal. Undergraduate researchers working with us in the lab cultivated audiences on Twitter using the #elitpathfinders hashtag (E-Lit Pathfinders Hashtag) and on Facebook using the e-lit Pathfinders page (Pathfinders — Home). Additionally, the video is broadcast live using YouTube via the Pathfinders e-lit YouTube channel ("Pathfinders e-lit"). Each of these three avenues for connecting with live audiences is monitored and moderated by an undergraduate researcher or a member of the ELL staff. These channels allow us to add live conversation to the Traversal that includes scholars, critics, and artists from around the world. After the event, the content of these three social media feeds, plus the photographs taken during the live event, are gathered and saved using the Storify service.

Performing our Traversals of e-lit live, online, and using social media channels adds a participatory aspect to the existing Pathfinders Traversal model. We are able to keep these seminal works alive by sharing their existence with a wider audience, capturing more of the depth and richness of the scholarly conversation surrounding these works, and recording the ensuing conversation for posterity.

In order to make the multi-layered activity of a live internet broadcast of a Traversal function, our undergraduate researchers come prepared to fill a variety of specific roles. The performance roles in front of the cameras and the technical roles behind the cameras are filled by faculty, staff, and outside experts. Thus, undergraduate researchers fill three other key roles. First, they research background material on the work being traversed. This enriches the social media streams with key context, background, and critical perspectives. The student researchers also curate the social media streams. On Facebook, Twitter, and the YouTube channel students (and occasionally faculty) monitor the conversation and post information from their research, adding to the recorded conversation. Finally, having prepared by researching in advance and through curating the live conversation streams, undergraduate researchers are primed to enrich the question and answer portion of the live Traversal.

4.1 Case

We explored this method for expanding the reach of e-lit to Sarah Smith's hypertext novel, *King of Space*. This novel, begun in 1988 and published in 1991 by Eastgate Systems, Inc., is a key example of early pre-web hypertext. It runs on Apple System Software 7x, 8x and 9x used on Macintosh Classics, Macintosh SEs, Macintosh LCs, and Macintosh Performas. Software requirements include Hypergate—an early hypertext system created by Mark Bernstein that was written in FORTH for the Macintosh operating system (Bernstein)—and requires Quicktime Movieplayer 2.x.It is a media-rich work consisting of 317 lexias and 25 different endings and involves numerous works of ASCII art produced by artist Matthew Mattingly, music composed by Michael Derzhinsky, and animations created by Mattingly, Bernstein, and others. Within the novel, one can also find several puzzles that must be solved and games readers can play.

As a work of literature, *King of Space* is noteworthy. It is the first work of born digital science fiction, predating John McDaid's *Uncle Buddy's Phantom Funhouse* by a year, and the first hypertext published as a literary work that blurs the line between literature and games.[4] The story involves a plague that can only be stopped through a sexual connection with the priestess. Seen through the lens of cultural theory, *King of Space* carries a strong feminist focus, exploring gender roles and dystopian worlds. The games and puzzles embedded in the work function as *agons* the reader must overcome in order to find success, which may be defined as engaging in the story long enough to save the world. In some cases where readers attempt to assume agency, Smith has purposely not allowed the opportunity. To make it successfully through the gauntlet of tests, then, constitutes a kind of heroism. It is also important to note that the work, created by a woman writer with an established reputation in the print world, also speaks to the fact that the field of electronic literature has long been well represented by women and was, early on, pioneered by women curious about the electronic medium, but without formal university training as computer programmers. Smith joins Judy Malloy, M. D. Coverley, Stephanie Strickland, Carolyn Guyer, Jane Yellowlees Douglas, Mary-Kim Arnold, Martha Petry, and others who were visual artists, poets, and novelists making the leap from print to digital at a time when the mainstream public were not yet online. Smith's own interest in creating a hypertext novel was heavily influenced by quilting, collage, and "choose your own adventure" games. We see these influences in the confluence of story, puzzle, and games in the work. Smith also views writing as a dialogue between readers' expectations and the author's vision and is particularly interested in how characters function in this kind of story, challenging the notion that characters needing to be consistent. Indeed, Smith's characters bleed into one another often (Smith 2017).

4.2 Implementation

The Electronic Literature Lab (ELL) at Washington State University, Vancouver, has been established to facilitate advanced study of born-digital literature. Our current project involves the documentation of pre-web works of electronic literature. This documentation provides scholars with access to pioneering work that otherwise would be difficult or impossible to achieve. Our process also serves to preserve the work, as it creates new discussions, descriptions, and criticism that are collected and archived. ELL provides an ideal space to undertake the project because it contains 61 vintage Macintosh & PC computers, dating back from 1977, vintage software, peripherals, and a library of over 300 works of electronic literature and other media. One of a handful of media archaeology labs in the U.S., it is used for the advanced inquiry into curating, preserving, and the production of born digital literary works and other media.

---

[4] The website for the Traversal performance is available here: http://dtcwsuv.org/wp/ell/2017/09/24/traversal-ofsarah-smiths-king-of-space/. The captured video recording of that broadcast is available here: https://youtu.be/kXJIcWctuDM, and the social media streams are preserved here: https://storify.com/nnschiller/king-of-spacea-live-elit-pathfinder-traversal.

The live internet Traversal of Sarah Smith's *King of Space* was broadcast on 29 September 2017.[4] The process of preparing for this Traversal began in mid-August, with Grigar arranging for the narrator to participate, and Dr. Amber Strother of WSU Pullman to do the performance. At this time the undergraduate researchers were given access to *King of Space* and the computer on which to read it so that they could familiarize themselves with the work before the Traversal. Grigar also began collecting the bibliography of criticism surrounding *King of Space*. Preparations also included assigning roles to the undergraduate researchers. As listed above, their roles included curating the Facebook live interactions on the Pathfinders page, curating the Twitter live interactions on the #elitpathfinders hashtag, and taking still photographs during the live Traversal.

At this time, our technical support professional Greg Philbrook began preparing our lab for the live internet Traversal. The preparation steps included he and Grigar choosing the computer that was best suited to handle the work and the video recording. While several machines in the ELL are capable of running the *King of Space* software, finding the one that offered the optimal monitor size, color display, and a minimum of light glare took a considerable amount of testing. Eventually, we settled on the Mac Performa Power PC 5215 CD, running MacOS 7.6.0. This machine showed off the visual and audio properties of the literature and also was best suited to being captured on video. One limitation of the Apple hardware of that era is a lack of an external video-out signal, requiring us to use a camera to capture the monitor. This introduces issues of framing the shot, reducing glare, and horizontal scrolling lines from the cathode ray tube technology of the monitor. Philbrook also set up additional camera feeds and microphone placements at this time. This arrangement allowed us to capture the narrator and also the audience during the live question and answer period following the reading. We used OBS studio by the Open Broadcaster Service to gather these feeds and pass them to YouTube for the broadcast (*Open Broadcaster Software*).

The week of the Traversal, Strouther came to ELL Team went through a rehearsal for the live Traversal. Technical details of camera angles and microphone placement were worked out, and intellectual details surrounding which hyperlink choices best show off the work in our limited window of time were also planned. An interview with the work's author, Sarah Smith, took place and was recorded in advance of the Traversal.

The day of the Traversal the undergraduate researchers, ELL faculty and staff, and Strother gathered in the lab. Those curating social media feeds had notes from their research and notes from Grigar's critical study on hand to feed content into the social media channels. While Strother performed the Traversal, Grigar moderated the YouTube chat and later the question and answer session; the undergraduate researchers documented the event on social media and with photography, mixing in prepared research on the work and its criticism with observations, comments, and interactions with other participants.

After the Traversal, the ELL faculty and staff reconvened to reflect on the event. We discovered that the use of live stream technology and social media did, in fact, extend the reach of the Traversal. The interactions gathered on Twitter differed from those gathered on Facebook. The chat conversation from the YouTube channel had the most interaction and the fastest paced conversation. Gathering Twitter and YouTube together, plus photographs on Storify was a useful way of providing a lasting documentation of the conversation. Having multiple channels open and monitored during the question and answer session allowed for a broader, more varied, and richer conversation. The final step in our project is to gather this data from all seven Traversals planned during the year into an open-source multimedia book, entitled *Rebooting Electronic Literature*, built on the Scalar platform and disseminating it widely via the internet.

4.3 Discussion

In retrospect, we discovered that the live internet broadcast of the Traversal did, in fact, provide contemporary scholars access to heretofore unavailable works of electronic literature. Sarah Smith's *King of Space*, as mentioned, has been out of circulation for over 10 years because it was neither migrated from floppy disk technology, nor updated to contemporary operating systems. However, since the live Traversal, we have had an average daily page view of 56.4. Daily unique visits to the site averaged 3.4. We also averaged a first-time visitor to the site every two days. We experienced on average 2.9 return visits per day. Thus, far we have had 3776 visitors to the site to view the Traversal and to experience *King of Space*.

Additionally, the live Traversal added value to the existing Pathfinders methodology. Having multiple paths for participants to interact with the event provided us with a rich transcript of conversation about *King of Space*. We were able to document and record this conversation and add it to the record available to scholars. Since we lack the rights to make *King of Space* available on the open internet, providing the conversations surrounding the work, its context, and its impact available on video and text documents the work and makes it less likely to be forgotten. The Pathfinders methodology has been proven to be an impactful and practical step we can take to document early works of e-lit. Live internet broadcasts of these Pathfinders Traversals extend the reach of this documentation process, making it more rich and including more voices in the story.

5 Final thoughts: best practices

The looming loss of early works of e-lit leads to our final comments about the best practices for preserving them.

First, the time to preserve is now. We cannot hesitate to begin this important work because the rate of obsolescence has increased. Second, to preserve effectively, we must use multiple methods: Emulate when we can; migrate when possible; and make the work available to the public, even if it means collecting vintage hardware and software for reading the works until which time other methods for preserving arise. We should follow Rinehart and Ippolito's notion and attend to the specificities of the works themselves when deciding how to preserve them (2013). Third, when archiving the original work, we should maintain the integrity of the work by keeping its components—floppy disks, author's papers, critical essays, and other contextualizing resources—together. Fourth, offer the public opportunities to access the work both on site and at a distance, as we are doing with the Electronic Literature Lab's open library, live Traversals, and open-source multimedia books. Fifth, document the works in Wikipedia and in databases like the Electronic Literature Organization's *Electronic Literature Directory* and ELMCIP's *Knowledge Base*. And finally, it is necessary to use open-source options for production and preservation to ensure accessibility over time. Following these suggestions, works such as Sarah Smith's *King of Space* can remain available to the public and achieve the recognition they deserve.

References

De Kosnik, A. (2016). *Rogue archives: Digital cultural memory and fandom*. Cambridge: MIT Press.

Dekker, Annet. (2013). On re-collection: New media, art, and social media: An e-mail interview with Richard Rinehart. In Annet Dekker (Ed.) Speculative scenarios. (pp. 88–93). Eindhoven: Baltan Laboratories.

Grigar, D., & Moulthrop, S. (2017). *Traversals the use of preservation for early electronic writing*. Cambridge: MIT Press.

Hayles, K. (2008). *Electronic literature: new horizons for the literary*. Notre Dame, Ind: University of Notre Dame.

Monaghan, P. (n.d.) Examination. A print version of the interactive poem was published (2002) *Dancing with Chaos*. Cliffs of Moher: Salmon Publishing, 20.

Moultrop, S., & Grigar, D. (2015). Pathfinders: Documenting the experience of early digital literature. Nouspace Publications. Retrieved December 4 2017 from http://scalar.usc.edu/works/pathfinders/index.

Obrist, H. U. (2007). The future is a dog. In *Everything you ever wanted to know about curating*. Berlin: Sternberg Press.

Rheingold, H. (2000). *The virtual community: Homesteading on the electronic frontier*. Cambridge: MIT Press.

Rumsey, A. S. (2016). *When we are no more: How digital memory is shaping our future*. New York: Bloomsbury.

Slattery, D. (2001) The Glide Project. Online documentation of the project available at https://elmcip.net/creative-work/glide-project and http://psychedelicsandlanguage.com/the-guild/diana-slattery-glide/, retrieved December 8, 2017.

Smith, S. (2017). Interview. Retrieved December 4, 2017 from http://scalar.usc.edu/works/rebooting-electronic-literature/interview-for-sarah-smiths-king-of-space?path=sarah-smiths-king-of-space.

Strickland, S. (1999). *True North*. Watertown: Eastgate Systems.

TXT Stories. (2017). Lazy Cat. Facebook. Retrieved December 12, 2017 from https://www.facebook.com/txtstories/videos/234390640463135/

Varela, F., Evan, T., & Eleanor, R. (1991). *The embodied mind: Cognitive science and human experience*. Cambridge: MIT Press.

West, S., & Ernesto L. (2009). Zoology. *Born Magazine*. Retrieved December 13, 2017 from http://bornmagazine.org/projects/zoology/

International Journal of Digital Humanities (2019) 1:59–70
https://doi.org/10.1007/s42803-019-00005-9

Anarchive as technique in the Media Archaeology Lab | building a one Laptop Per Child mesh network

libi striegl[1] · Lori Emerson[2]

Published online: 1 April 2019
© Springer Nature Switzerland AG 2019

Abstract

The Media Archaeology Lab (MAL) at the University of Colorado at Boulder (U.S.A.) acts as both an archive and a site for what the authors describe as 'anarchival' practice-based research and research creation. 'Anarchival' indicates research and creative activity enacted as a complement to an existing, stable archive. In researching the One Laptop Per Child Initiative, by way of a donation of XO laptops, the MAL has devised a modular process which could be used by other research groups to investigate the gap between the intended use and the affordances of any given piece of technology.

Keywords Archive · Anarchive · Mesh network · Media lab · Media archaeology · Practice-based research · Research creation

1 Introduction

What follows in part one is an overview of the philosophy and holdings of the Media Archaeology Lab (MAL), based at the University of Colorado at Boulder (U.S.A), along with a summary of its key ongoing activities. We discuss the MAL in terms of conventional notions of the archive and more anarchic notions of the anarchive as developed by Siegfried Zielinski, University of Toronto's WalkingLab, and Concordia University's Senselab. Part two of our article focuses exclusively on our One Laptop Per Child (OLPC) XO Mesh Network Project and the four-part set

Chapter 5 was originally published as Striegl, L. & Emerson, L. International Journal of Digital Humanities (2019) 1: 59–70. https://doi.org/10.1007/s42803-019-00005-9.

✉ libi striegl
  striegl@gmail.com; libi.striegl@colorado.edu

✉ Lori Emerson
  lori.emerson@gmail.com; lori.emerson@colorado.edu

[1] Intermedia Arts, Writing, and Performance Program, University of Colorado at Boulder, Boulder, CO, USA

[2] Department of English and Intermedia Arts, Writing, and Performance Program, University of Colorado at Boulder, Boulder, CO, USA

of guidelines we have developed as a result of this project and as a way of documenting our anarchival process. Though our anarchival process is a living document and thus subject to change and revision, our guidelines serve as an initial point of consideration for future case studies. By approaching the OLPC XO collection anarchivally, we suggest a novel approach to assessment and to knowledge creation related to this specific technology, while also suggesting how these guidelines might be developed to approach other technologies.

2 The Media Archaeology Lab as archive and anarchive

In his essay 'AnArcheology for AnArchives: Why Do We Need—Especially for the Arts—A Complementary Concept to the Archive?' Siegfried Zielinski, who is sometimes aligned with a somewhat softer practice or a mode of thinking called media archaeology, eloquently clarifies what a classic archive is: channeling Michel Foucault, the archive is, in short, 'the externalization of historical consciousness, thereby documenting a consciousness fundamentally tied to power. The utterances, objects, and artefacts produced by artists and thinkers closely involved with the arts are liable to end up in these archives. Once this happens, archivists, librarians, and curators transform heterogeneous objects into structures to whom they are and will remain profoundly alien' (116). The 'anarchive,' however, is, Zielinski posits, 'a complementary opposite and hence an effective alternative to archive... Following a logic of plurality and wealth of variants, they are particularly suited to handle events and movements; that is, time-based sensations. Just as the anarcheological sees itself first and foremost as an activity, anarchives are principally in an active mode' (121). While the foregoing has helped us think through how to handle experiments with still-functioning but obsolete networks in the MAL, Zielinski also asserts that artists and researchers like us need both archives and anarchives:

> archives that collect, select, preserve, restore, and sort in accordance with the logic of a (dispositive) whole, and the autonomous, resistant, continually reactivated *anarchives* geared toward individual needs and work methods. It is the utopia, the non-place, which in an ongoing process reshapes and reinterprets the materials from which memories are made. Anarchives necessarily challenge, indeed provoke, the archive: otherwise, they would be devoid of meaning. Caring for anarchives may help prevent the many idiosyncratically designed particular collections from changing into a rule-bound administrative apparatus. It may even enable us to celebrate the past as a regained present. (122)

Thus, since 2009, when we founded the Media Archaeology Lab, the lab has become known as both an orderly and an unruly place. On the one hand, the MAL's extensive collection of still functioning media from the late nineteenth century through the twenty-first century has been carefully accessioned and catalogued, and we have also created disk images of all our valuable pieces of early digital art and literature. If you visit the lab, you will be greeted by roughly one hundred and thirty years' worth of media to turn on, play with, open up, create with, move around, and juxtapose with other media. Our oldest media objects range from a camera from 1880, a collection of early twentieth-century magic lanterns, and an Edison diamond disc phonograph player from 1912. Our more recent media range from the desktops, laptops, luggables, portables, and game consoles from the mid-1970s through the early 2000s. We also have a collection of printed matter and software from the 1950s through the 2000s. Highlights of the collection include: a 1976 Altair 8800b; a 1981 desktop computer from Sweden; a 1984 Vectrex game console; a 1986 desktop from East Germany; and a rare 1987 'advanced work processor' called the Canon Cat computer.

On the other hand, the MAL changes from year to year, depending on who is in the lab and what donations have arrived at our doorstep, and thus it undoes many assumptions about what archives as well as labs should be or do. As a testament to the flexibility and open-endedness of the MAL, in the last three years (coinciding with the opening of the new Intermedia Arts, Writing, and Performance PhD program at CU Boulder) the lab's vitality has grown substantially because of the role of three PhD students affiliated with the program. These students have been invited to develop their own unique career trajectories in and through the lab. One student, who wishes to obtain an academic position after graduation, has created a hands-on archive of scanners in conjunction with a dissertation chapter, soon to be published as an article, on the connections between the technical affordances of scanners and online digital archives. Another student, who wishes to obtain a curatorship after graduation, founded an event series called MALfunctions, which pairs nationally and internationally recognized artists with critics on topics related to the MAL collection; this student also arranges residencies at the lab for these visiting artists/critics who, in turn, generate technical reports on their time spent in the MAL; furthermore, as a result of her work with this event series, she has been invited to serve as a curator for an annual media arts festival at the Boulder Museum of Contemporary Art. Finally, another student (and a coauthor of this essay), who wishes to pursue a career in alternative pedagogical practice outside of higher education, has started a monthly retro games night for members of the CU Boulder community; she also is running monthly workshops teaching students and members of the public how to fix vintage computers and game consoles and the basics of surveillance and privacy.

Thus, unlike archives or labs that are structured hierarchically and driven by a single person with a single vision, the MAL takes many shapes. It is, as we write above, an archive for original works of early digital art/literature and their original platforms; it is also an apparatus through which we come to understand a complex history of media and the consequences of that history; it is a site for artistic interventions, experiments, and projects; it is a flexible, fluid space where students and faculty from a range of disciplines can undertake practice-based research; it is a space where graduate students come for hands-on training in fields ranging from digital humanities, literary studies, media studies, and curatorial studies to community outreach and education. In other words, the MAL is an intervention in the notions of 'archive' and 'lab' insofar as it is a place where, depending on your approach, you will find opportunities for research and teaching in myriad configurations and a host of other, less clearly defined activities made possible by a collection that is both object and tool.

The MAL has also evolved into a 'real life' and virtual community enterprise: it has an international advisory board of scholars, archivists, and entrepreneurs; faculty fellows from across the CU Boulder campus; and a regularly rotating cohort of undergraduate interns, graduate research assistants, post-graduate affiliates, and volunteers from the general public who help with class tours and guest visits to the lab. We also host media studies reading groups, artist residencies, an event series called MALfunctions, retro game nights, and workshops on how to fix old or new devices and even on how to build mesh network, as we discuss in part two. The more MAL becomes a communal enterprise, the more it also appears open and accessible to all kinds of people who themselves may have no background in programming or tinkering or making or building, but who understand that we are increasingly compelled to have some understanding of how our everyday technologies work and how we might build alternatives. The objects in the MAL demonstrate how determinisms (ideological and otherwise) are built into technologies of the past, and they do this partly as a result of hands-on interactions with them and partly as a result of experience with the ways in which objects in the lab depart from our present-day expectations. They show how technological determinisms are historical, and therefore changeable, according to the values and concerns we develop.

What follows is a description of one particular archival/anarchival project on which we have been working in the MAL since 2017. By presenting this project, we wish not only to describe thoroughly one possible activity one might undertake archivally/ anarchivally in the lab, but also to explore the ways in which such an activity has the potential to guide other hands-on experiments with obsolete technology. In other words, while we are suggesting a novel approach to assessment and knowledge creation related to this specific technology, we hope this can serve as a model to approach other technologies within and beyond the MAL.

3 Archiving and anarchiving the MAL's collection of OLPCs

In early 2017, the MAL received a donation of twenty OLPC XO laptops, opening up an avenue for hands-on research into and critical consideration of the history, implementation, and outcomes of the OLPC project.

The OLPC initiative was founded in 2005 by then MIT Media Lab Director Nicholas Negroponte with the following mission: 'to create educational opportunities for the world's poorest children by providing each child with a rugged, low-cost, low-power, connected laptop with content and software designed for collaborative, joyful, self-empowered learning' [OLPC n.d.-e]. The goal was to design and manufacture laptops which could be sold *en masse* to governments or Non-Governmental Organizations involved in educational programs for $100, approximately 1/10th the cost of the average laptop at the time. The project was originally funded by member organizations including eBay, Red Hat, Quanta, and Google [OLPC n.d.-g]. As the project continued, the price never actually dropped to $100 and the initiative faced backlash from one-time member Intel and a dramatic drop in overall funding.

Thus, the OLPC project was immediately polarizing. Positive responses came from within the tech industry, evidenced by the support of the member organizations willing to give funding to the initiative. Several governments also responded positively with a willingness to sign up for the laptop distribution program, including Uruguay, Rwanda, and Peru. Negative responses came from the tech industry and from diplomats and leaders from countries in the target market. Marthe Dansokho of Cameroon was quoted at the 2005 World Summit on the Information Society held in Tunisia as saying, 'What is needed is clean water and real schools.' At the same Summit, Mohammed Diop of Mali stated, 'It is a very clever marketing tool. Under the guise of non-profitability hundreds of millions of these laptops will be flogged off to our governments' [Smith]. Bill Gates was skeptical of the project when it was proposed at Davos [Olson] and Lee Felsenstein, in a blog post written shortly after the initiative was founded, noted that 'By marketing the idea to governments and large corporations, the OLPC project adopts a top-down structure. So far as can be seen, no studies are being done among the target user populations to verify the concepts of the hardware, software and cultural constructs' [Felsenstein]. Criticism notwithstanding, beginning in 2007, laptops were distributed in 42 countries [OLPC n.d.-a].

Philosophically, the OLPC project was based on an educational foundation derived from the work of Seymour Papert. 'Constructionism' was name of the philosophy Papert developed around principles of student-centered, active learning; Papert's philosophy, in turn, was based on the work of Jean Piaget and his notions of Constructivist ontology. The active, discovery-based, unstructured learning process advocated by Papert formed the central tenet of the hands-off methods central to the OLPC initiative. This hands-off method drives the belief that the XO laptops, through their careful design, can be handed to children in any situation, who will simply figure out how the devices work and progress via self-guided learning without the aid of a teacher. Negroponte also took inspiration from Sugata Mitra's 'Hole-in-the-wall' project, which called for learning with no or minimal interaction from an instructor [Venkatraman]; Mitra's project inspired Negroponte to pursue implementation plans which included possible helicopter drops of XO laptops in remote locations [OLPC News].

Even though the OLPC project is effectively over, research on the overall effectiveness of the initiative is ongoing. Most studies have so far suggested that the success of the implementation depends on whether devices are properly integrated into classrooms, whether there is appropriate teacher education with regard to laptop use and pedagogical deployment, and whether there is a general enthusiasm around the project in the target community.

Thus, since these devices have what one might call 'contextual baggage' as part of their associated global education project, their presence in the broader MAL collection has special significance as a clear illustration of the nature of top-down technological solutions to global problems. By providing opportunities for active exploration, the MAL opens up all devices in its collection to a consideration of their complexity through an investigation of their affordances. As we point out above, by design the MAL is both an archive housing these and other devices and a lab for experimental work and knowledge creation. It provides space for archiving but also for moving beyond and through the archive (Fig. 1).

At first glance, the XO collection exists as a static set of objects - nothing more than a pile of plastic and electronics in bright and ostensibly friendly colors sitting in a corner of the lab. In other words, these devices fit neatly into the least generous definition of archive as a collection of things in their original state which are usually only considered in terms of their place in whatever has been deemed 'history.' The aforementioned is true of any object in the MAL. If they are not activated, they are lifeless. Furthermore, while the XO collection could be used to illustrate the laptops' original intended use, thereby demonstrating their capacity within that sphere (for example, as an educational tool for children in underserved communities and

Fig. 1 A part of the MAL OLPC XO collection in its inactive state. The collection contains an additional 6 computers and accessories

developing countries), if the collection of XO laptops is only activated in this way it runs the risk of simply replicating the outcomes for which the OLPC project's initial implementation has been criticized. The archival impulse in this scenario is necessarily backwards-looking, where any attempts to reframe or reimagine the devices are bound to be purely abstract in the sense that they would merely serve the original intentions and even ideological purpose of the OLPC project.

Thus, the MAL's research on the XO laptops is intended to move beyond simple situational replication and into active critique. In other words, we are constantly seeking ways to activate our collection which will enable us to examine the hardware and software independently of their original associations. By reflecting on the relationship of the technology to its broader socio-political context, we are able both to provide space for critique and to create pathways for future action. While the impulse is normally to dismiss a piece of technology entirely when the broader project of which it is part is unsuccessful or problematic, we are suggesting that the alternative is to reframe the technology in terms of its real potential and address how its associated project fell short of this potential. The challenge is to accept the technology for what it can do and compare these capabilities with what the technology was designed to do.

3.1 The Anarchive and the counter-archival impulse

Our desire to do something new with the laptops, as opposed to preserving them in place, was, again, a decidedly counter-archival one. Preserving in place, in the case of the XO laptops, seemed to give implicit approval to the OLPC project as a whole without offering any space to negotiate and understand the project's successes and failures, both ideologically and technologically. Instead of figuratively and metaphorically placing the history of these devices on a shelf, ready to be abstracted and transported into a conventional narrative, we wanted to take the opportunity to confront the project's history by experimenting with the devices' aforementioned real potential activated via its functionalities; for example, the XO laptop is particularly well suited to low and/or variable power consumption and mesh networking. Also, by expressing the capabilities of the hardware and software within the scope of what they seem well suited for rather than within the scope of what they were intended for, we hope to find a perspective from which accurately to critique a project like OLPC, which had both complex intentions and outcomes.

3.2 Inspiration

We want to be clear that our OLPC project is not intended to be scientific and it refuses a prescriptive methodology in favor of offering guidelines which we hope can be adapted to the circumstances of any particular research group. By proposing an explicitly open-ended and modular anarchival process for the lab, we are suggesting a way of channeling the counter-archival impulse.

For our purposes, we are revising University of Toronto WalkingLab's definition of the anarchive as 'an activity that resists mere documentation and interpretation in favour of affective and material processes of production, where archival "technicities" create new compositions and new nodes of research' [WalkingLab]. Combining this with the notions expressed by Zielinski, we are declaring that the anarchive is deliberate activity which resists collection, documentation, and abstraction in favor of affective, concrete knowledge production wherein the archive is activated in order to create new directions for critique and research.

We have also adapted a description from SenseLab (based at Concordia University in Montréal, Canada) of their anarchiving process as a basis from which to construct our own process of approaching the XO laptops. SenseLab's definition begins with the following assertions:

1. The anarchive is best defined for the purposes of the Immediations project as a *repertory of traces* of collaborative research-creation events. The traces are not inert, but are carriers of potential. They are reactivatable, and their reactivation helps trigger a new event which continues the creative process from which they came, but in a new iteration.
2. Thus the anarchive is not documentation of a past activity. Rather, it is a *feed-forward mechanism* for lines of creative process, under continuing variation.

And the authors continue, concluding with the following:

7. Approached anarchivally, the product of research-creation is process. The anarchive is a technique for making research-creation a *process-making engine*. Many products are produced, but they are not *the* product. They are the visible indexing of the process's repeated taking-effect: they embody its traces (thus bringing us full circle to point 1). [SenseLab]

Once again, the aim of this project is to construct a range of situations and interactions with the OLPC XO's which take advantage of the particular innate qualities of the OLPC XO hardware in order to imagine alternative potential uses. Iterating different versions of these interactions/situations will, ideally, generate a course of action for an anarchiving process which extends beyond the OLPC project. With the formation of a process which is fundamentally both iterative and generative, we hope that future projects carried out in the lab will build upon this anarchiving framework.

3.3 Direction

The questions we have sought to answer over the course of the project are: what relationship does a technology have to its intended deployment? Does everything need to be preserved in its original state? Can the process of engaging with the technology be preserved without the content? And, is it critically productive to interrogate the functional reality of an object and re-deploy it for new (potentially better suited) ends? In answering these questions within the framework proposed, the goal is both to examine this particular example of technology and also to create a framework for a process-based examination of technologies which can be transferred to other devices held in similar archives.

The questions we have sought to answer require both that we examine the technology itself and work outwards; they also require that we examine the history and context of the technology within the context of the project for which it was designed and deployed. As such, initially we surveyed the technical specs of the hardware and software package that make up the XO. This survey was undertaken both by examining the laptops physically and interacting with them as a user, and also by accessing various online documentation about the device. This was a necessary step in order to understand the value of the device as it stands, rather than resting on the assumptions gleaned from press coverage as well as personal and academic accounts. In addition, we researched both the OLPC initiative as it was first conceived, the immediate and ongoing critical response to the project, and the outcomes thus far from its various implementations. The OLPC project is at present largely defunct, but the XO laptops are still in use in several countries, including Uruguay and Ethiopia, and they are still being deployed in these contexts by various non-governmental entities and other organizations with an educational mission. The research we conducted has largely been through reports available publicly, though some anecdotal information has been collected as well, including the origins of the MAL collection. The MAL collection was donated by one of the entities referenced above, a church mission group which purchased the devices for use in Ethiopia. This contextual research was necessary to understand the archive from which we were drawing, through which we were moving, and from which we were exiting.

From these initial explorations, we were able to derive the first two guidelines for our anarchival process:

1. Become familiar with the context of the archived technology and understand the intended manifestation of the technology, both of which are necessary in order to move beyond them.
2. Understand the technology itself. Conduct hands-on research in order to determine the technology's capabilities and failings. This might take the form of using the device as a primary computer for an extended period of time. Conduct hands-off research as a supplement to this process, especially if there is something one cannot learn by hands-on use. This might take the form of

reading manuals or other documentation. Document what is discovered during hands-on versus hands-off research.

3.4 Learning the technology

In terms of software, the XO laptops were designed with the idea that the user not require fluency in any particular computer language and not even have to have any previous experience with computers. Surprisingly, in our own informal studies conducted in and around the MAL, we found the foregoing generally holds true. We gave XOs to people with varying degrees of computer literacy and they were all able to navigate the basic functions of the device within a very short period of time. Text documents, camera, and games are all readily findable within a few minutes of opening the laptop. In fact, we observed that the way in which all of our testers are accustomed to the standards of computer layout and interface normalized by Windows and Apple ecosystems is a hindrance, as these users were forced to overcome their own presuppositions about interface design in order to familiarize themselves with the laptops. However, we also noted in our users' interactions that there were some pieces of information about the devices not easily obtained by interaction alone and this required investigation in the secondary documentation available online. Because open source is one of the tenets of the OLPC project, the documentation of hardware and software specifications is extensive (Fig. 2).

In terms of hardware, the XO laptops were also designed to be easy and intuitive to navigate, durable, and connectable. The devices also require little power and have variable power consumption which is directly tied to the software activities and the hardware use. Devices have a wifi module which, in conjunction with the Sugar OS, is tailored towards transmission. In addition, devices which are in low power mode or even powered off can still be used as transmitters, all of which makes the laptops ideal for mesh networking.

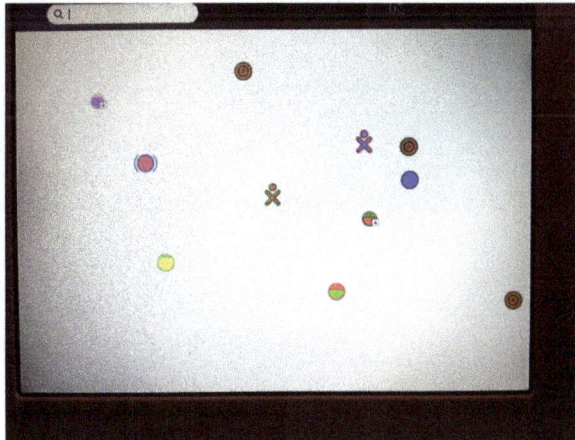

Fig. 2 The Sugar interface in 'Neighborhood' mode. The small 'person' icons indicate nearby XO laptops with open connections. The solid circles indicate available internet connections, the solid circles with parentheses around them indicate a connection in progress, the circles with a line across them indicate internet connections requiring a password, and the concentric circles indicate mesh networking Channels

Broadly speaking, a mesh network is a dynamic, nodal networking model that exists as a complement to the traditional single-access-point network familiar to most internet users. More specifically, a mesh network is an ad hoc, node-to-node network connection whereby each node provides and accesses a signal, as opposed to a direct connection with a single signal source. The XO laptops were designed for mesh networking in order to amplify an internet signal in areas with minimal connectivity, and the devices could use a single access point (ethernet line, satellite phone connection, landline) to provide internet access to many devices. The XO laptops can also connect to one another wirelessly even when no internet signal is available to facilitate data sharing on a local network (Fig. 3).

3.5 Active process

The anarchive pertains to events rather than objects. It extends outside of the archive and exists in addition to it. Thus, for our purposes, we defined a third step in our process as follows:

3. Determine a path by which you can escape the archive using the technology you are activating. Follow that path to its logical conclusion and re-trace it with variations if necessary, for as long as necessary. This escape and activation might range from playful interactions to more rigorous hardware or software hacking. The active process is the anarchive. The anarchive may have byproducts (including documentation), but these byproducts are not the anarchive. Document whatever seems appropriate. Save the residue of all experiments wherever appropriate

Based on the information gathered during our survey of the physical capabilities of the XO laptops, we are in the process of creating a cross-campus mesh network using

Link Status		Profiles	Available Network	WPS	Information
Associated	SSID	Channel	Network Type	Encryption	BSSID
	olpc-mesh	1	AdHoc	No Encryption	022c7c77d339
	xfinitywifi	11	Infrastructure	No Encryption	000d679768c2
	CableWiFi	11	Infrastructure	No Encryption	000d679768c3
	UCB Wireless	6	Infrastructure	No Encryption	0015c7fc4360
	UCB Guest	6	Infrastructure	No Encryption	0015c7fc4362
	eduroam	6	Infrastructure	WPA2-PSK AES	0015c7fc4363
		6	Infrastructure	No Encryption	0015c7fc4361

Fig. 3 Available networks list showing the olpc-mesh AdHoc network available for connection on a MacBook Pro

solely these devices which act as communication nodes and transfer points. In the case of our OLPC Mesh Network project, the event or active process is the individual instantiations of network connectivity and the interactions made possible therein are the byproducts. When we treat the XO laptops as the objects in this case, it becomes clear they are ideal facilitation devices for the networking event rather than containers for it. If a network is not initiated and a place for connectivity is not created, the devices return to the archive and are no longer participants in the anarchival process. They can, however, always be reengaged for new instantiations of the network.

We have so far formed active networks in both formal and informal sessions. Each network activation builds upon previous activations. Thus, while our first session involved two devices and two individuals working simultaneously in a shared text document, by the fifth session, the laptops had been 'abandoned' in a building with their network active so that users would interact with the network as they encountered it. Every instance of the network has involved a shared text document because this has proven the best method for provoking and promoting interactions that will leave evidence of the network's existence. However, just as the nature of the network is ephemeral and ad-hoc, the evidence of the network is fleeting. If it is not preserved at regular intervals during the event, it is possible for a participant to erase all traces of their participation or all traces of any participation. In this case, the anarchive carries out its function as an external energetic force around the archive, escaping the function of the archive as a located, documented, and catalogued entity. In other words, the counter-archival impulse expressed earlier is continued through these anarchival activities, wherein preservation neither is the goal nor is desirable.

Given our research thus far, we have decided that future network events should be broader and should take place outside rather than inside various campus buildings. Exploiting the maximum range of the XO's wireless unit and taking advantage of the unit's ruggedness, we plan to conduct two network events, one involving facilitators guiding interactions with the network and one involving laptops that are simply left for passersby to investigate. These two modes of interaction are based directly upon the contextual research on the intended implementation of the laptops and the studies on post-implementation success of the project. From our plans for these next network activations, we have devised a final step for our anarchiving process:

4. Resolve the archive and the anarchive, if possible. Use the results of the events to address the context of the archive. This might take the form of repeating the activities with the original intended user base for the technology

We have not yet reached the point of resolving the archive and the anarchive. In spite of this, the anarchival process is in constant conversation with the archive and with the contextual information surrounding the physical manifestation of the archive. Without consideration of the history held within the archive, the next path for anarchival activity would not be so clear.

4 Conclusions

Our research into the OLPC remains incomplete, as our anarchival activity around the OLPC Mesh Network Project is ongoing. Though our four-step anarchival process is a living document and as such is subject to change and revision, our guidelines serve as an initial point of consideration for future case studies. The anarchival process presented serves as an extension of the archival function served by the Media Archaeology Lab and a supplementary activity which enlivens the archive as it stands. By approaching the OLPC XO collection anarchivally, we are suggesting a novel approach to assessment and knowledge creation related to this specific technology. We are also developing a model for approaching other technologies within or beyond the MAL.

References

Bender, W. (2012). *Learning to change the world: The social impact of one laptop per child.* New York: Palgrave Macmillan.

Felsenstein, L. (2005, November 10). Problems with the $100 Laptop. *The Fonly Institute.* Retrieved from http://www.fonly.typepad.com/fonlyblog/2005/11/problems_with_t.html.

McArthur, V. (2009, September). *Communication Technologies and Cultural Identity: A Critical Discussion of ICTs for Development* Paper presented at the IEEE Toronto International Conference: Science and Technology for Humanity, 2009, Toronto, Canada, 910–914. https://doi.org/10.1109/TIC-STH.2009.5444367.

Media Archaeology Lab (n.d.). Retrieved from http://mediaarchaeologylab.com. [Last accessed 21 February 2018].

OLPC (n.d.-a). *About The Project > Countries. laptop.org.* Retrieved from http://laptop.org/about/countries.

OLPC (n.d.-b). *Laptop.* Retrieved from http://laptop.org/en/laptop/index.shtml.

OLPC (n.d.-c). *Laptop Hardware > Specs.* Retrieved from http://laptop.org/en/laptop/hardware/specs.shtml.

OLPC (n.d.-d). *Mission.* Retrieved from http://laptop.org/en/vision/mission/index.shtml.

OLPC (n.d.-e). *Vision.* Retrieved from http://laptop.org/en/vision/index.shtml.

OLPC (n.d.-f). *Vision > History.* Retrieved from http://laptop.org/en/vision/project/index.shtml.

OLPC (n.d.-g). *Vision > Mission > FAQ.* Retrieved from http://laptop.org/en/vision/mission/faq.shtml.

Olson, P (2006, March 16). Gates Pours Water on $100 Laptop. *Forbes.* Retrieved from https://www.forbes.com/2006/03/16/gates-laptop-microsoft-cx_po_0316autofacescan06.html#42282ce43e38.

SenseLab (n.d.). Anarchive – Concise Definition. Retrieved from http://senselab.ca/wp2/immediations/anarchiving/.

Smith, S. (2005, December 1). The $100 laptop – is it a wind-up? *CNN.* Retrieved from http://edition.cnn.com/2005/WORLD/africa/12/01/laptop/.

Venkatraman, V. (2011, December 7). I want to give poor children computers and walk away. New Scientist. Retrieved from https://www.newscientist.com/article/mg21228425.500-i-want-to-give-poor-children-computers-and-walk-away.

Vota, W. (2006, November 17). An implementation miracle. *OLPC News.* Retrieved from http://www.olpcnews.com/implementation/plan/implementation_miracle.html.

WalkingLab (n.d.). Walking Anarchive. Retrieved from https://walkinglab.org/portfolio/walking-anarchive/.

Zielinski, S. (2015). AnArcheology for AnArchives: Why do we need—Especially for the arts—A complementary concept to the archive? (Winthrop-young, G., trans.). *Journal of Contemporary Archaeology, 2*(1), 1–147. https://doi.org/10.1558/jca.v2i1.27134.

International Journal of Digital Humanities (2019) 1:71–84
https://doi.org/10.1007/s42803-019-00006-8

RESEARCH ARTICLE

The invention and dissemination of the spacer gif: implications for the future of access and use of web archives

Trevor Owens[1] · Grace Helen Thomas[1]

Published online: 5 April 2019
© This is a U.S. government work and not under copyright protection in the U.S.; foreign copyright protection may apply 2019

Abstract

Over the last two decades publishing and distributing content on the Web has become a core part of society. This ephemeral content has rapidly become an essential component of the human record. Writing histories of the late 20th and early 21st century will require engaging with web archives. The scale of web content and of web archives presents significant challenges for how research can access and engage with this material. Digital humanities scholars are advancing computational methods to work with corpora of millions of digitized resources, but to fully engage with the growing content of two decades of web archives, we now require methods to approach and examine billions, ultimately trillions, of incongruous resources. This article approaches one seemingly insignificant, but fundamental, aspect in web design history: the use of tiny transparent images as a tool for layout design, and surfaces how traces of these files can illustrate future paths for engaging with web archives. This case study offers implications for future methods allowing scholars to engage with web archives. It also prompts considerations for librarians and archivists in thinking about web archives as data and the development of systems, qualitative and quantitative, through which to make this material available.

Keywords Web archiving · Computational scholarship · Cryptographic hash · Digital history

'The Web Is Ruined and I ruined it.' This is the title of author and Web Designer David Siegel's 1997 post to XML.com (Siegel 1997). Siegel, the author of the book *Creating*

Chapter 6 was originally published as Owens, T. & Thomas, G. H. International Journal of Digital Humanities (2019) 1: 71–84. https://doi.org/10.1007/s42803-019-00006-8.

The following research represents the opinions, perspectives and ideas of the authors. It does not necessarily represent the perspectives of any institutions with which they are affiliated.

✉ Grace Helen Thomas
   grth@loc.gov

   Trevor Owens
   trow@loc.gov

[1]   U.S. Library of Congress, Washington, DC, USA

  Springer

Killer Websites (Siegel, 1996), went on to explain his role in what he describes as 'The Roots of HTML Terrorism.' (Siegel 1997) Specifically, he contends that 'The hacks I've espoused, especially the single-pixel GIF, and using frames and tables to do layout, are the duct tape of the Web.' All of these elements of design went out of fashion. As he explains, 'I ruined the Web by mixing chocolate and peanut butter so they could never become unmixed. I committed the hangable offense of mixing structure with presentation.' In particular, he advocated the use of these single-pixel, clear GIF files as a way of building page layouts. These kinds of technical discussions of design practices in web history are invaluable resources for understanding the records of the web (Owens 2015). One of his self-proclaimed offenses, 'the single-pixel GIF,' became a subject of analysis and study by digital artist and folklorist Olia Lialina in a 2013 online exhibit (Lialina 2013).

As part of an ongoing effort to explore and explain the early history of the web, Lialina produced the online exhibit illustrated below. This presentation, *clear.gif*, shows a series of transparent GIFs wrapped in elaborate frames. Widely referred to as 'spacer' GIFs, these single-pixel, transparent GIFs were used first and foremost as a way of controlling the placement and presentation of content on a website. They were invisible, or rather transparent, i.e. whatever was behind them showed through. However, they still took up space. So a designer could encode into their HTML document any number of spacer GIFs to appear in a row in order to control the placement of any given element on a page. This provided a means of controlling exactly where visual elements would appear on a given web page. As is evident in Fig. 1, they only become visible when broken, when the link to the image file no longer resolves.

These tiny files, the presence of which is only conspicuous when they are no longer present, are invaluable aids which help us understand the history of the web. Simultaneously, exploration of The study of these files, furthermore, offers insight toward the future of enabling scholarly research on the history of the web. In our explanation of the findings of this investigation, we identify key ways of working with records of the web, and born-digital collections more broadly, which can inform our future understanding of our digital past. The single-pixel GIF is an element of design, invisible like so many other aspects of design on the web, but still encoded in highly structured ways.

In an interview about her ongoing work to explore and understand the early web, in particular the Geocities archive, Lialina explains, 'I remember, everybody who made pages in the 1990s had cgif, maybe it was called clear gif, some people would call it

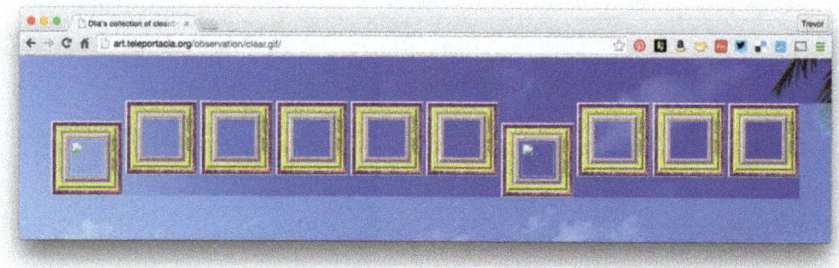

Fig. 1 Screenshot of *clear.gif* online exhibit

zero-dot-gif, but it was this transparent one that would help you to make layouts.' (Johnson 2011). Her exhibit functions as a way of drawing attention to this practice, but it also provides a point of entry to begin to explore the form and function of the history of these images in the history of web design.

In 2006, Jesper Rønn-Jensen, asked exactly this kind of question as a blog post: *Who Invented the Spacer Gif* (Rønn-Jensen 2006). Rønn-Jensen is an early web developer who has remained passionate and outspoken about the history of web design and development. In an update to the post, Rønn-Jensen notes that Siegel claimed credit in personal email correspondence with him. Specifically, Siegel claimed 'I invented it all by myself in my living room.' But at that point, another designer, software developer Joe Kleinberg, chimed in and claimed that he was really the one who had invented it (Rønn-Jensen 2007). What answers do web archives and other born-digital archives offer to such questions? Furthermore and in some ways more interestingly, in what ways might we be able to track the emergence and decline of something like the single-pixel GIF?

Cultural heritage organizations such as the Internet Archive, the British Library, the Library of Congress, and hundreds of others across the globe are working to collect and preserve the web. Many of these institutions now have significant holdings documenting more than two decades of the web's history. In what follows, we approach these collections as a means of exploring the ways in which we can ask and answer such questions concerning web archives.

Before diving into specific questions regarding single-pixel GIFs, we contextualize this work in ongoing discussions about the future of access and use of digital collections. Cultural heritage institutions are increasingly exploring ways of thinking about enabling computational scholarship to think of their collections as data. Much of these conversations are about digitized collection materials, but we now have access to massive corpora of born-digital material, These born digital collections are functionaly born computable for digital scholarship.

Within that section, we briefly introduce computational scholarship and how approaching digital collections as data sets results in new kinds of research. We then provide examples of ongoing projects which focus on applying computational scholarship to web archives as a model of treating web archives collections as data to support new and evolving kinds of research.

Next, we present the findings of our efforts to trace the history of single-pixel GIFs as far back as the first instances appearing in the Internet Archive and Library of Congress Web Archives. Then, we share the findings of the use of computational scholarship, more specifically distant reading, on the UK Web Archive, headquartered at the British Library, to map the patterns of single-pixel GIFs over a 15-year period of web harvesting. Finally, using our methods as a case study, we discuss the findings of an approach based on tracing tiny files through terabytes of messy web archives data and the implications of these findings for researchers and digital library practitioners.

1 Situating web archives in trends in online collections

Without realizing it, humanists have been using computational methods to carry out their research for decades by using full-text search to explore electronic databases

(Underwood 2014) and, prior to this, with the advent of the computer, grappling with how to integrate computational analysis into historical inquiry, if at all (Anderson 2008). In other words, much of current scholarship is already computational, but many people are unaware of the role that computation plays in their research and discovery process. Over the course of the last twenty years, a more sophisticated approach to computational research has developed for humanists who are working with cultural heritage collections and imposing pattern and relevance algorithms directly onto the contents they are studying.

'Distant reading' has evolved into its own methodology of studying texts at scale (Jockers 2013), especially for text-based collections. Letting a computer 'read' hundreds of thousands of novels in seconds has significantly expanded the types of questions we can ask about collections, beyond keyword and word co-occurrence patterns. For example, text mining can identify linguistic patterns, highlight and map named entities (Finkel et al. 2005), compare authors' styles, create connected network graphs, and generate interrelated topics (Blei et al. 2003) over a collection or corpus. These methods have been applied to a collection of twenty thousand novels to predict trends in the literary world (Archer and Jockers 2016) and to thousands of articles from eighteenth-century (Newman and Block 2006) and nineteenth-century (Smith et al. 2013) newspapers to discover trends in news coverage and reprinting over time and geographic location.

The work has continued with specifically non-text-based collections. Scholars have used similar distantly-consumptive analytic methods on their recorded sound (Clement et al. 2016), image (Lorang et al. 2015), audio-visual, visual, and crowdsourced collections, whether the content in the collection began as digital items or had been digitized. Indeed, the expansion of these methods has itself resulted in the need for libraries, archives, and museums increasingly to rethink the modes of access they provide to collections. Computational scholarship is powered by corpus level engagement with works and artifacts as data.

The Library of Congress Collections as Data events and the related Always Already Computational initiative have stimulated conversation concerning access for digital collections and helped articulate visions for multi-modal access to digital collections (Mears 2017). The series brought together experts and practitioners creating digital collections and using digital collections in an effort to highlight common themes throughout the process. Major takeaways included a need for iterative processes with the goal of providing digital collections with better access, form, and quality (Padilla 2017).

To date, much of the work on broad access to digital collections has focused on digitized content. However, work on web archives is one significant exception. The Wayback Machine, the platform developed by the Internet Archive to provide access to web archives, has long been the primary means of entry to viewing web archives content. Alternatively, archives may use other, similar playback software, such as the community-driven open-source OpenWayback[1] or pywb,[2] a version of Wayback written in the programming language Python. It is important to note that the Wayback

---

[1] See the wiki for OpenWayback at https://github.com/iipc/openwayback/wiki

[2] See the documentation for pywb at https://pywb.readthedocs.io/en/latest/manual/apps.html#wayback-pywb.

Machine and other, similar efforts are not *the* archive. Rather, as software, the Wayback Machine, OpenWayback, and pywb provide windows onto the resources stored in any web archive.

With basic computer and internet literacy, one is able to navigate through archived web content on the Wayback Machine much like browsing the live web. However, as web archives have grown exponentially from gigabytes to petabytes, clicking through weekly captures of one section of one website gives users only a tiny fraction of the archive's content and even of that particular website over time. The sheer amount of web archive data now necessitates computational methods to detect patterns across the archived web and highlight areas of the archive in which to dig deeper.

In the autumn of 2016, the Library of Congress commissioned a pilot project simulating a potential researcher using LC web archives (Gallinger and Chudnov 2016). The LC web archiving team provided more than five terabytes of web archives content by means of a secure cloud platform to enable bulk use and analysis. The Web ARChive file format,[3] or WARC, is the standard aggregate file for harvested web content. It combines multiple resources as content blocks within each WARC, as well as associated metadata for each resource. WARC files are well suited for use in a playback mechanism like the Wayback Machine, but the structure and scale of these files is often challenging for researchers to work with directly.

Utilizing the cloud infrastructure and distributed computing provided by the third-party service, the contractors generated derivatives of the WARC files: Web Archive Transformation (WAT) files. WAT files are a slimmed version of WARC files which consist only of metadata for each resource contained in a WARC file, excluding the resource itself. This metadata includes the referring URI, the resource URI, MIME type, a timestamp of harvest, and the size of the resource. WAT files are a lightweight option for dealing with web archive resource metadata, taking up less than 20 % of the space of a WARC file.[4] For the pilot project, the contractors ultimately used the referring URIs and resource URIs to create link analysis visualizations in order to map how each website domain in the collection linked externally to other website domains.

Network analysis is a common way for researchers to explore web archives and for institutions practicing web archiving to begin understanding the breadth of their own collections[5] or perform quality review and completeness checks. This type of analysis over web archives provides a snapshot in time, i.e. a high-level view of a subset of the archive.

In order to arrive at a deeper understanding of researchers' needs, the British Library's UK Web Archiving Team hosted ten researchers on campus in 2014 under the Big UK Domain Data for the Arts and Humanities (BUDDAH) project. These researchers aimed to complete case studies while collaborating with the UK Web Archiving Team as a long term project. As a result, the case studies highlighted ways in which communication between the Web Archiving Team, project managers, and

---

[3] See the file format description at https://www.loc.gov/preservation/digital/formats/fdd/fdd000236.shtml.
[4] See the Internet Archive documentation at https://webarchive.jira.com/wiki/spaces/ARS/pages/90997503/WAT+Overview+and+Technical+Details.
[5] See the UK Web Archive Link Analysis visualization https://www.webarchive.org.uk/ukwa/visualisation/ukwa.ds.2/linkage and the ongoing Web Archives for Longitudinal Knowledge (WALK) Project by partners at the University of Waterloo, the University of Alberta, and York University http://webarchives.ca/ for more information.

  Springer

researchers would be improved and more intuitive interfaces and datasets could be created for the researchers.[6]

To this end, there have been efforts to lower the barrier of entry to WARCs and analysis of web archives content. The Mellon-funded Archives Unleashed Toolkit (AUT),[7] which grew out of Warcbase (Lin et al. 2017), is currently the most robust system providing streamlined access to web archives data for researchers. AUT consists of web archives data loaded onto a high-performance computing platform, with data analysis interfaces at the ready. Similarly, Web Archiving Systems API, or WASAPI (Bailey and Taylor 2017), is an effort funded by the Institute of Museum and Library Services (IMLS), which seeks to map an interoperable API-based model for access to web archives data.

The existence and evolution of these efforts gesture toward a future in which we move increasingly away from one-at-a-time views of rendered web pages toward a model of treating web archives as digital corpora. It took tremendous effort to make something like the Google Ngram viewer to make sense of the noise in digitized texts. In contrast, libraries, archives and museums have billions of born-digital files in their web archives which, as born-digital objects, are born ready for computational scholarship.

Having provided this context and background, we return now to the questions raised at the beginning of this essay. Traces of the single-pixel GIF in web archives will offer some insights into the potentials of this mode of engaging with web archives.

2 Explorations in the history of the single-pixel GIF

What can we understand about the history of the single-pixel GIF when we begin by approaching web archives computationally? Part of the initial impulse to conduct this research was Lialina's online exhibit of single-pixel GIFs. If we take these hand-picked and curated examples of single-pixel GIFs as an initial source, we can begin to characterize them and, in turn, use that characterization to query web archives.

Lialina's exhibition links to a series of live manifestations of these images, presented in the list below. Of particular note, these are each specific locations on the web where one can find, or could once find, a copy of a spacer GIF. After the last forward slash in each of the URLs, we find the filename and extension. One of the exhibited works comes directly from Siegel's site (killersites.com), but in each of them, even just at the filename level, we can see the different names these files take on:

http://www.geocities.com/clipart/pbi/c.gif
http://pic.geocities.com/images/pixel.gif
http://www.google.com/clear.gif
http://killersites.com/killerSites/resources/dot_clear.gif
http://visit.geocities.yahoo.com/visit.gif
http://blingee.com/images/spaceball.gif
http://www-cdr.stanford.edu/~petrie/blank.gif
http://img.artlebedev.ru/;-)/n.gif
https://mail.google.com/mail/images/cleardot.gif
http://www.google.com/images/cleardot.gif

---

[6] For final reports from the BUDDAH project, see the blog https://buddah.projects.history.ac.uk/2016/04/.
[7] http://archivesunleashed.org/about-project/.

2.1 Characterizing/identifying files

Below we have characterized each of the files using two methods. First, by querying their instances on the Wayback Machine, we have identified the earliest date for which the Internet Archive and the Library of Congress have captures of each respective resource in the specified location. Second, we have computed a SHA-1 cryptographic hash for each file. A cryptographic hash function is an algorithm which takes a given set of data (such as a file) and computes a sequence of characters which can then serve as a unique identifier for that data. Even changing a single bit in a file will result in a different sequence of characters. For a sense of just how high that confidence can be, it is worth noting that a cryptographic hash offers more confidence as a characterizer of individualization than a DNA test does for uniquely identifying a person (Kruse II and Heiser 2001, p. 89).

URL	Earliest LC	Earliest IA	SHA-1	Match
http://www.geocities.com/clipart/pbi/c.gif	2/8/02	10/13/99	356F32DA60A0387E36ED94 B0CB3D0A0394D90B60	
http://pic.geocities.com/images/pixel.gif	2/23/02	3/2/00	328E472721A93345801E D5533240EAC2D1F8498C	1
http://www.google.com/images/cleardot. gif	7/2/02	5/10/00	56D45F8A17F5078A20A F9962C992CA4678450765	2
http://www.google.com/clear.gif	2/22/02	8/5/00	317496A096D6C86486A71 D4521994BCD171A6BB3	
http://killersites. com/killerSites/resources/dot_clear.gif	8/5/09	6/20/03	328E472721A93345801E D5533240EAC2D1F8498C	1
https://mail.google. com/mail/images/cleardot.gif	1/28/08	4/5/06	56D45F8A17F5078A20A F9962C992CA4678450765	2
http://visit.geocities.yahoo.com/visit.gif	none	7/3/06	FAA81452F0C19B304B89 F0086F85A2941A57C32D	
http://blingee.com/images/spaceball.gif	10/3/07	1/18/07	2DAEAA8B5F19F0BC209 D976C02BD6ACB51B00B0A	3
http://www-cdr.stanford. edu/~petrie/blank.gif	6/16/09	6/12/07	9D01CC5DC8E042C0D4AD6 CFB8B3AC38E84A5EF9F	
http://img.artlebedev.ru/;-)/n.gif	none	12/5/13	2DAEAA8B5F19F0BC209 D976C02BD6ACB51B00B0A	3

Of these, the earliest recorded capture of any of the single-pixel GIFs is the Geocities Clipart link. With that noted, this only tells us when that file was acquired by respective institutions, not necessarily when it was created. This is a recurring pattern which we will encounter as we work through our analysis. A central challenge in interpreting the contents of web archives is retaining a certain level of skepticism: to what extent are any research findings mapping trends in web history, versus trends in how the web was collected? This is a topic, we futher explore later.

Significantly, by hashing the files, we have found seven distinct files out of the original ten. The chart above is coded to show three sets of duplicate files (coded '1,' '2,' and '3' in the 'Match' column) and four unique files. The files within each duplicate set are bit-for-bit identical (i.e. the file coded with '1' is identical to the other file coded with '1'). In most cases where this occurred, one could deduce that the files with identical hash values are themselves historically related. In other words, one file is likely a later, identical copy of the original. However, in this unique case, given the miniscule file size, we cannot assume any interrelation of identical files. A tiny transparent image file does not lend much to the original maker's unique creativity, and it is possible that several users created identical files using identical processes.

2.2 Single-pixel GIF trends across corpora

Given that we have distinct, digital fingerprints for each of these single-pixel GIFs in the form of their SHA-1 hash values, it becomes possible to query an entire corpus of a web archive to determine where and when files with the same hash value were collected.

To date, the UK Web Archiving program remains unique in that it stores a copy of all the content it has collected in a high-performance distributed computing system. As a result, it is possible to run queries across the entirety of the content of their web archive. Andrew Jackson, the technical leader for the UK Web Archives, generously scanned the UK Web Archive for appearances of these seven hash values. Jackson then published the scripts and data resulting from this query (Jackson 2015).

The charts below display the number of times each of the seven distinct single-pixel GIFs from the Geocities data set appeared in the UK Web Archive collections over time. The first initial pass at the findings shows that there are three extant examples of GIFs in the archive dating from 1996: two instances of blank.gif, three instances of pixel.gif, and 46 instances of spaceball.gif. Hence, we can conclude that spaceball.gif was the earliest widely used or at least widely collected example of single-pixel GIFs. This year is significantly earlier than the first instance of each GIF from the Geocities data set previously discussed (Fig. 2).

Each of the seven unique GIFs studied here existed in the UK Web Archive by 1997. Yet, as the charts show, they made their way across the web and through time in strikingly varied ways. Cleardot.gif (a category documented in two distinct, original Google URLs) emerges as the most widely collected GIF out of the seven. In 2008, the British Library collected and documented the presence of more than one million copies of cleardot.gif (1,062,943 copies). This collection results in a fascinating spike, while the other six GIFs nearly vanish from the archive after having had a large presence in 2006 and 2007. Clear.gif had the earliest significant spike in 1998, and the usage of dot_clear.gif/pixel.gif shot up to nearly 200,000 entries (combined total) in 2004. Blank.gif resurfaced in 2010 and all seven GIFs have low representation in 2009. To begin understanding the trends of single-pixel GIFs over time, it is important to consider whether the GIFs themselves had distinct histories and to examine the details of those histories, separately from collection practices.

Exploration of the histories of each of these individual files through independent searching reveals the varied ways in which these files have been developed and used. As a post by Martin Brinkmann from 2007 documents, spaceball.gif was used by Flickr, the community-driven website launched in 2004 hosting photographs and images, to prohibit easy download of the image files by individuals or crawlers. When a user would attempt to right click and download an image file, they would instead be

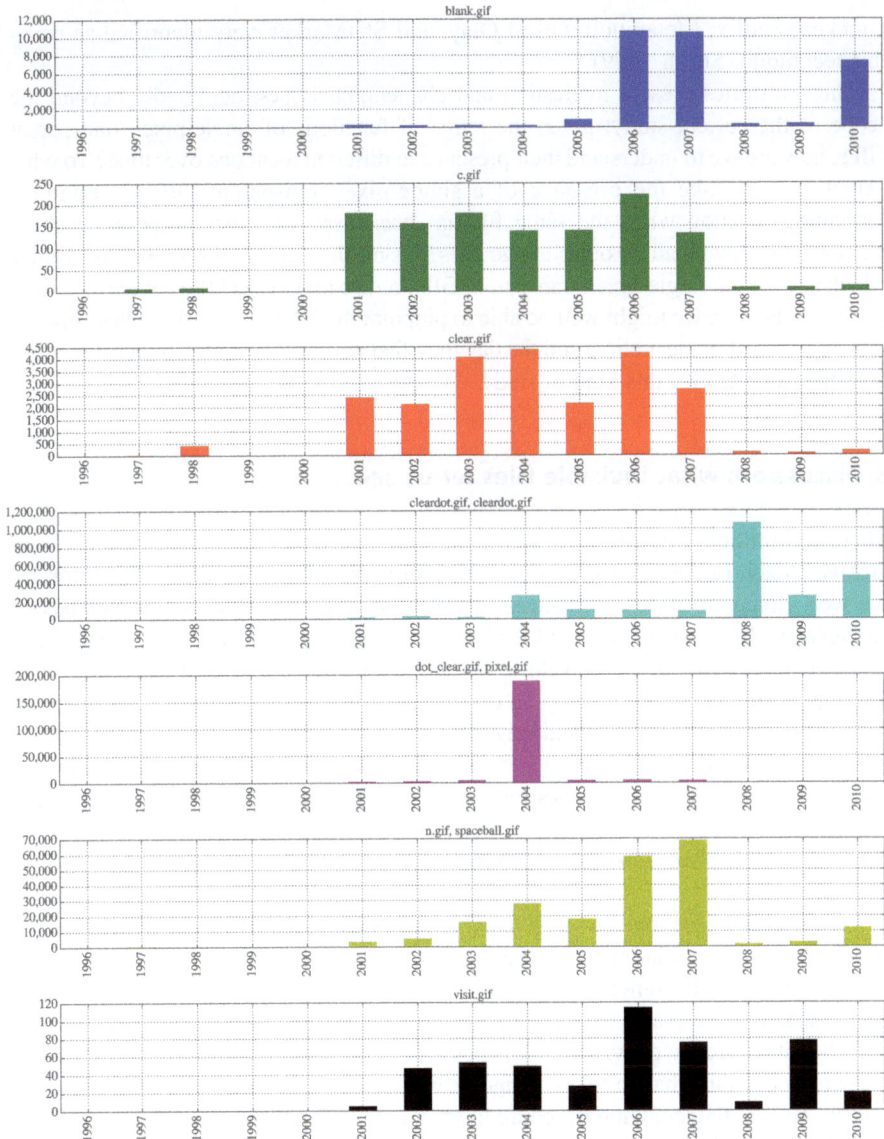

Fig. 2 Appearances of the seven distinct GIFs in the UK Web Archive from 1996 to 2010

tricked into downloading a tiny, transparent GIF which had been invisibly masking the underlying displayed image (Brinkmann 2007).

Similarly, cleardot.gif (much like spaceball.gif) appears to serve a distinctly different purpose from a spacer GIF solely used for formatting. Often referred to as 'web beacons' or 'web bugs,' these files are widely known to be used as a means of surveillance and tracking. Specifically, their tiny size and invisibility means that they load quickly, without being detected. Each time one of these files loads, it results in a ping back to the source. Indeed, the URL https://mail.google.com/mail/u/0/images/cleardot.gif is an example of this (pabouk 2013). Critiques of these methods go back to at least late 1999, when sites for companies including

Quicken, FedEx, Metamucil, Oil of Olay, and StatMarket were identified as using this technique (Smith 1999).

These histories present interesting and challenging issues, admittedly beyond the scope of the current study: given the range of functions of single-pixel, transparent GIFs, how are we to understand their presence in different locations over time? To what extent can we take the presence of a single-pixel transparent GIF as serving a formatting function when the same file has been used for other purposes, such as blocking the download of other image files? Using the data, is it possible to identify which uses of the single-pixel, transparent GIF predate other uses? If we were to zero in on that early year, we might well be able to pinpoint the URL that each of these images first appeared at in the archive and the day they first appeared, which would constitute a possible next step for this kind of study.

3 Discussion: what invisible files let us see

There are millions of copies of single-pixel, transparent GIFs in the world's web archives. Each one is a trace of a practice and method of presenting information on the web. Some are traces of changes in web design. Some are traces of methods of surveillance. By working back and forth between the URLs for these tiny, functionally invisible images and their hash values, we have begun to map some of this history. The findings of this preliminary mapping offer a range of considerations for the future of access and use of web archives and the history of the web. They suggest requirements for a better understanding of crawling and collecting practices, new methods for characterizing and indexing files, and issues for the interpretation of born-digital collection data.

3.1 Seeing web history or web archiving history?

A web crawler whose job is to archive particular websites makes appraisal decisions in a different way than a human archivist processing a donated collection. Both processes include having all documents in front of the archivist and the crawler, and both must decide which to keep and which to pass over. However, all of the rules for a crawler must be set before the crawl starts. It is possible to change the crawler behavior during the crawl, but this change takes a significant amount of effort and ongoing quality review. To avoiding crawling the entire Internet every time, the rules tell a crawler what to archive and what to avoid. Restricted areas can include entire domains or a regular expression for all URLs with the string 'login,' for example.

For this study, it is possible that any dramatic drop in GIF appearances, such as in 1999 and 2000, could reflect the choice of a web archivist to exclude single-pixel, transparent GIFs from the crawl entirely. This decision may have been made for any number of reasons, including space constraints or a simple belief that single-pixel, transparent GIFs were unnecessary to store in the archival record. It is also possible that the program stopped archiving a site or many sites which contained a large number of these single-pixel, transparent GIFs. Collateral content, or superfluous content the crawler ends up harvesting during a crawl, is unavoidable given the nature of the web. If most of the single-pixel GIFs were crawled as collateral content, the exclusion of certain websites may have caused a reduction in their appearances.

80

3.2 Approaching web archives as data corpora

It is imperative for libraries and archives to consider the end *data* utilized by researchers in the future when building digital *collections* in the present. Part of this practice requires web archivists to create scope and content notes and keep records of crawl decisions as they are made and as crawls are performed. Content processing done by the web archivists to understand their own collections as data can help with this. If an archivist saw these dramatic drops in appearances of single-pixel, transparent GIFs as a result of crawling practices, the archivist could file the information and share it with a researcher attempting to understand the collection in the future.

This study looks at transparent GIFs appearing in two specific collections, Olia Lialina's exhibit of transparent GIFs from the Geocities archive and the UK Web Archive. These two collections make up a small percentage of content in web archives throughout the world, web archives which have had varying crawl practices over time (Milliganet al. 2016). We took a look at the history of seven transparent GIFs in data resulting from harvesting done by the UK Web Archiving Team. We have not looked at the complete history of all single-pixel GIFs as they appeared on the live web over time (Brügger 2017).

With appropriate technical infrastructure, this same study could be completed on any organization's web archives. Since each one of these entities will have different crawl practices, multiple web archiving initiatives collecting the same websites is invaluable to researchers studying the web. As the crawl becomes more comprehensive, we can begin to see how the findings of case studies like these are influenced by crawling practices (crawl frequency, crawl depth, deduplication, etc.) and whether the findings are indicative of web usage trends throughout time. Decoupling these concepts is essential for an understanding of the practice of web archiving and the history of the web, respectively, and can only be done through multiple archives.

When we approach each institution's web archives as corpora it becomes increasingly clear that there is significant value in having a range of organizations engaged in web archiving Ideally, they are engaging in these practices with a range of tools. The trends in the appearance of these files raise all kinds of questions. For instance, what conclusions do we reach when we apply similar methods to different kinds of files? In other words, what do trends in identical copies of files themselves tell about the movement, dissemination, and popularity of practices and approaches? There is informational content in the files, but the history of the appearance of a given file in a given place also has potential informational value.

3.3 Characterizing files as key to future modes of access

Knowing the specific URLs at which files exist is also invaluable to the study of web history. The case of single-pixel GIFs illustrates the significant value of modes of characterizing and identifying files using other methods. The ability to hash a file and use that digital fingerprint to see where else it, or files created through identical processes, exists in web archives is immensely powerful. Who would have imagined there were millions of copies of one of these tiny files captured in the UK Web Archive in one particular year? When we discover that two URLs held identical files at a particular date, we can start to track and trace the replication and movement of information. Importantly, this is all derivative information about the content. Even in a situation in which archives can't offer global access to the content itself, non-consumptive hashes could very well be provided for this kind of work.

While hashes are exciting, it is important to remember that there are many other ways of characterizing similarity. An alternative approach to this kind of research could involve simply identifying all the '.gif' files in a web archive that are particularly small and visually inspecting them to identify potential other candidates for different, unique single-pixel GIFs. When one moves further into hash-based approaches to the study of files, it will be critical to remember that minor changes in a file are going to give it a new hash. With that noted, this only further points to the need to root the future of the study of web archives in the ability to compute against the files in these corpora.

3.4 Implications for digital library infrastructure

Access issues highlighted in the computational scholarship are a sobering reminder that 'digital' or 'digitized' doesn't not necessarily mean immediately ready for computational scholarship. Different kinds of questions require data to be prepared, processed, and made accessible in a number of ways. While digital material, rather than analog, is one step closer to becoming data, there is still work to be done to strategically arrange the content for a future of computational scholarship. Furthermore, there are specific necessary affordances in technical architecture in order to enable researchers to compute against a corpus.

As the Library of Congress pilot project showed, cracking open complex WARC files to perform high-level analyses of the archive takes computing power that many researchers, and even institutions, do not always have at their disposal. The present study was, in large part, possible because a copy of the UK Web Archive is maintained and managed on a high-performance distributed computer system and because its archivist was willing to field a request to search across this web archive corpus to answer this particular question. Most web archives are not currently configured in a manner which enables researchers to compute against their content as a corpus.

In order for this kind of research to become more of a reality, library institutions will first have to explore having compute-on-demand capabilities for their entire corpus of web archives and, more broadly, other large, born-digital and digitized collections. This has significant implications for the future of infrastructure. It largely requires either establishing local high-performance computing environments or a shift to approaching access systems that rely on cloud computing environments for access copies of content. Models that involve caching portions of content and working across multiple levels of tiered storage media simply will not be able to facilitate this kind of data corpus use of querying collections.

4 Conclusion: researchers and web archivists embracing distant Reading

The single-pixel, transparent GIF seems to exemplify the essence of insignificance. The files are tiny and invisible. However, the history of these files reveals a great deal about the history of web design, tracking, and surveillance. Sometimes they are spacer GIFs, sometimes they are web bugs, and sometimes they are web beacons. While we have not offered conclusive answers to any of the questions about their history, we have explored single-pixel, transparent GIFs as a case study to shed light on future methods of studying the history of the web through born-digital web archives collections.

The future of the study of the web and the future of collecting the web are intertwined. When we step back and see the patterns that emerge by looking at the hashes of a small set of files in the UK Web Archive, we immediately are prompted to raise two questions: What does this tell us about the history of the web? What does this tell us about the history of web archiving practices? Researchers, now and in the future, will want to approach web archives collections by pivoting between distant reading and close reading. The pairing of distant and close reading as a method of studying the archived web is the only way of conceptualizing the sheer scale of the archived web and performing meaningful research.

However, these methods will also help iteratively to build better, more comprehensive, and more curated web archives throughout the world. The scale of a web archive is also a challenge for the archivists charged with curating and maintaining it. Yet, the same tools used by researchers can be used by web archivists and practitioners in the field to understand their archives or, sometimes more importantly, what is missing from their archives. As practitioners come to understand their archives in greater detail, this knowledge will inform future preservation practices and will provide immediate assistance in provenance for researchers utilizing the data.

Since the scale of web archives does not lend itself to traditional page-through reading and distant reading will become a necessity of close reading, the burden is on digital librarians to rethink the nature and structure of digital libraries, digital content, and web archives infrastructure. This could mean putting more resources into development of tools outside of web page rendering mechanisms, such as streamlined creation and delivery of data sets or web archives content derivatives. Overall, detailed collection notes, especially crawling, scoping, and other specific decisions made over time, are crucial to improving the system and furthering research.

References

Anderson, I. (2008). History and computing. *Making History*. Retrieved from http://www.history.ac.uk/makinghistory/resources/articles/history_and_computing.html.

Archer, J., & Jockers, M. L. (2016). *The bestseller code: Anatomy of the blockbuster novel*. New York: St. Martin's Press.

Bailey, J., & Taylor, N. (2017). *Web Archiving Systems APIs (WASAPI) for systems interoperability and collaborative technical development*. Paper presented at the CNI Fall 2017, Washington DC, US.

Blei, D. M., Ng, A. Y., & Jordan, M. I. (2003). Latent dirichlet allocation. *Journal of Machine Learning Research, 3*(Jan), 993–1022.

Brinkmann, M. (2007). How to avoid saving spaceball.gif at Flickr. *gHacks Tech News*. Retrieved April 25, 2018 from https://www.ghacks.net/2007/09/29/how-to-avoid-saving-spaceballgif-at-flickr/.

Brügger, N. (2017). The archived website and website philology. *Nordicom Review, 29*(2), 155–175. https://doi.org/10.1515/nor-2017-0183.

Clement, T. E., Auvil, L., & Tcheng, D. (2016). *High performance sound technologies for access and scholarship*. Retrieved from http://hdl.handle.net/2152/33295.

Finkel, J. R., Grenager, T., & Manning, C. (2005). Incorporating Non-local Information into Information Extraction Systems by Gibbs Sampling. In *ACL-05 - 43rd Annual Meeting of the Association for*

Computational Linguistics, Proceedings of the Conference (pp. 363–370). Michigan: AnnArbor. https://doi.org/10.3115/1219840.1219885.

Gallinger, M., & Chudnov, D. (2016). *Library of Congress lab: Library of Congress digital scholars lab pilot project report*. Washington, DC: The Library of Congress Retrieved from http://digitalpreservation. gov/meetings/dcs16/DChudnov-MGallinger_LCLabReport.pdf.

Jackson, A. (2015). Tracing clear.gif: Jupyter Notebook. UK Web Archive Github Repository. https://nbviewer.jupyter.org/github/ukwa/halflife/blob/master/clear/tracingclear.gif.ipynb.

Jockers, M. L. (2013). *Macroanalysis: Digital methods and literary history*. Urbana: University of Illinois Press.

Johnson, P. (2011). Digital folklore with Olia Lialina & Dragan Espenschied: The transcript. Retrieved from http://artfcity.com/2011/05/13/digital-folklore-with-olia-lialina-dragan-espenschied-the-transcript/.

Kruse, W. G., II, & Heiser, J. G. (2001). *Computer forensics: Incident response essentials*. Boston: Addison–Wesley Professional.

Lialina, O. (2013). Olia's collection of clear/blanc/0/transparent/cover/beacon GIFs. Retrieved from http://www.collection.evan-roth.com/olia_lialina/clear.gif/.

Lin, J., Milligan, I., Wiebe, J., & Zhou, A. (2017). Warcbase: Scalable analytics infrastructure for exploring web archives. *Journal on Computing and Cultural Heritage (JOCCH), 10*(4), 22.

Lorang, E. M., Soh, L.-K., Datla, M. V., & Kulwicki, S. (2015). Developing an image-based classifier for detecting poetic content in historic newspaper collections. *D-Lib Magazine, 21*(7/8). https://doi.org/10.1045/july2015-lorang.

Mears, J. (2017). Read collections as data report summary. Retrieved April 25, 2018 from https://blogs.loc.gov/thesignal/2017/02/read-collections-as-data-report-summary/.

Milligan, I., Ruest, N., & Lin, J. (2016). Content Selection and Curation for Web Archiving: The Gatekeepers vs. The Masses. In *Proceedings of the 16th ACM/IEEE-CS on Joint Conference on Digital Libraries* (pp. 107–110). New York, NY, USA: ACM. https://doi.org/10.1145/2910896.2910913

Newman, D. J., & Block, S. (2006). Probabilistic topic decomposition of an eighteenth-century American newspaper. *Journal of the Association for Information Science and Technology, 57*(6), 753–767.

Owens, T. (2015). *Designing online communities: How designers, developers, community managers, and software structure discourse and knowledge production on the Web*. New York: Peter Lang.

pabouk. (2013). How does Google's cleardot.gif track email recipients with a generic URL? *Super User*. Retrieved April 25, 2018 from https://superuser.com/questions/658098/how-does-googles-cleardot-gif-track-email-recipients-with-a-generic-url.

Padilla, T. (2017). On a collections as data imperative. Retrieved April 25, 2018 from http://digitalpreservation.gov/meetings/dcs16/tpadilla_OnaCollectionsasDataImperative_final.pdf.

Rønn-Jensen, J. (2006). Who invented the spacer.gif? Retrieved from http://justaddwater.dk/2006/03/03/who-invented-the-spacergif/.

Rønn-Jensen, J. (2007). Who invented the spacer.gif (Part 2). Retrieved from http://justaddwater.dk/2007/02/11/who-invented-the-spacergif-part-2/.

Siegel, D. (1997). The Web is ruined and I ruined it. *XML.Com*. Retrieved from https://www.xml.com/pub/a/w3j/s1.people.html.

Smith, R. M. (1999). The Web Bug FAQ. Retrieved April 25, 2018 from https://w2.eff.org/Privacy/Marketing/web_bug.html.

Smith, D. A., Cordell, R., & Dillon, E. M. (2013). Infectious texts: Modeling text reuse in nineteenth-century newspapers. In *Big Data, 2013 IEEE International Conference on* (pp. 86–94). IEEE.

Underwood, T. (2014). Theorizing research practices we forgot to theorize twenty years ago. *Representations, 127*(1), 64–72. https://doi.org/10.1525/rep.2014.127.1.64.

International Journal of Digital Humanities (2019) 1:85–111
https://doi.org/10.1007/s42803-019-00007-7

RESEARCH ARTICLE

Web archives as a data resource for digital scholars

Eveline Vlassenroot[1] · Sally Chambers[2] · Emmanuel Di Pretoro[3] ·
Friedel Geeraert[4] · Gerald Haesendonck[5] · Alejandra Michel[6] · Peter Mechant[1]

Published online: 8 March 2019
© Springer Nature Switzerland AG 2019

Abstract

The aim of this article is to provide an exploratory analysis of the landscape of web archiving activities in Europe. Our contribution, based on desk research, and complemented with data from interviews with representatives of European heritage institutions, provides a descriptive overview of the state-of-the-art of national web archiving in Europe. It is written for a broad interdisciplinary audience, including cultural heritage professionals, IT specialists and managers, and humanities and social science researchers. The legal, technical and operational aspects of web archiving and the value of web archives as born-digital primary research resources are both explored. In addition to investigating the organisations involved and the scope of their web archiving programmes, the curatorial aspects of the web archiving process, such as selection of web content, the tools used and the provision of access and discovery services are also considered. Furthermore, general policies related to web archiving programmes are analysed. The article concludes by offering four important issues that digital scholars should consider when using web archives as a historical data source. Whilst recognising that this study was limited to a sample of only nine web archives, this article can nevertheless offer some useful insights into the technical, legal, curatorial and policy-related aspects of web archiving. Finally, this paper could function as a stepping stone for more extensive and qualitative research.

Keywords Web archives · Digital scholarship · Curation of digital collections · Copyright · Technology for web archiving

Chapter 7 was originally published as Vlassenroot, E., Chambers, S., Pretoro, E. D., Geeraert, F., Haesendonck, G., Michel, A. & Mechant, P. International Journal of Digital Humanities (2019) 1: 85–111. https://doi.org/10.1007/s42803-019-00007-7.

✉ Eveline Vlassenroot
  Eveline.Vlassenroot@UGent.be

✉ Sally Chambers
  Sally.Chambers@UGent.be

Extended author information available on the last page of the article

1 Setting the scene: Archiving the web as a historical source

The history of web archiving goes back more than 20 years, with the first initiatives launched in 1996 by the Internet Archive, the National Library of Australia and Sweden (Schroeder and Brügger 2017). France was also a pioneer in the field with the National Library of France (BnF) undertaking its first web archiving experiments in 1999 (BnF 2014). However, web archiving has roots in a wider digital preservation movement, which emerged in the 1980s–1990s. Led by memory institutions, the aim of this movement was to develop strategies to respond to the rise of digital technologies and in particular address their ability to capture and preserve digital artefacts as 'records of social phenomena' (Schneider and Foot 2008). As web archiving is still a nascent field, clear definitions are sometimes difficult to find. For this reason, the phrase 'web archiving' is often used interchangeably with 'web preservation,' without any clarification or distinction between the two. For example, the International Internet Preservation Consortium (IIPC)'s definition of web archiving includes both terms: 'Web archiving is the process of collection portions of the World Wide Web, preserving the collections in an archival format, and then serving the archives for access and use' (IIPC 2017). 'Web archiving', therefore, refers to the whole process, whereas 'web preservation' is one of the steps in the process of archiving the web. Web preservation is a crucial step as, in the words of Reyes Ayala, it is 'the process of maintaining internet resources in a condition suitable for use' (2013: 1). A website can be captured and stored, but the preservation of this content ensures it will still be accessible over time. Given this long-term perspective, web archiving requires a strategic approach as much is required in terms of technologies, systems, policies, procedures and resources to make web archiving more than merely harvesting and storing online content.

For digital scholars in the social sciences and humanities, web archives are increasingly recognised as an essential source for studying cultural and social phenomena of recent decades (Schneider & Foot 2005). Some examples include: Brügger et al. (2017), who have been studying the evolution of national domains; Helmond et al. (2017), who used the Internet Archive Wayback Machine for empirically surveying the historical dynamics of social media industry partnerships and partner programmes; Chakraborty and Nanni (2017), who used archived websites as primary sources to examine activities of scientific institutions through the years, or Weber (2017), who traces the tumultuous history of news media on the web through an examination of archived news media content maintained within the Internet Archive. Furthermore, in the BUDDAH (Big UK Domain Data for the Arts and Humanities) project, a number of bursaries were awarded to researchers for carrying out research in their subject area using the UK web archive (BUDDAH 2014). At the European level, RESAW, the Research Infrastructure for the Study of Archived Web Materials, has been established 'with a view to promoting the establishing of a collaborative European research infrastructure for the study of archived web materials' (RESAW 2012).

Legal issues have implications for web archiving as they influence selection policies and users' access to archived online content:

1. Copyright legislation.[1]
2. Personal data protection as web archiving is likely to imply personal data processing. However, it is important to keep in mind that the General Data Protection Regulation (GDPR) authorises legal derogations from the rights of the data subjects when personal data are processed for historical or scientific purposes and for archiving purposes in the public interest.
3. The legal framework on authenticity and integrity of online content as web archives could be used before courts for probative reasons.
4. The issue of illegal contents violating public policy and their potential interest for researchers due to the automatic nature of web archiving tools.
5. Legally delimiting the national scope of competence in a web archiving context with unclear digital boundaries. Indeed, regarding potential overlap between legislation on legal deposit and on public records, it is important to have clear criteria to determine the country and the national heritage institution in charge of the archiving of a particular website.
6. Legislation concerning reuse of public sector information.

As the web has evolved from a publishing to a communication medium, it now presents a vast collection of primary sources for our past. This wealth of diverse information provides the necessary conditions for the emergence of web archiving as a truly interdisciplinary field, bringing together practitioners and scholars from different backgrounds: humanities, social sciences, computer and information sciences, libraries, archives, etc. (Ogden et al. 2017). However, the sheer quantity of information, and the constant evolution of the web, complicate its preservation and make diachronic study for researchers very challenging (Chakraborty and Nanni 2017). As Laursen notes: 'Curators do what they can to capture what they can, and their practices and opportunities change over time' (2017: 220).

The following sections report the findings of a review of web archiving activities in Europe. After a short description of our research methodology, we discuss the aspects of web archiving that affect the users of web archives. First, the web archiving selection process is analysed from an operational point of view, including an in-depth analysis of legal deposit legislation. The different ways in which the concept of a 'national web' is defined and the different selection strategies used by the studied web archiving institutions are explored. Second, the differences in policies regarding access to web archives are analysed, taking into account the legal framework with regard to copyright and the inclusion of illegal content in web archives. On an operational level, the user-friendliness of the studied web archives is explored based on an analysis of the available search functionalities. The role of metadata, and the importance of obtaining a thorough understanding of user needs and requirements are stressed. Third, the 'hands-on' or technical aspects of working with web archives are introduced and some of the challenges and main techniques to keep in mind when working with web archives are discussed. Our explorative analysis of European web archives ends with a discussion underlining four important considerations for digital scholars.

---

[1] For instance, obtaining prior authorisation of right holders, creating new exceptions for reproduction or communication to the public for archiving purposes and obtaining a fair balance between the public interest in preserving information of cultural or historical significance and the interests of rights holders.

2 Methodology

The research methodology consisted of three phases. In the first phase, a secondary research approach (also known as desk research) was taken. This involved summarising, collating and/or synthesising documentation related to existing web archiving projects. A number of web archiving initiatives were selected and analysed in depth. These included the National Library and National Archive of the Netherlands, the Royal Danish Library (Netarkivet), the National Library of Ireland, the National Library of France (BnF), the National Library of Luxembourg, the British Library, The National Archives UK and Arquivo.pt. in Portugal. With regard to the selection of our sample of web archiving initiatives, a number of characteristics were taken into account:

–   Established web archiving initiatives
–   Web archiving initiatives in countries where both the national library and the national archives are involved in web archiving (as the PROMISE project is a collaboration between the Belgian Royal Library and State Archives, useful lessons could be drawn from countries where both institutions engage in web archiving)
–   Web archiving initiatives in countries with multiple official languages
–   Web archiving initiatives in countries of different sizes
–   Combination of web archiving initiatives relying on external service providers and initiatives that manage all aspects of the process in-house.

Not all of these features are applicable to each initiative; the main aim was to study a representative mix of web archiving initiatives, based on the above characteristics.

The main research question for this study is: how are other European national libraries and national archives engaging in web archiving and how are the web archiving processes organised? The web archives were studied from a legal, technical and operational point of view. The aim was to create an overview of the web archiving processes in place in each of the institutions covering a) the selection (selection policy, legal framework), b) the web archiving process itself (crawling, quality control, indexation, preservation and storage) and c) access to, and use, of the web archive (policies, search functionalities and legal framework). Operational questions such as the composition of the web archiving teams in terms of professional profiles or the storage requirements in terabytes (TB) or petabytes (PB), were also included in the mix.

In the second research phase, interviews were conducted with representatives from the aforementioned institutions. The aim of the interviews was to fill in the gaps that remained on the specific initiatives following the literature review so that a complete overview of the web archiving activities was obtained for each of the institutions. All participants were interviewed either in face-to-face meetings or by conference call. The interviews were semi-structured, using both closed and open questions. Some interviewees already provided written replies to (some) of these questions beforehand, in which case the interview consisted mainly of follow-up questions. Interviewees included a mix of archivists, librarians, IT specialists, managers, digital curators and researchers (see Appendix A).

The third and final research phase encompassed further validation and synthesis. The answers to the questions that were obtained during the literature review, and in the interviews, were integrated. On the basis of which, comparisons were drawn, thereby obtaining an answer to the research questions and creating an overarching view of the selected web archiving initiatives. This allowed to us to distil the relevant aspects that are important for digital scholars.

3 Selection of content for web archives

3.1 How is web archiving framed by the law?

In all of the countries where our selected European web archiving institutions are based, the National Library is legally responsible for preserving and opening up cultural and historical heritage to the public, even if they have no legal deposit law (e.g. The Netherlands). There is a lot of information available online; thus, institutions believe that the preservation of online cultural heritage is naturally part of their legal mandate. In addition to the mandate to preserve a nation's heritage, there are two legal ways to enable web archiving: on the one hand, legal deposit legislation; on the other hand, legislation on public archives.

The majority of countries have gradually modified their national legal deposit legislation in order to widen it to the Internet and thus allow the collection and preservation of online information.[2] In Ireland, this process is ongoing as the legal deposit legislation is now under review to broaden its scope to include online contents (Ryan 2017). As Maria Ryan (2017) stated: 'The Irish situation is difficult because Irish Legal Deposit legislation does not extend to digital or online publications. The legislation is under review at the moment'.

The scope of this legislation is often very broad in regard to determining which websites should be archived. However, national legislation generally excludes personal correspondence and private spaces available on intranets, for privacy reasons.

Still, a minority of countries do not have any legal texts relating to legal deposit (at least, to the web legal deposit).[3] In these countries, the deposit of websites of cultural and/or historical significance to the National Library is in principle done on a voluntary basis (Beunen and Schiphof 2006, p. 18; Kunze and Power n.d., p. 2). Indeed, in the absence of a legal obligation to deposit publications, the consent of website owners is necessary.[4] These right holders are, therefore, able to refuse web archiving.

In the Web 2.0 world, obtaining the prior consent of each right holder is impracticable, especially since their identification can be very difficult. Therefore, heritage

---

[2] It is the case for France with the DADVSI Law (see « Loi n° 2006–961 du 1er août 2006 relative au droit d'auteur et aux droits voisins dans la société de l'information »), for Luxembourg (see « Loi luxembourgeoise du 25 juin 2004 portant réorganisation des instituts culturels de l'Etat »), for United Kingdom (see « Legal Deposit Libraries (Non-Print Works) Regulations of 5th April 2013 »), For Denmark (see "Danish Act n° 1439 on Legal Deposit of Published Material of 22nd December 2004").

[3] For instance, The Netherlands, Portugal and Switzerland (at the federal level).

[4] Prior authorization of the right holders is not necessary for websites that have fallen into the public domain or that were made available under the system of Creative Commons License (Beunen and Schiphof 2006, p. 16).

institutions acting in countries that do not have legislation for the web legal deposit do not always ask the permission from the websites owners before proceeding to collect their website, preferring to take a pragmatic approach. On the one hand, they either notify the website owner of their intention to archive their website and if he/she does not object, they consider that the website owner implicitly consents to the archiving.[5] As Kees Teszelszky states:

> The biggest problem for web archiving in the Netherlands and for our national library is that we do not have a legal deposit like you have in Belgium. [...] So then we decided [...] to [use] the opt out method. So if we want to archive the website, [...] we do not ask permission, we say we are going to archive and if people are not reacting on our wish, then we are archiving. (Teszelszky 2017a)

On the other hand, they either choose to archive all websites included in their selection policy without prior notification, but allow the website owner to object to the archiving by using Robot Exclusion Protocols.[6] In any case, these heritage institutions are generally very cautious. In this way, they develop a very effective takedown policy in the event of subsequent objections by website owners, through the removal of the archived content from their database.

There are a number of advantages for heritage institutions of relying on legal provisions that enable them to frame their web archiving activities in order to solve the aforementioned difficulties. Firstly, legislation on web legal deposit has the advantage of offering greater legal certainty and facilitating the web archiving by forcing the website owners to comply with the legal deposit obligation. Indeed, such legislation means that heritage institutions are not required to ask for prior permission from website owners (Beunen and Schiphof 2006). Without that legislation, the owners' consent would be required, because the archiving of a website composed of various protected contents[7] necessarily triggers an act of reproduction,[8] likely to infringe copyright. Alongside a web legal deposit obligation, some countries created some copyright exceptions covering activities intrinsically linked to web archiving and access.[9] It is, in fact, technically impossible to archive a website without reproducing it. In this way, these kind of exceptions have proved unavoidable in order to permit acts of reproduction (Graff and Sepetjan 2011: 179–180). Secondly, some countries have a legal provision allowing the heritage institution responsible for web archiving to require

---

[5] This approach is the one of the National Library of The Netherlands (KB Nederland, n.d.-b and n.d.-d).

[6] This approach is the one of Arquivo.pt. in Portugal (Arquivo.pt, n.d.-c).

[7] Let us indicate that websites are composed of a set of elements that can be each protected by copyright (original texts, images, search engine, database, etc.) and may each have a different right holder (KB Nederland n.d.-e). We also have to underline the fact that websites can also be composed of elements protected by other rights such as trademark law, database right, neighboring rights and image right (KB Nederland n.d.-b).

[8] Act for which the consent of the right holders is in principle required.

[9] In France, the DADVSI Law has introduced an exception allowing acts of reproduction and communication related to the web legal deposit (see French Heritage Code, art. L132–4 to L132–6). In the United Kingdom, Sections 19 to 31 of the Legal Deposit Libraries (Non-Print Works) Regulations of 5th April 2013 and Section 44A of the Copyright, Designs and Patents Act of 15th November 1988 allow the realization of certain activities related to web legal deposit without that they violate copyright.

domain names management bodies to help them identify website owners.[10] Thirdly, some legislations go even further by allowing heritage institutions to require website owners to give the passwords and access keys necessary for collecting their website.[11] This makes it considerably easier for the heritage institutions to obtain the web material covered by legal deposit.

Concerning the criteria for deciding the scope of the national web archive at the national level, we noticed some similarities in the choices made by the studied countries with legal deposit legislation. Considering that online information falls within the scope of competence of one state or another, there are three main principles to be followed. Firstly, a state considers itself competent to archive online contents published within its national domain name. Secondly, a state also considers itself competent to archive online contents published on other domain names if one of these additional conditions is met: if the website was registered to the national body responsible for managing domain names or by a citizen of the state; if the content of the website is related to the state (i.e. concerns the general affairs of the state); if the content of the website was drafted by a citizen of the state or in the national territory. Luxembourg also has an additional criterion which was not found elsewhere: if the production of the publication has been supported by the state. Thirdly, the language of the content is an additional criterion. However, this criterion only applies to countries with a single national language but does not work for countries with multiple national languages that are also national languages of other countries.

In countries without legal deposit legislation for online content, the scope is defined in a similar way. In Ireland, in addition to the national top level domain, web material that is of Irish interest, has heritage value and that treats a subject of interest, is also considered to be within scope (National Library of Ireland 2017a). In Portugal, the top level domain of all Portuguese speaking domains, except for the Brazilian domain, are included, as are websites on other domain names that are of broad interest to the Portuguese community. While in The Netherlands, websites about Dutch language, history and culture on both the national domain, and other domain names, are within the scope of the project (Arquivo.pt n.d.-c; Sierman and Teszelszky 2017).

There is a marked difference between public record legislation that regulates the activities of national archives and legal deposit legislation that frames the missions of national libraries. Where web legal deposit legislation exists (UK, France, Denmark, …) numerous detailed provisions are included to frame web archiving activities. For instance, the text of the UK legal deposit legislation[12] comprises of more than 20 legal provisions, specifically related to web legal deposit. However, in public records legislation, the same text that applies to classic public records also applies to online public records, meaning that there are no specific legal provisions where web archiving is concerned, except for in the Library and Archives of Canada Act. The legal text on

---

[10] For instance, in France, Article L132–2-1 of the French Heritage Code authorize the "Bibliothèque Nationale de France" to turn to domain names management bodies or to the Higher Audiovisual Council to identify the publishers and producers of websites. There is also a similar legal provision in Denmark (See Danish Act n° 1439 on Legal Deposit of Published Material of 22nd December 2004, §11).

[11] It is the case in France (see French Heritage Code, art. R132–23-1, II), United Kingdom (see Legal Deposit Libraries (Non-Print Works) Regulations of 5th April 2013, Section 16 (4)) and Denmark (see Danish Act n° 1439 on Legal Deposit of Published Material of 22nd December 2004, §10).

[12] The Legal Deposit Libraries (Non-Print Works) Regulations 2013

public records therefore applies to websites of public institutions only because the notion of "records" is broadly defined (for instance, as 'all types of medium').

3.2 How is web archived content selected?

Our analysis shows a great deal of variation when it comes to selection strategies and criteria. Furthermore, the terminology for describing the web archiving approach, differs between web archiving initiatives. As can be seen in Table 1, in the case of Arquivo.pt., two main strategies can be distinguished: broad crawls (covering top-level domain crawls (e.g. .be, .fr) and relevant content outside of the national domain(s)) and selective crawls (thematic or events-based collections, for example). The selection policy of national archives with regard to web archiving differs in the sense that it is mostly limited to the public records of governmental organisations. For national libraries, the scope of collection is broader as web archiving is seen as part of the legal deposit legislation or as a complement to the more traditional electronic or paper collections of publications in countries without legal deposit legislation.

All national libraries and Arquivo.pt. in Portugal combine broad crawls with selective crawls, except for the National Library of France (BnF) where a representative sample of the web is taken instead of a complete top level domain crawl and the National Library of The Netherlands, where only a selective approach is taken Table 1.[13]

Different methods are used to identify the content that does not reside under URLs of the national domain. The British Library, for example, uses Geo-IP localisation to locate information on servers in the UK or make use of UK postal addresses (Hockx-Yu 2014). At the Royal Danish Library a specific system has been developed to identify this content. As Jakob Moesgaard explained:

> We've built a system that basically looks at everything we harvest. It looks at all the links that point out [...] and then it analyses the content on all of those pages. [...] It scans for regular expressions that cover Danish phone numbers and [...] we try to have this sort of validation process ranking [...] to see if [...] it looks Danish enough for us to trust that we should automatically add it to the archive. (Moesgaard and Larsen 2017a, b)

In the case of selective crawls, there are different ways of determining these collections. Some institutions have defined overarching selection criteria for these collections. The British Library, for example, focuses on websites that publish research, reflect the diversity of lives, interests and activities in the UK and demonstrate web innovation for the UK Web Archive (UK Web Archive n.d.-a). In general, websites deemed of interest to the nation are included in the selection, meaning websites that are representative of the diverse society, or that are linked to the history and culture of a nation. It is interesting to note that the popularity, uniqueness or the degree of innovation of websites is sometimes also taken into account, as well as websites that publish research (KB Nederland n.d.-a; National Library of Ireland 2017a; Maurer and Els 2017a; Gomes 2017b).

---

[13] Sierman and Teszelszky 2017; BnF 2017a, b; Maurer and Els 2017a; UK Web Archive (n.d.-a); Hockx-Yu 2014; Brügger et al. 2017; Arquivo.pt n.d.-c; Ryan 2017; National Library of Ireland 2017a, b.

Table 1 Overview of general selection strategies for web content

Country	Institution	Broad crawl	Selective crawl
The Netherlands	National Library	No	Yes
France	National Library	No (Representative sample)	Yes
Luxembourg	National Library	Yes	Yes
UK	British Library	Yes (non-print legal deposit)	Yes (open UK web archive)
Denmark	Royal Danish Library	Yes	Yes
Portugal	Foundation for Science and Technology (FCT) (Arquivo.pt)	Yes	Yes
Ireland	National Library	Yes	Yes

Another way to create selective collections is to build them based on specific themes, events or even emergencies (mostly focusing on natural disasters or other unforeseeable events). There is a large variety in how thematic collections are defined. They can, for example, be centred around the different collection departments in the institution, as is the case in the National Library of France (BnF 2017a) or focus on other themes such as literary collections or health and social issues amongst others, which is the case in the National Library of Ireland (National Library of Ireland (n.d.-d)). Event-based collections on the other hand are more coherent between institutions. Most often they are about events such as elections (national or local), commemorations, referendums or sporting events such as the Olympics.

With regard to social media, a number of web archiving initiatives include them in their collections. From a technical point of view, archiving social media is challenging (e.g. due to the vast amount of data generated or changing access policies), which explains why increasingly sophisticated proprietary and open source software and services are available to support social media archiving. The policies with regard to social media differ widely between institutions. Table 2 provides an overview of which institution preserves which social media.[14] The most popular social media platforms captured by the studied web archiving initiatives are Twitter, YouTube and Facebook. The social media accounts that are captured, in general focus on important people, organisations and events such as political parties, politicians, newspapers, journalists, athletes, other celebrities, etc. In the case of Arquivo.pt. no special efforts are made to harvest social media, although their web archive does contain some material stemming from Facebook and Twitter (Gomes 2017b). The National Library of the Netherlands is also not currently harvesting social media, but they have it included in their 10-year plan. At the National Archive of The Netherlands social media are not yet included in their collection either, but tests have been scheduled in 2018 to archive social media (Teszelszky 2017a; Posthumus and van Luin 2017a*)*.

---

[14] Tanésie et al. 2017; Maurer and Els 2017b; British Library 2017a; British Library (n.d.-b); National Archives (n.d.-a); Netarkivet.dk 2017; Moesgaard and Larsen 2017a

Table 2 Overview of social media included in web archives

Country	Institution	Facebook	Twitter	YouTube	Instagram	Flickr
France	National Library	(used to, not anymore)	Yes	No	No	No
Luxembourg	National Library	Yes	Yes	Yes	Yes	No
UK	British Library	Yes	Yes	No	No	No
UK	National Archives	No	Yes	Yes	No	No
Denmark	Royal Danish Library	Yes	Yes	Yes	Yes	No
Ireland	National Library	No	Yes	Yes	No	(starting in 2018)

Some institutions also make use of certain exclusion criteria, some of which concern the legality of the content. The national legislations are unanimous on what constitutes illegal content: child pornography, hate, xenophobic or racist speech, speech inciting to violence, etc. Some institutions take specific measures to exclude this content automatically. The National Library of France, for example, makes use of a filtering tool (Tanésie et al. 2017). Additional exclusion criteria are sometimes in place, for instance, excluding content that is already included in other web archives or material that cannot be captured for technical reasons (KB Nederland (n.d.-d); Moesgaard and Larsen 2017a). In the case of The National Archives UK, additional selection criteria have been developed for Twitter content, for example, tweets written by the selected government organisations are included, but retweets or tweets sent from non-governmental accounts to government accounts are excluded (National Archives (n.d.-a)).

When digital scholars use web archives for their research, it is important that they take into account how the archived web content is selected and who is responsible for making that selection. In some institutions specific collection specialists are responsible for making the selection, while in other cases, selection is a responsibility that is shared between a large number of people, each devoting only a limited amount of time to selecting the content. This is, for instance, the case at the National Library of France (BnF 2016) where the selection is done transversally, meaning that each department contributes to the web archiving by entering URLs into the system (Tanésie et al. 2017).

Furthermore, some institutions collaborate with external partners. The National Library of Ireland sometimes contacts specialists in the field. For their collection on the Irish elections, they contacted political analysts, lecturers and journalists in order to obtain their feedback on what should be included in the collection (Ryan 2017).

The role of digital scholars, along with the general public, in the selection of content for web archives is a topic worthy of consideration. For example, engagement from the digital scholars as well as the general public is already being sought: the national libraries of France, The Netherlands, Luxembourg, Denmark and Ireland, and Arquivo.pt., all provide a way for people to make suggestions for websites to be included in the selection (BnF 2017c; KB (n.d.-d); BnL n.d.; Netarkivet.dk 2016a; Ryan 2017; Arquivo.pt (n.d.-e)).

As 'all web archives to a greater or lesser degree can only suggest comprehensiveness', (Koerbin 2017: 194) web archiving institutions have a very important role to play as facilitator. They should ensure that sufficient information about the web archiving context is made available so that researchers can find the answers to the questions evoked by Webster (2017: 175–176): 'Why has this content been archived, by whom and on whose behalf?' There is a clear demand for this information. Sara Aubry of the National Library of France (BnF) stated:

> This is information researchers increasingly request meaning that they wish to understand the context of the production of the archive in order to gain insight into whether [a resource] was archived as part of a selective crawl or of a broad crawl, if it was part of a specific project, how long the crawl lasted, [...], so really everything about the context of the capture. (Tanésie et al. 2017, translated from French)

However, even though the importance of this contextual information is understood, it is sometimes not made available. From a research perspective, this lack of contextual information is problematic.

Finally, the web archiving process itself has an impact on what digital scholars can do with the material:

> The purpose, strategies and technology of an archive affect what is archived and the manner in which it can be accessed, and in this way influence the possibility of constructing a research object on the basis of the material in the archive. (Nielsen 2016)

It is important that digital scholars keep these various aspects in mind, when they undertake their research using data from web archives.

4 Consultation, access and ease of use of web archives

4.1 How to consult and access web archived content?

It is essential to underline that access conditions differ widely between web archives as can be seen in Table 3. Some of the web archives are freely accessible online such as Arquivo.pt. in Portugal or the web archive developed by the National Library of Ireland[15] (Arquivo.pt n.d.-a; National Library of Ireland n.d.-a). For the national libraries, this mission of making national heritage accessible to the public is complementary to their national heritage preservation mandate. However, granting such access to the public must comply with the legal provisions related to copyright. Indeed, the vast majority of archived online content is protected by copyright and, while it is clear that their mere archiving is not likely to cause too much damage to right holders, this is not the case when making this content available to the public (Beunen and Schiphof 2006).

As a result, in a number of web archives, only specific parts of the collections are freely accessible. In the case of the British Library, the Open UK web archive and the

---

[15] In the case of the National Library of Ireland, this only counts for the web archive collections that were based on a selective policy. Access conditions to the web material collected during the top-level domain crawl that started in 2017 were not yet defined at the time of the interview.

  Springer

JISC UK web domain dataset for example are freely accessible, whereas the UK non-print legal deposit web archive is not (UK Web Archive (n.d.-b); British Library (n.d.-b)). At the National Archive of the Netherlands, a specific status for access is assigned to each archived website: open, restricted or offline (Posthumus and van Luin 2017b). Some web archives, which are not freely available, are only accessible on the premises of the library from specific workstations. In the case of the UK non-print legal deposit web archives, the law also specifies that only one user can access a certain piece of online content at any given time.[16] A reader card needs to be obtained in some cases to gain access to the reading rooms as is the case in the National Library of The Netherlands (KB Nederland (n.d.-e)). At the National Library of France (BnF)[17] however, the legislation is more flexible: accredited users are allowed to bring their own laptop to connect to the network. At the Royal Danish Library remote access is provided for PhD-level researchers (Moesgaard and Larsen 2017b). Some web archives are also only open to researchers and others are not accessible at all, as is the case for the web archive of the National Library of Luxembourg where the technical infrastructure is not yet in place (Maurer and Els 2017a). However, in most cases, the access restrictions are in place because of copyright reasons. As Webster states: 'A common feature of most web archiving backed by legal deposit legislation is some sort of restrictions on the access afforded to the end user of the archive' (Webster 2017: p. 180) Table 3.

The British Library found a way to avoid certain access restrictions with their interface SHINE of which the beta version was launched in December 2017 (UK Web Archive (n.d.-d)). Their archive is open to anyone, but for content that is not publicly available, only the metadata is shown (Webber 2017). Other web archiving specialists showed interest in the SHINE interface, Yves Maurer from the National Library of Luxembourg stated that:

> The SHINE interface of the UK British Library would be very useful for digital humanities researchers, for sociologists, political scientists maybe or even journalists. (Maurer and Els 2017a)

In the context of access to web archives, it is important to keep in mind the interests of rights holders. Table 4 provides an overview of how the studied institutions allow web archives to be used. Some countries are keen to put in place a fair balance between the interests of website owners and the interest of the public to access archived online content. Indeed, some heritage institutions respect a kind of 'embargo' on access (meaning that content can only be made accessible to the public at the end of a certain period) upon a duly justified request of right holders. For instance, in the United Kingdom right holders have the opportunity to submit a written request to the deposit library to prevent readers' access for a renewable period of three years in order to protect their commercial interests. The British Library grants this 'embargo' request if it considers that providing access to readers during the specified period would unreasonably prejudice the interests of right holders (see Legal Deposit Libraries (Non-Print Works) Regulations of 5th April 2013, Section 25). Arquivo.pt. in Portugal also makes use of an automatic 'embargo' for all online publications. They are attentive to the interests and rights of authors by respecting an access

---

[16] See Legal Deposit Libraries (Non-Print Works) Regulation of 5th April 2013, Section 23.

[17] See French Heritage Code, art. R132–23-2.

Table 3 Overview of access methods to the web archives

Country	Institution	Access method			Who has access?
		Open & freely accessible online	Physical access on location		
The Netherlands	National Library	No	Yes		Everyone with a paid library card. Big data researchers can gain access after a meeting and having signed a contract.
The Netherlands	National Archive	Yes (for websites with an 'open' status)	Yes (for websites with a 'restricted' or 'offline' status)		'Open' & 'offline' status websites: everybody. Some items are 'restricted', which means you need a special permission (a research proposal is required to obtain this permission or proof that the subject of the archived content is dead). Together with the special permission a signed form is needed stating you understand your own responsibilities under the privacy-law.
France	National Library	No	Yes (but also from within the 26 partner libraries)		Authorized users of the BnF (18 years or older and for university studies, professional or personal research. For the latter two categories, interviews are conducted before accreditation is given.)
Luxembourg	National Library	No	No		No public system yet.
UK	British Library	Yes (for the UK web archive)	Yes (for the legal deposit UK web archive and JISC domain dataset)		Everyone with a reader's pass.
UK	National Archives	Yes	No		Everyone
Denmark	Royal Danish Library	Yes (only for researchers conducting research on a Ph.D-level or above)	Yes (only for researchers)		Only for research purposes after filling an application form that needs to be evaluated.
Portugal	Foundation for Science and Technology	Yes	No		Everyone
Ireland	National Library	Yes	No		Everyone

The information included in this table can be found in: KB Nederland (n.d.-e); Posthumus and van Luin 2017b; BnF 2017c; Maurer and Els 2017b; UK Web Archive (n.d.-c); British Library (n.d.-a); Webber 2017; National Archives (n.d.-b); Moesgaard and Larsen 2017b; Arquivo.pt (n.d.-b); National Library of Ireland 2017a, b embargo period of one year after the collection of the website to avoid that the archived content competes with the online website (Gomes 2017a) Table 4.

Finally, web archives raise the question of how to proceed in relation to illegal content. Since most of web archiving procedures are automatic, it is inevitable that sometimes so-called 'illegal' content is collected. This was also noted by the National Library of France (BnF) where Sara Aubry stated:

> We will not collect them, we will not take active steps to collect [illegal content] in the context of selective crawls [thematic or events-based collections, for example]. In the broad crawls [covering the capture of a representative sample of the French web], however, we will not refrain from collecting them. (Tanésie et al. 2017, translated from French)

Table 4 Overview of allowed use of the web archives

Country	Institution	Functionalities
The Netherlands	National Library	Copy only for themselves.
The Netherlands	National Archive	Not specified.
France	National Library	Short quotations and screenshots only for teaching and research. Forbidden to download archived files and other technical restrictions may prevent copying of texts or screenshots.
Luxembourg	National Library	No functionalities as no access is currently provided.
UK	British Library	Printing of material in the legal deposit UK web archive is allowed, but very limited.
UK	National Archives	Most Crown copyright material within the Web Archive can be used without formal permission under the terms of the Open Government Licence. Where the copyright of material is owned by a third-party, it is the responsibility of the user to obtain the necessary permission for re-use.
Denmark	Royal Danish Library	Possible to make a copy of the website for personal use, display the archive or websites from the archive for teaching (non-public classes or courses). Use in public, scientific and television presentations and for scientific publications is also possible but with certain restrictions.
Portugal	Foundation for Science and Technology (FCT) (Arquivo.pt)	Access is intended to support work of an educational, scientific or research nature. Use for commercial purposes is strictly forbidden.
Ireland	National Library	Available for the purposes of research and private study only. For publication the permission is needed from the National Library. When copyright exists and is not held by the National Library, the copyright holder's permission is also needed.

The information included in this table can be found in: KB Nederland (n.d.-e); BnF (2017c); Maurer and Els 2017b; UK Web Archive (n.d.-c); National Archives (n.d.-a); Netarkivet.dk 2016b; Arquivo.pt (n.d.-d); National Library of Ireland (n.d.-b); National Library of Ireland (n.d.-c)

If web archives contain illegal content, heritage institutions usually ensure that these archived web pages are not made accessible to the public. Nevertheless, such contents might be of interest for digital scholars and researchers in certain disciplines to understand and analyse the history and the culture of the country. To paraphrase Valérie Schafer; having, for example, access to past Neo-Nazi websites, which, in fact, contain hate speech, is of utmost importance, both for the study of digital cultures and of history in general (Tanésie and Aubry 2017).

4.2 What makes a web archive easy to use?

Once users have obtained access to a web archive, archived websites are often not easily discoverable via the available search and browse methods (see Table 5). This inhibits use (Dooley 2016). Two main challenges were revealed to ensure discoverability in the context of a web archive; the lack of descriptive metadata guidelines and the lack of a clear understanding of user needs and behaviour (Dooley et al. 2017). It is necessary to address these two challenges in order to guarantee the discoverability of web archives.

The lack of descriptive metadata guidelines related to web archiving is also problematic for initiatives where the aim is to link different web archives, as is the case for the National Coalition for Digital Preservation (NCDD) in The Netherlands. The NCDD is working on promoting cooperation and creating an inventory of which material is present in which web archive (NCDD n.d.). Related to this initiative, Teszelszky (2017a) said: 'If we want to have a national web collection, we need to use the same software. We need to have common standards and that's something that

Table 5 Overview of search options in the web archives

Country	Institution	Search options			
		URL	Full-text	Topical browsing	Alphabetic browsing
The Netherlands	National Library	Yes	No	No	No
The Netherlands	National Archive	No	No	No	No
France	National Library	Yes	Yes	Yes	No
Luxembourg	National Library	Not open for the public yet.	Not open for the public yet.	Not open for the public yet.	Not open for the public yet.
UK	British Library	Yes	Yes	Yes	No
UK	National Archives	Yes	Yes	No	Yes
Denmark	Royal Danish Library	Yes	Yes	No	No
Portugal	Foundation for Science and Technology	Yes	Yes	No	No
Ireland	National Library	Yes	Yes	No	Yes

The information included in this table can be found in: Teszelszky 2017b; Posthumus and van Luin 2017b; BnF (2017c); Maurer and Els 2017b; UK Web Archive (n.d.-b); The National Archives n.d.; Gomes 2017b; National Library of Ireland (n.d.-a)

will be worked on'. Increasing standardisation of metadata management would, there-fore, be advantageous for the users.

The second most frequently mentioned challenge is the need for a better under-standing of user needs and behaviour to ensure discoverability for archived websites (Costa and Silva 2010; Dougherty et al. 2010). Many web archiving institutions do not have accurate statistics on the number of visitors of their web archive. Often the number of visitors to the web archive are merged with the number of visitors of the whole website (as is the case at the National Archive of the Netherlands) or in other cases the internal use of the staff was included (as is the case at the National Library of the Netherlands). Furthermore, numbers like these do not indicate who these visitors are; why they are visiting; what they expect to find; what they take away with them and whether they experienced any degree of satisfaction. As Maria Ryan (2017) of the National Library of Ireland stated: 'It's difficult to get good analytics on web archive users, due to the fact the selective web archive can be accessed remotely'. In the case of Arquivo.pt., efforts are made to target the right people to stimulate them to make use of the web archive. In this regard, they have a well-defined communication strategy in place to encourage researchers and academia to use their collections. For example, they organise contests offering prize money to researchers working with their collections (Gomes 2017b). That user engagement is also considered an important matter at the British Library is underscored by the fact that they have a 'Web Archiving Engagement Manager' for the web archive (British Library 2017b). This contrasts with other web archiving initiatives that find it hard to attract users:

> Not many people are using our web archive. I think we have 100 visitors a year
> [...] We only see this year that these kind of researchers come to our web archive
> because some websites are not in the Internet Archive. (Teszelszky 2017a)

In general, most interfaces of web archives afford a form of URL search (either searching for an exact URL or a specific part of a URL), combined with full-text searches. The URL approach has been dominant for years (Ben-David and Huurdeman 2014) but, recently, full-text search is also supported by most of the web archives. Research by Costa and Silva (2010) shows that users prefer full-text search to URL search. However, some web archives have also permitted other types of searches for some time now. In such web archives, the user can also explore topical collections or undertake alphabetical browsing (see Table 5).

5 Overview of tools used in web archiving

This section briefly describes web archives from a technical viewpoint. In particular, it discusses software tools involved in the process of gathering web content and analysing this content that might be relevant for digital scholars. Not all available tools are described, however, nor are the long-term preservation systems or the back-ends of archives.

Web archiving starts with harvesting or crawling websites, which means trying to get a copy of websites. Since web content is diverse—static pages, dynamic pages, multimedia, social media, etc.— different harvesting tools focus on different types of content. Typically they produce output that can be stored or archived, for instance, as a directory structure on disk, mimicking the original website or as Web Archive (WARC) files (ISO 2017).

HTTrack (Roche 2018) copies the website(s) to disk so the user can simply open it in a browser. It uses a single thread so one instance is only suited for limited crawls. Webrecorder (Webrecorder n.d.) uses a browser to harvest content of websites, hereby addressing typical issues of other harvesting tools: dynamic content, flash, multimedia, etc. It 'records' web pages as the user browses them, so it is suited for very selective, high quality crawling. Although it requires some technical skills to install, an online demo is available. The content is saved in the WARC format.

Wget (Free Software Foundation 2017) and the similar tool Wpull (Foo 2016) are versatile command line tools that have built-in web crawling functionality, comparable to HTTrack. They can write to a directory structure or to WARC files. Wpull is better suited for large crawls because it stores detected URLs to disk as opposed to WGet which stores them in often limited computer memory, and it offers deduplication (i.e. crawls a page only once). Both tools are rather easy to install and to run; the art is to compose the right commands to instruct them. Grab-site (Grab-site GitHub 2018) provides a graphical interface for Wpull.

Social media require specialised tools to capture their content because of their very dynamic nature. Capturing content is typically done programmatically using Application Programming Interfaces or APIs, offered by the social media providers. F(b)arc (Fbarc GitHub 2018) is a command line tool that can be used to archive data using the Facebook Graph interface. Twarc (Twarc GitHub 2018) is a command line tool and library that makes using the Twitter APIs easy. It can be used to archive data, detect trends, search friends, etc. Social Feed Manager (Social Feed Manager 2018) can harvest data from Twitter, Tumblr, Flickr, and Sina Weibo.

Web archiving organisations tend to use more advanced tools, which often require technical skills to install and use. Heritrix (Webarchive.jira.com, July 2016) is a general purpose web crawler designed with web archiving in mind. It can be configured for broad crawls or targeted crawls, on one machine or in clusters, it can be extended with custom code, etc. It is suited for large scale crawling activities, but less so for dynamic pages or social media. It produces WARC files. The NetarchiveSuite (Rosenthal 2017) is built with Heritrix at its core, but provides extra functionality in the area of deployment, long term preservation and access. Brozzler (Brozzler GitHub 2018) uses the engine of the Chrome browser to harvest pages, which offers the same advantages Webrecorder offers, but it requires no user interaction during crawling. It can be set up on a cluster.

Besides tools to get the data, there are also tools for doing something with the data. Tools to view the archived websites include Webrecorder Player (Webrecorder Player for Desktop GitHub 2018), OpenWayback (IIPC 2018), pywb (Pywb GitHub 2018) and WAIL (Web Archiving Integration Layer) (Kelly 2017). Webrecorder Player is relatively easy to install and use and can open content from ARC, WARC and HAR (http Archive) files. OpenWayback reads and indexes WARC files and lets users browse or search the archived content in a web browser. Pywb offers OpenWayback functionality, but it also enables web pages to be recorded while the user surfs the web. It is the software used in Webrecorder and Webrecorder Player. Note that OpenWayback and pywb require technical skills to set up. WAIL is an easy-to-use tool with a graphical user interface that combines Heritrix for capturing websites and OpenWayback for viewing the captured content.

Several tools and libraries exist to *enable* processing archived data, but don't *do* a lot of actual processing. Tools that can read and write data, or validate and extract metadata from WARC files include JWAT (Clarke 2016), node-warc (Node-warc GitHub 2018), WARCAT (WARCAT GitHub 2017) (Web ARChive (WARC) Archiving Tool), warcio (Warcio GitHub 2017) and warctools (Warctools GitHub 2016). These tools often require programming skills to write software that processes the data itself.

Some tools go a step further and provide a framework for analysing web archives. The Archives Unleashed Toolkit (AUT), part of the Archives Unleashed Project (Archives Unleashed Project 2018), provides a flexible data model for storing and managing raw content as well as metadata and extracted knowledge. Although basic programming or scripting skills are required, a lot of built-in functions (including, extracting links, popular images, and named entity extraction) help the writing of powerful code. A version running in the cloud, providing a user interface, is currently being developed. A tool similar to AUT is ArchiveSpark (ArchiveSpark GitHub 2018). This tool focuses somewhat more on entity recognition and linking than AUT. Another difference is that ArchiveSpark extensively uses CDX files, which are indexes generated from WARC files to speed up some processing. Both tools are built using the Apache Spark analytics engine, enabling a plethora of (big) data processing and analysis tools on top of their own functionality.

A last aspect worth mentioning is how to access publicly available archived data from organisations. As described before, most organisations make this data accessible by means of a web page. However, there is a standardized way of getting web resources near a given timestamp, with a specific URL: Memento (Van de Sompel et al. 2013). It is not necessary to know which organisation holds the data, as long as it runs a Memento aware web service. Organisations supporting Memento are Arquivo.pt., National Library of Ireland, UK Government Web Archive, UK Web Archive, Internet Archive and many more (Kremer 2016). OpenWayback and pywb for instance are tools that provide Memento functionality. A number of Memento clients exist, as standalone libraries or browser plugins, which can be used to access data in this way. A demo is available online.[18]

6 Discussion and conclusion

Our explorative analysis of European web archives for use by digital scholars underlines four important considerations:

(1) Digital scholars need to investigate why, by whom and on whose behalf web archiving is being done. This is important because it '(…) serves to orient users as to some of the questions they should be asking of their sources, and of the institutions that provide them' (Webster 2017: 176). With regard to why the content in question has been archived, it has been shown that the selection is based on a variety of strategies and criteria. Sometimes the collection scope is

---

[18] See http://timetravel.mementoweb.org/

defined by law as is the case in countries with legal deposit legislation; in other cases, the scope is defined by the heritage institution itself. In the case of national libraries and Arquivo.pt., it has been shown that two main approaches exist: broad crawls and selective crawls although some institutions combine both. Broad crawls cover top-level domain crawls and relevant content outside of the national domain(s) and selective crawls mostly focus on specific events, themes or emergencies. When it comes to social media in the studied web archives, it has been demonstrated that approaches differ widely: some institutions do not (yet) include any social media content, while others cover several platforms. Twitter, Facebook and YouTube are the social network platforms that are most often included by web archives.

Who does the web archiving is another important factor from the user perspective. Sometimes specific collection specialists are responsible, whereas in other cases, selection is a responsibility that is shared collectively by a large number of people. A number of institutions also work together with external experts for the selection of web content and most of the studied initiatives offer the public the possibility to submit suggestions to be included in the web archive.

The context in which web archiving has taken place is, therefore, very important for researchers as it has a significant impact on its use as a source in scholarly studies (Webster 2017).

(2) Access conditions differ widely between web archives and the vast majority of archived online contents is protected in order to respect the legal provisions relating to copyright. Once access to the archive is gained, most web archive interfaces only afford simple tools (e.g. URL or full-text searches). Researchers also need to take into account the integrity and authenticity of the information captured (which is strongly linked with quality assurance and metadata management procedures of the webarchive). Nielsen remarks that the 'ongoing efforts that are being made to enhance access to the archives' (2016: 22) also reveal new challenges. For example, full-text keyword search provides different possibilities for finding material, but can potentially create challenges for digital scholars such as data overload and the task of filtering out the relevant results by themselves. The latter is difficult as most digital scholars are so accustomed to seeking information through querying search engines, such as Google, where the results are ordered by relevance, which means they expect to find information in web archives in the same way (Costa and Silva 2011).

Ultimately, digital scholars need data-level access to web archives to undertake analysis using digital tools and methods. A pioneer in this area is Ian Milligan, who made, in the context of the Web Archives for Longitudinal Knowledge project (WALK n.d.), a number of datasets available, including information about those datasets and how to cite them. It is anticipated that data-level access to web archives will increase in the future (Lin et al. 2017). Digital scholars will thus need to become aware of the characteristics of web archive search results and of the fact that they can be sometimes problematic. For example, web archive search results will often be very numerous, neither ordered by relevance nor importance and full of irrelevant material and false returns (Deswarte 2015). The tools and the interfaces offered by web archives are very much in an early stage of development and web archivists are only beginning to tackle the strengths and weaknesses of both their data and interfaces.

Another challenge identified is the need for a better understanding of user needs and behaviour because of the lack of available resources of web archiving institutions. However, a variety of studies have investigated the practices of web archiving and researchers using web archives. Studies done by BUDDAH underlined, amongst other issues, the lack of guidance for humanities researchers: 'A shared conceptual framework of the web archives research process is essential to systematize practices, advance the field, and to welcome new entrants to this area. [...] Such a framework would be structurally useful to describe any research that investigates social questions based on web archives' (Maemura et al. 2016: 3251–3252). Web archiving institutions could play a role in providing this guidance for researchers.

(3) With regard to legal frameworks for web archiving, it is important for digital scholars to understand the general legal frameworks governing web archiving. Increasingly, many European countries have extended their legal deposit legislation to include web archiving. While this means that national libraries have a formal mandate to archive the web content of their nation, there are still challenges to providing access to this content, for example, for research use. Sometimes this access can, for example, only be provided on-site within a national library. For countries where there is no legal deposit legislation in place, a number of, often pragmatic solutions—such as approaching website owners to ask permission to archive their website content—are in place to enable cultural heritage organisations to archive websites. It should also be important to have in mind that the General Data Protection Regulation (GDPR) gives the Member States the possibility to put in place a softened regime when personal data are processed in specific contexts such as archiving in the public interest, historical or scientific research and statistical purposes

(4) Using web archives as a basis for research requires, perhaps even more than other digital research materials, a relatively high level of technical knowledge. Not only is it important to understand the context in which the websites were archived (e.g. how they were selected, when and with tools were they archived), but there are also technical challenges to accessing this content (e.g. full-text search is not always readily available), and understanding the file formats (e.g. WARC) that have been used for web-archiving. However, thanks to the increasing community that is building around web-archiving (e.g. IIPC) and research using web archives (e.g. RESAW), the expertise, tools and knowledge are also growing.

Given the importance of legislative, technical and policy-related elements linked to the creation of a web archive as a research object, it is paramount to provide adequate information and documentation about this context to the users of the web archive in order to open up the black box of web archiving. The Portuguese web archive can be considered a good example in this context as videos are created that shed light onto the inner workings of the web archive, thereby furthering transparency (Arquivo.pt 2018). The features and history of a web archive are pertinent to all its users. It is particularly relevant in order to evaluate the web archive as a data source. As Laursen states: 'In short, the story of an archive is relevant for the trustworthiness of the archive' (2017: 223). We have shown that many challenges are associated with web archiving. However, some of the greatest challenges, seen from the user's perspective, come down to two factors. Firstly, that it is impossible to save everything, and that the choices made are significant for the research object. As Masanès states: 'Web archiving is often a matter of choices, as perfect and complete archiving is unreachable' (Masanès 2005: 77). Secondly, in most cases the object researchers are attempting to preserve when creating a web archive will be distorted by the actual archiving process (Nielsen 2016). It could be argued that it is unlikely, if not impossible, that we can preserve all of the attributes and functionality of digital materials. However, little is known about the levels of loss that are acceptable for digital scholars (Harvey 2005).

7 Limitations and future research

Although this research produced useful insights on how European web archiving initiatives select and open up archived web content, the research design had some limitations. Most importantly, this study was limited to a sample of only nine web archives, eight of which are managed by heritage institutions. This is not meant to be a representative sample for the web archiving landscape, as it only includes European web archives. In addition all these web archives are members of the International Internet Preservation Consortium (IIPC), except for the National Archive of the Netherlands.

Despite these limitations, this article can function as a point of departure for more extensive and qualitative research. With regard to selection, research into the retrieval of examples of the earliest web pages of a national web domain would be very interesting, as would studies about how to ensure the representative inclusion of web material about and from minority groups in web archives. Furthermore, the different models of collaboration with partners external to national heritage institutions for selection, such as digital scholars and members of the general public, could also be an interesting research subject. From an access perspective, it could be worthwhile to explore how secure remote access to web archives could be provided for researchers, in compliance with the related legal provisions.

Furthermore, research related to data-level access to web archives would be another valuable research area, backed by a solid evidence-base from user studies. From a legal point of view, future research can center around two legal developments that will impact web archiving: on the one hand, the impact of the GDPR on the legislation of the various EU member states; on the other hand, the reform of copyright exceptions and limitations at the European level. From a technical point of view, it has been noted that 'the archive separates itself increasingly from the live web the archive tries to preserve' (Laursen and Møldrup-Dalum 2017: 216) and that further research into the development of solutions and tools for the various technical challenges web archives are confronted with is, therefore, essential.

Acknowledgements The research outlined in this article was conducted in the context of the PROMISE-project. This project received funding from the Belgian Science Policy Office (BELSPO) in December 2016, through their Belgian Research Action through Interdisciplinary Networks (BRAIN) research programme, for a 24-month period. The project was initiated by the Royal Library of Belgium and the State Archives of Belgium and the project consortium also includes the universities of Ghent and Namur and the Information and Documentation School of the Brussels-Brabant Institute of Higher Education (HE²B IESSID). We would like to thank the interviewees and their colleagues for taking the time to answer our many questions.

List of institutions and representatives consulted

- National Library of The Netherlands: Kees Teszelszky (Researcher web archiving, Digital Preservation Department)
- National Archive of The Netherlands: Antal Posthumus (Adviser recordkeeping, Directie Infrastructuur & Advies) and Jeroen van Luin (Acquisition and Maintenance of Digital Archives)
- National Library of France (BnF): Pascal Tanésie (Assistant to the head of the department of digital legal deposit), Sara Aubry (Web Archiving Project Manager, IT department) and Bert Wendland (IT Department)
- National Library of Luxembourg: Yves Maurer (Webarchiving Technical Manager) and Ben Els (Digital Curator)
- The Royal Danish Library: Jakob Moesgaard (Specialkonsulent, Department of Digital Legal Deposit and Preservation) and Tue Hejlskov Larsen (IT analyst)
- The UK National Archives: Tom Storrar (Head of Web Archiving) and Claire Newing (Web Archivist)
- The British Library: Jason Webber (Web Archiving Engagement and Liaison Manager)
- Arquivo.pt.: Daniel Gomes (Head of Arquivo.pt, the Portuguese web-archive, Advanced Services Department)
- National Library of Ireland (NLI): Maria Ryan (Web Archivist)

References

Archives Unleashed Project. (2018). *The Archives Unleashed Project*. Retrieved from http://archivesunleashed.org/. Last accessed on 20/04/2018.

ArchiveSpark GitHub. (2018). Helgeho/ArchiveSpark: *An Apache Spark framework for easy data processing, extraction as well as derivation for Web archives and archival collections, developed by the Internet Archive and L3S Research Center*. Retrieved from https://github.com/helgeho/ArchiveSpark. Last accessed on 20/04/2018.

Arquivo.pt. (2018). *Arquivo.pt (Portuguese web-archive): official playlist*. Retrieved from https://www.youtube.com/playlist?list=PLKfzD5UuSdETtSCX_TM02nSP7JDmGFGIE. Last accessed on 12/02/2018.

Arquivo.pt. (n.d.-a). *Arquivo.pt*. Retrieved from http://www.arquivo.pt. Last accessed on 22/01/2018.

Arquivo.pt. (n.d.-b). *Knowledge*. Retrieved from https://www.fccn.pt/en/knowledge/arquivo-pt/. Last accessed on 20/10/2017.

Arquivo.pt. (n.d.-c). *Crawling and archiving Web content*. Retrieved from http://sobre.arquivo.pt/en/help/crawling-and-archiving-web-content/#qe-faq-2416. Last accessed on 20/10/2017.

Arquivo.pt. (n.d.-d). *Terms and conditions*. Retrieved from http://sobre.arquivo.pt/en/about/terms-and-conditions/. Last accessed on 31/01/2017.

Arquivo.pt. (n.d.-e). *What is Arquivo.pt - the Portuguese Web Archive?* Retrieved from http://sobre.arquivo.pt/en/help/what-is-arquivo-pt/. Last accessed on 20/10/2017.

Ben-David, A., & Huurdeman, H. (2014). Web archive search as research: Methodological and theoretical implications. *Alexandria, 25*(1–2), 93–111.

Beunen, A. & Schiphof, T. (2006). *Legal aspects of web archiving from a Dutch perspective* (report commissioned by the National Library in The Hague).

BnF. (2014). *Historique de l'archivage web*. Retrieved from http://www.bnf.fr/fr/professionnels/archivage_web_bnf/a.depot_legal_internet_histoire.html#SHDC__Attribute_BlocArticle1BnF. Last accessed on 22/01/2018.

BnF. (2016). *BnF Collecte de web (BCWeb)*. Retrieved from https://collecteweb.bnf.fr/login.html. Last accessed on 04/02/2018.

BnF. (2017a, February). *Collectes ciblées de l'internet français*. Retrieved from http://www.bnf. fr/fr/collections_et_services/anx_pres/a.collectes_ciblees_arch_internet.html. Last accessed on 16/12 /2017.

BnF. (2017b). *Internet archives*. Retrieved from http://www.bnf.fr/en/collections_and_services/book_press_ media/a.internet_archives.html. Last accessed on 21/09/2017.

BnF. (2017c). *Guide des archives de l'Internet* [Brochure]. Retrieved from http://www.bnf. fr/documents/guide_archives_internet.pdf. Last accessed on 20/09/2017.

BnL. (n.d.). *Appel à participation - Bibliothèque nationale de Luxembourg*. Retrieved from: http://crawl.bnl. lu/2017/06/appel-a-participation-bibliotheque-nationale-de-luxembourg-web-archive/. Last accessed on 26/01/2018.

British Library. (2017a, April 18). *The challenges of web archiving social media* [web log message]. Retrieved from http://blogs.bl.uk/webarchive/2017/04/the-challenges-of-web-archiving-social-media.html. Last accessed on 30/10/2017.

British Library. (2017b, May 17). *Web Archiving Engagement Manager*. Retrieved from https://www.bl. uk/people/experts/jason-webber. Last accessed on 04/02/2018.

British Library. (n.d.-a). *UK web archive*. Retrieved from https://www.bl.uk/collection-guides/uk-web-archive. Last accessed on 31/10/2017.

British Library. (n.d.-b). *Explore the British Library. Non-print legal deposit: FAQs*. Retrieved from http://www.bl.uk/catalogues/search/non-print_legal_deposit.html. Last accessed on 31/10/2017.

Brozzler GitHub. (2018). *internetarchive/brozzler: brozzler - distributed browser-based web crawler*. Retrieved from https://github.com/internetarchive/brozzler. Last accessed on 20/04/2018.

Brügger, N., Laursen, D., & Nielsen, J. (2017). Exploring the domain names of the Danish web. In N. Brügger & R. Schroeder (Eds.), *The web as history. Using web archives to understand the past and present* (pp. 62–80). London: UCL Press.

BUDDAH, Big UK Domain Data for the Arts and Humanities. (2014) *Bursaries*. Retrieved from https://buddah.projects.history.ac.uk/news/bursaries/ . Last accessed on 04/02/2018.

Chakraborty, A., & Nanni, F. (2017). The changing digital faces of science museums: A diachronic analysis of museum websites. In N. Brügger (Ed.), *Web 25. Histories from the first 25 years of the world wide web* (pp. 157–174). New York: Peter Lang.

Clarke, N. (2016). *JWAT*. Retrieved from https://sbforge.org/display/JWAT/JWAT. Last accessed on 20/04 /2018.

Costa, M. & Silva, M. (2010). Understanding the information needs of web archive users. In *Proceedings of the 10th International Web Archiving Workshop* (pp. 9-16).

Costa, M. & Silva, M. (2011). Characterizing search behavior in web archives. In *Proceedings of the 1st International Temporal Web Analytics Workshop*.

Deswarte, R. (2015). *Revealing British euroscepticism in the UK web domain and archive case study*. Retrieved from http://sas-space.sas.ac.uk/6103/#undefined. Last accessed on 25/01/2018.

Dooley, J. (2016 October). *Metadata to meet user needs*. Presented at the OCLC Member Forum. Los Angeles.

Dooley, J. M., Farrell, K. S., Kim, T. & Venlet, J. (2017). Developing web archiving metadata best practices to meet user needs. *Journal of Webstern Archives, 8*(2), Art. 5, 15 pp.

Dougherty, M., Meyer, E. T., Madsen, C., van den Heuvel, C., Thomas, A., & Wyatt, S. (2010). *Researcher engagement with web Archives: State of the art*. London: JISC.

Fbarc GitHub. (2018). *justinlittman/fbarc: A commandline tool and Python library for archiving data from Facebook using the Graph API*. Retrieved from https://github.com/justinlittman/fbarc. Last accessed on 20/04/2018.

Foo, C. (2016). *Welcome to Wpull's documentation! - Wpull 2.0.1 documentation*. Retrieved from https://wpull.readthedocs.io/en/master/#. Last accessed on 20/04/2018.

Free Software Foundation. (2017) *Wget - GNU Project - Free Software Foundation*. Retrieved from https://www.gnu.org/software/wget/. Last accessed on 20/04/2018.

Gomes, D. (2017a, November 30). *Web preservation demands access*. Retrieved from http://www.dpconline. org/blog/idpd/web-preservation-demands-access. Last accessed 14/12/2017.

Gomes, D. (2017b, November 24) *Personal interview via Zoom with Daniel Gomes /Interviewers: Sally Chambers, Friedel Geeraert, Gerald Haesendonck, Alejandra Michel and Eveline Vlassenroot*. [M4A file].

Grab-site GitHub. (2018). *ludios/grab-site: The archivist's web crawler: WARC output, dashboard for all crawls, dynamic ignore patterns*. Retrieved from https://github.com/ludios/grab-site. Last accessed on 20 /04/2018.

Graff, E. & Sepetjan, S. (2011). Le dépôt légal en France. *Les cahiers de la propriété intellectuelle*, 2011/1, 179–180.

Harvey, D. R. (2005). *Preserving digital materials*. München: KG Saur.

Helmond, A., Nieborg, D., & van der Vlist, F. N. (2017). The political economy of social data: A historical analysis of platform–industry partnerships. In *Proceedings of the 8th International Conference on Social Media & Society* (SMSociety 17) New York: ACM Press. https://doi.org/10.1145/3097286.3097324.

Hockx-Yu, H. (2014). *Archiving social media in the context of non-print legal deposit*. Paper presented at IFLA, Lyon.

IIPC. (2017). *Why archive the web?* Retrieved from http://netpreserve.org/web-archiving/. Last accessed on 22 /01/2018.

IIPC. (2018). *OpenWayback*. Retrieved from http://netpreserve.org/web-archiving/openwayback/. Last accessed on 09/02/2018.

ISO. (2017). *Information and documentation - WARC file format (ISO 28500:2017)*.

KB Nederland (n.d.-a) *Selectie bij webarchivering*. Retrieved from https://www.kb.nl/organisatie/onderzoek-expertise/e-depot-duurzame-opslag/webarchivering/selectie-bij-webarchivering. Last accessed on 19/12 /2017.

KB Nederland (n.d.-b). *Legal issues*. Retrieved from https://www.kb.nl/en/organisation/research-expertise/long-term-usability-of-digital-resources/web-archiving/legal-issues. Last accessed on 22/09/17.

KB Nederland (n.d.-c). *Web archiving*. Retrieved from https://www.kb.nl/en/organisation/research-expertise/long-term-usability-of-digital-resources/web-archiving. Last accessed on 22/09/17.

KB Nederland (n.d.-d) *KB-webarchief: veelgestelde vragen*. Retrieved from https://www.kb.nl/organisatie/onderzoek-expertise/e-depot-duurzame-opslag/webarchivering/kb-webarchief-veelgestelde-vragen. Last accessed 08/12/2017.

KB Nederland (n.d.-e) *Gebruiksvoorwaarden webarchief Koninklijke Bibliotheek*. Retrieved from https://www.kb.nl/bronnen-zoekwijzers/databanken-mede-gemaakt-door-de-kb/webarchief-kb/gebruiksvoorwaarden-webarchief-koninklijke-bibliotheek. Last accessed on 08/12/2017.

Kelly, M. (2017). *Web Archiving Integration Layer (WAIL)*. Retrieved from https://machawk1.github.io/wail/. Last accessed on 20/04/2018.

Koerbin, P. (2017). Revisiting the world wide web as artefact: Case studies in archiving small data for the National Library of Australia's PANDORA archive. In N. Brügger (Ed.), *Web 25. Histories from the first 25 years of the world wide web* (pp. 191–206). New York: Peter Lang.

Kremer, I. (2016). *About the Time Travel Service*. Retrieved from http://timetravel.mementoweb.org/about/. Last accessed on 20/04/2018.

Kunze, S. & Power, B. (n.d.). *The 1916 Easter Rising Web Archive* Project, p. 2. Retrieved from https://archivedweb.blogs.sas.ac.uk/files/2017/06/RESAW2017-PowerKunze-The_1916_Easter_Rising_web_archive_Project.pdfp_.pdf. Last accessed on 2/11/2017.

Laursen, D., & Møldrup-Dalum, P. (2017). Looking back, looking forward: 10 years of web development to collect, preserve and access the Danish web. In N. Brügger (Ed.), *Web 25. Histories from the first 25 years of the world wide web* (pp. 207–228). New York: Peter Lang.

Lin, J., Milligan, I., Wiebe, J., & Zhou, A. (2017). Warcbase: Scalable analytics infrastructure for exploring web archives. *Journal on Computing and Cultural Heritage, 10*(4), 1–30. https://doi.org/10.1145/3097570.

Maemura, E., Becker, C., & Milligan, I. (2016). *Understanding computational web archives research methods using research objects*. In James Joshi, George Karypis, Ling Liu, et al., *2016 IEEE International Conference on Big Data* (Big Data)(pp. 3250–3259).

Masanès, J. (2005). Web archiving methods and approaches: A comparative study. *Library Trends, 54*(1), 72–90.

Maurer, Y. & Els, B. (2017a, November 24). *Personal interview via GoToMeeting with Yves Maurer and Ben Els/Interviewers: Emmanuel Di Pretoro, Friedel Geeraert, Gerald Haesendonck, Eveline Vlassenroot*. [M4A file].

Maurer, Y. & Els, B. (2017b, November 24). *Written answers given by the Bibliothèque nationale de Luxembourg via Google Docs before the personal interview with Yves Maurer and Ben Els/ Interviewers: Emmanuel Di Pretoro, Friedel Geeraert, Gerald Haesendonck, Eveline Vlassenroot*.

Moesgaard, J. & Larsen, T. H. (2017a, November 30). *Personal interview via GoToMeeting with Jakob Moesgaard & Tue Hejlskov Larsen/Interviewers: Emmanuel Di Pretoro, Friedel Geeraert, Gerald Haesendonck, Sally Chambers and Alejandra Michel*.

Moesgaard, J. & Larsen, T. H. (2017b, November 30). *Written answers given by the Danish Royal Library via Google Docs before the personal interview with Jakob Moesgaard & Tue Hejlskov Larsen/Interviewers: Emmanuel Di Pretoro, Friedel Geeraert, Gerald Haesendonck, Sally Chambers and Alejandra Michel.*

National Archives. (n.d.-a). How to use the web archive. Retrieved from http://www.nationalarchives.gov.uk/webarchive/information/. Last accessed on 19/10/2017.

National Archives. (n.d.-b). *UK Government web archive.* Retrieved from http://www.nationalarchives.gov.uk/webarchive/. Last accessed on 31/10/2017.

National Library of Ireland. (2017a). *NLI Review 2016.* Retrieved from https://www.nli.ie/GetAttachment.aspx?id=011e629f-1a5a-4cde-91d7-8a62ccf84bef. Last accessed 9/10/2017.

National Library of Ireland. (2017b). *Web Archive FAQ & Resources.* Retrieved from https://www.nli.ie/en/web-archive-faq.aspx. Last accessed on 9/10/2017.

National Library of Ireland. (n.d.-a) *NLI Web Archive: A record of the online life in Ireland.* Retrieved from http://collection.europarchive.org/nli. Last accessed on 1/02/2018.

National Library of Ireland. (n.d.-b). *Rights and Reproductions.* Retrieved from https://www.nli.ie/en/rights-reproductions.aspx. Last accessed on 31/01/2018.

National Library of Ireland. (n.d.-c). *Web Archive.* Retrieved from https://www.nli.ie/en/web_archive.aspx. Last accessed on 31/01/2018.

National Library of Ireland. (n.d.-d). *Web archive collections.* Retrieved from http://www.nli.ie/en/udlist/web-archive-collections.aspx. Last accessed on 20/10/2017.

NCDD. (n.d.). *Expertgroep webarchivering.* Retrieved from http://www.ncdd.nl/kennis-en-advies/expertgroepen/expertgroep-webarchivering/. Last accessed on 08/12/2017.

Netarkivet.dk. (2016a). *Selektive høstninger.* Retrieved from http://netarkivet.dk/om-netarkivet/selektive-hostninger_2016/. Last accessed on 31/10/2017.

Netarkivet.dk. (2016b). *Adgang til Netarkivet.* Retrieved from http://netarkivet.dk/adgang/. Last accessed on 31/01/2018.

Netarkivet.dk. (2017). *Brugermanual til Netarkivet.* Retrieved from: http://netarkivet.dk/wp-content/uploads/2015/03/Netarkivet_Strategi_Langtidsbevaring_1.0_150115.pdf . Last accessed on 1/02/2018.

Nielsen, J. (2016). *Using web archives in research - an introduction.* Retrieved from http://www.netlab.dk/wp-content/uploads/2016/10/Nielsen_Using_Web_Archives_in_Research.pdf. Last accessed on 18/01/2018.

Node-warc GitHub. (2018). *N0taN3rd/node-warc: Parse And Create Web ARChive (WARC) files with node.js.* Retrieved from https://github.com/N0taN3rd/node-warc. Last accessed on 20/04/2018.

Ogden, J., Halford, S. & Carr, L. (2017). Observing web archives. The case for an ethnographic study of web archiving. *WebSci. June* (25-28). https://doi.org/10.1145/3091478.3091506.

Posthumus A. and van Luin, J. (2017a, December 6). Personal interview via UC4all with Antal Posthumus and Jeroen van Luin/Interviewers: Eveline Vlassenroot and Friedel Geeraert.

Posthumus A. and van Luin, J. (2017b, December 6). *Written answers given via Google Docs by the National Archive before the personal interview with Antal Posthumus and Jeroen van* Luin/Interviewers: Eveline Vlassenroot and Friedel Geeraert.

Pywb GitHub. (2018). *webrecorder/pywb: Core Python Web Archiving Toolkit for replay and recording of web archives https://pypi.python.org/pypi/pywb.* Retrieved from https://github.com/webrecorder/pywb. Last accessed on 20/04/2018.

RESAW (Research Infrastructure for the Study of Archived Web Materials). (2012). *About RESAW.* Retrieved from http://resaw.eu/about/. Last accessed on 04/02/2018.

Reyes Ayala, B. (2013). *Web archiving bibliography 2013.* Texas: UNT Digital Library.

Roche, X. (2018). *HTTrack Website Copier.* Retrieved from http://www.httrack.com/. Last accessed on 20/04/2018.

Rosenthal, C. (2017, July). *NetarchiveSuite.* Retrieved from https://sbforge.org/display/NAS/NetarchiveSuite. Last accessed on 20/04/2018.

Ryan, M. (2017, November 16). *Personal interview via GoToMeeting with Maria Ryan/Interviewers: Gerald Haesendonck, Alejandra Michel and Eveline Vlassenroot.* [M4A file].

Schneider, S. M., & Foot, K. A. (2005). Web sphere analysis: An approach to studying online action. In C. Hine (Ed.), *Virtual Methods - Issues in Social Research on the Internet.* Oxford: Berg Publishers, 157–171.

Schneider, S., & Foot, K. (2008). Archiving of internet content. In W. Donsbach (Ed.), *The international encyclopedia of communication.* Oxford: Blackwell. https://doi.org/10.1002/9781405186407.wbieca051.

Schroeder, R., & Brügger, N. (2017). Introduction: The web as history. In N. Brügger & R. Schroeder (Eds.), *The web as history. Using web archives to understand the past and present* (pp. 1–19). London: UCL Press.

Sierman, B., & Teszelszky, K. (2017). How can we improve our web collection? An evaluation of web archiving at the KB National Library of the Netherlands (2007-2017). *Alexandria, 27*, 94–107. https://doi.org/10.1177/0955749017725930.

Social Feed Manager. (2018). *Social Feed Manager*. Retrieved from https://gwu-libraries.github.io/sfm-ui/. Last accessed on 20/04/2018.

Tanésie, P. & Aubry, S. (2017, December 12). Le dépôt légal du web à la BnF : organisation, procédures et outils. Presentation given at the Bibliothèque nationale de France, Paris.

Tanésie, P., Aubry, S., Wendland, B. (2017, December 12), *Personal interview at the BnF with Pascal Tanésie, Sara Aubry & Bert Wendland/Interviewers: Sally Chambers, Rolande Depoortere, Friedel Geeraert, Alejandra Michel, and Eveline Vlassenroot* [mp3 file].

Teszelszky, K. (2017a, November 8). *Personal interview via GoToMeeting with Kees Teszelszky/Interviewers: Gerald Haesendonck, Alejandra Michel and Eveline Vlassenroot*. [M4A file].

Teszelszky, K. (2017b, November 8). *Written answers given via Google Docs by the KB Nederland before the personal interview with Kees* Teszelszky/Interviewers: Gerald Haesendonck, Alejandra Michel and Eveline Vlassenroot.

The National Archives. (n.d.). *UK Government Web Archive*. Retrieved from http://www.nationalarchives.gov.uk/webarchive/. Last accessed on 1/02/2018.

Twarc GitHub. (2018). *DocNow/twarc: A command line tool (and Python library) for archiving Twitter JSON*. Retrieved from https://github.com/DocNow/twarc. Last accessed on 20/04/2018.

UK Web Archive. (n.d.-a). *About*. Retrieved from https://www.webarchive.org.uk/ukwa/info/about. Last accessed on 30/10/2017.

UK Web Archive. (n.d.-b). *Browse*. Retrieved from https://www.webarchive.org.uk/ukwa/browse. Last accessed on 1/02/2018.

UK Web Archive. (n.d.-c). *Frequently asked questions*. Retrieved from https://www.webarchive.org.uk/ukwa/info/faq. Last accessed on 30/10/2017.

UK Web Archive. (n.d.-d). *SHINE*. Retrieved from https://www.webarchive.org.uk/shine. Last accessed on 05/02/2018.

Van de Sompel, H., Nelson, M.L., Sanderson, R. (2013). *RFC 7089: HTTP Framework for Time-Based Access to Resource States—Memento*. Retrieved from http://tools.ietf.org/rfc/rfc7089.txt. Last accessed on 20/04/2018.

WALK (Web Archives for Longitudinal Knowledge). (n.d.). *Datasets*. Retrieved from: http://webarchives.ca/datasets. Last accessed on 04/02/2018.

WARCAT GitHub. (2017). *chfoo/warcat: Tool and library for handling Web ARChive (WARC) files*. Retrieved from https://github.com/chfoo/warcat. Last accessed on 20/04/2018.

Warcio GitHub. (2017). *webrecorder/warcio: Streaming WARC/ARC library for fast web archive IO https://pypi.python.org/pypi/warcio*. Retrieved from https://github.com/webrecorder/warcio. Last accessed on 20/04/2018.

Warctools GitHub. (2016). *internetarchive/warctools: warctools*. Retrieved from https://github.com/internetarchive/warctools. Last accessed on 20/04/2018.

Webber, J. (2017, November 16). *Personal interview via GoToMeeting with Jason Webber/Interviewers: Sally Chambers, Gerald Haesendonck, Alejandra Michel and Eveline Vlassenroot*. [M4A file].

Weber, M. S. (2017). The tumultuous history of news on the web. In N. Brugger & R. Schroeder (Eds.), *The web as history. Using web Archives to understand the past and the present* (pp. 83–100). London: UCL Press.

Webrecorder. (n.d.). Collect & revisit the web. Retrieved from https://webrecorder.io/. Last accessed on 19/02/2019.

Webrecorder Player for Desktop Github. (2018). *webrecorder/webrecorderplayer-electron: Webrecorder Player for Desktop (OSX/Windows/Linux). (Built with Electron + Webrecorder)*. Retrieved from https://github.com/webrecorder/webrecorderplayer-electron. Last accessed on 20/04/2018.

Webster, P. (2017). Users, technologies, organisations: Towards a cultural history of world web archiving. In N. Brügger & N. (Eds.), *Web 25. Histories from 25 years of the world wide web* (pp. 175–190). New York: Peter Lang.

Affiliations

Eveline Vlassenroot[1] · Sally Chambers[2] · Emmanuel Di Pretoro[3] · Friedel Geeraert[4] · Gerald Haesendonck[5] · Alejandra Michel[6] · Peter Mechant[1]

Emmanuel Di Pretoro
edipretoro@he2b.be

Friedel Geeraert
Friedel.Geeraert@kbr.be

Gerald Haesendonck
Gerald.Haesendonck@UGent.be

Alejandra Michel
alejandra.michel@unamur.be

Peter Mechant
Peter.Mechant@UGent.be

[1] imec-mict-UGent, Ghent, Belgium

[2] Ghent Centre for Digital Humanities, UGent, Ghent, Belgium

[3] URF-SID, Haute École Bruxelles-Brabant, Bruxelles, Belgium

[4] Royal Library and State Archives of Belgium, Brussel, Belgium

[5] Department of Electronics and Information Systems, Ghent University - imec – IDLab, Ghent, Belgium

[6] NADI/CRIDS, UNamur, Namur, Belgium

International Journal of Digital Humanities (2019) 1:113–131
https://doi.org/10.1007/s42803-019-00008-6

RESEARCH ARTICLE

A landscape of data – working with digital resources within and beyond DARIAH

Tibor Kálmán[1] · Matej Ďurčo[2] · Frank Fischer[3] · Nicolas Larrousse[4] ·
Claudio Leone[5] · Karlheinz Mörth[2] · Carsten Thiel[5]

Published online: 3 April 2019
© Springer Nature Switzerland AG 2019

Abstract

The way researchers in the arts and humanities disciplines work has changed significantly. Research can no longer be done in isolation as an increasing number of digital tools and certain types of knowledge are required to deal with research material. Research questions are scaled up and we see the emergence of new infrastructures to address this change. The DigitAl Research Infrastructure for the Arts and Humanities (DARIAH) is an open international network of researchers within the arts and humanities community, which revolves around the exchange of experiences and the sharing of expertise and resources. These resources comprise not only of digitised material, but also a wide variety of born-digital data, services and software, tools, learning and teaching materials. The sustaining, sharing and reuse of resources involves many different parties and stakeholders and is influenced by a multitude of factors in which research infrastructures play a pivotal role. This article describes how DARIAH tries to meet the requirements of researchers from a broad range of disciplines within the arts and humanities that work with (born-)digital research data. It details approaches situated in specific national contexts in an otherwise large heterogeneous international scenario and gives an overview of ongoing efforts towards a convergence of social and technical aspects.

Keywords Research infrastructure · Digital humanities · Arts and humanities · Sustainability · DARIAH · FAIR principles

1 Introduction

Funding agencies, on both the European and national levels, increasingly require that research data and publications produced in publicly funded research projects be

Chapter 8 was originally published as Kálmán, T., Ďurčo, M., Fischer, F., Larrousse, N., Leone, C., Mörth, K. & Thiel, C. International Journal of Digital Humanities (2019) 1: 113–131. https://doi.org/10.1007/s42803-019-00008-6.

✉ Tibor Kálmán
   tibor.kalman@gwdg.de

Extended author information available on the last page of the article

published in an open access format. Policy recommendations on research data management are being revised in the context of Open Science (European Commission 2018). It has become a common practice for researchers to publish their research data in an open-access fashion, using free or permissive licenses. In the arts and humanities in particular, however, data sharing and reuse among researchers is not a commonly established practice. Even if researchers in these disciplines published their data in European repositories and archives, this data is often hard to find, access, or reuse. Even if there were an increased awareness of the need and benefit of sharing resources within the disciplines of the arts and humanities, much needs to be done to make it an integral part of an everyday research practice.

The sharing of resources is an inherently complex phenomenon that involves many different actors and is influenced by many factors. Challenges to the level of the data itself are well summarised by the FAIR principles, which comprise of stable identifiers, rich, broadly disseminated metadata, widely adopted formats, vocabularies and protocols (Wilkinson et al. 2016). These requirements need to be supported by an appropriate technical infrastructure: (a) stable *repositories for depositing* and publication of the data; (b) means for broad *dissemination* of metadata, most notably the Open Archives Initiative's Protocol for Metadata Harvesting (OAI-PMH) in combination with large-scale aggregators; (c) *authentication and authorisation* infrastructure (AAI), allowing for fine-grained handling of permissions and (d) *interoperability* between tools, i.e., support for established formats and availability of well-defined APIs and import/export functionality to ensure permeability and an easy data flow within the research process. These technical requirements need to be underpinned by policy measures: *promotion of standards* and permissive intellectual property rights (IPR) for research seconded by clear *licensing*. It is also important to establish academic gratification for the creation and publication of research data and software, as well as to appreciate its value as research output and enable a proper *academic contribution*. The latter point is particularly crucial: while the other aspects could be considered as, primarily, enabling factors, the gratification aspect constitutes a strong incentive for researchers to willingly share their work.

All of these measures need to be accompanied by appropriate training and outreach campaigns, raising awareness and ensuring the transfer of this kind of knowledge. Both scholars and students and the interested public need to have the opportunity to acquaint themselves with digital methods, technologies, formats and best practices. Ideally, this should take place in intensive, small-scale, hands-on settings, which focus on individual aspects, up-to-date online training material, comprehensive documentation, and opportunities for on-demand personal consultations with experts.

The sharing of resources should not be seen as a mere handover of data, but rather as an integral aspect of working with digital resources, interwoven with all the various stages of the research data lifecycle, from creation and curation to dissemination of digital resources for reuse and knowledge acquisition. It naturally affects and is affected by all stakeholders in the research area. While the decision of individual scholars to share the resources they created is the *conditio sine qua non*, it is crucial to embed the resource in a fruitful, supportive broader environment that ensures all the above-mentioned enabling factors. The traditional institutional context might be the home organisation of the scholar, but given the global challenge to increase the accessibility of research data, the issue at stake cannot be addressed by individual institutions anymore and requires joint efforts on many levels, involving entities from the individual research groups up to European and global institutions. Research infrastructure consortia feature a multi-layered structure, ranging from topic-specific working groups and national consortia to the governing bodies on a European level. They are in an ideal position to tackle these multifaceted challenges. Not only do they represent their respective community, but they are also an integral part of it, possessing a deep understanding of research practices in the field.

This article gives an overview of the ongoing developments and reflects on the current discourse within and beyond the DARIAH research infrastructure. It is structured as follows: First, we present the DARIAH initiative in detail, including the reasons for its initiation and its unique position in the European context. We then shift our focus to describe different national chapters of DARIAH and their take on dealing with (born-)digital research data collections in a heterogeneous research environment. By helping to moderate the change of scientific practices in the humanities, we aim to make it easier to integrate digital and technical aspects into research workflows in disciplines that were previously rather 'untechnical'. Some remarks on our work towards a convergence of social and technical aspects of this endeavour will conclude the article.

2 DARIAH – A digital and distributed infrastructure for the arts and humanities

A research infrastructure can serve as the basis for offering services and resources for the sharing and management of data and for the management of associated legal and organisational issues. Developing such a sustainable research infrastructure, which integrates existing resources, tools and services to broaden the possibilities of a truly open science, and promotes the acceptance of digitally-enabled approaches is also the *raison d'être* of the DARIAH initiative.

DARIAH is short for Digital Research Infrastructure for the Arts and Humanities. This pan-European organisation aims at enabling and supporting digital research methods and teaching across the arts and humanities (DARIAH 2018). DARIAH-EU, as the umbrella organisation is called, was founded in the framework of the European Strategic Forum for Research Infrastructures (ESFRI) and first appeared on the ESFRI roadmap in 2006 as one of six projects for the humanities and social sciences (European Roadmap for Research Infrastructures 2006: 33). Within the ESFRI, the legal form of European Research Infrastructure Consortium (ERIC) has been developed to enable the funded European research alliances to operate on a stable, long-term basis. After a long preparation phase, the DARIAH-ERIC was established by the European Commission in August 2014. To date, 17 countries— Austria, Belgium, Croatia, Cyprus, Denmark, France, Germany, Greece, Ireland, Italy, Luxembourg, Malta, Poland, Portugal, The Netherlands, Serbia and Slovenia—have become DARIAH members, and the list of cooperating partners in these and other countries is growing. Six further candidate countries are expected to become members by 2020.

In practice, DARIAH is a vivid marketplace of ideas and know-how, where people from different countries and disciplines can meet and collaborate, help and learn from each other. It addresses the aforementioned challenges in many different ways. Mainly through its individual partners, DARIAH provides the necessary basic technical infrastructure and specialised tooling to underpin the whole research process; be it virtual research environments (VRE) for co-creation and publication, repositories for long-term preservation and publication of research data, general publication platforms, or generic project-management solutions, allowing efficient communication in highly distributed collaboration setups. Around these technical efforts, DARIAH also organises numerous training and outreach events to raise awareness and transfer practical skills for digital methods to the scholarly community.

On the European level, DARIAH uses its unique position and capacity to push forward necessary policy work that makes the handling and especially sharing of research resources easier. It propagates the utilisation of standards to address the problem that large parts of the produced research data are neither visible, nor reusable (legally or technically). This is why DARIAH engages in the Open Science Policy Platform (OSPP) (Edmond 2018). In the framework of the ongoing project DESIR (DARIAH ERIC Sustainability Refined, see CORDIS 2018), DARIAH has identified six dimensions of sustainability that it seeks to strengthen: dissemination, growth, technology, robustness, trust, education. Up until the projected end of DESIR in December 2019, we will see international workshops and other types of dissemination events to initiate collaborations and further educational work, and the existing services will be enhanced with a focus on entity-based search, scholarly content management, visualisation and text-analytic services. Furthermore, DARIAH collaborates with other SSH infrastructures such as CESSDA (Consortium of European Social Science Data Archives, see CESSDA 2018), CLARIN (Common Language Resources and Technology Infrastructure [see CLARIN 2018]), and the emerging research software engineering community. The aim is to find a common understanding of how to sustain research software, to address specific challenges of research infrastructures, and to develop a unified technical reference (Kalman et al. 2018). It is a declared task in the DARIAH Strategic Action Plan, released in November 2017, to help developing sustainability models for Digital Humanities (DH) projects and their data collections, especially to ensure the longevity of such projects after the direct funding period has run out (DARIAH 2017).

In the future, DARIAH aims at working towards a more resilient, robust setup of the technical infrastructure, making datasets and services more independent from individual providers through stronger cooperation between partners of the consortium, and with e-Infrastructures like EGI (EGI 2018), EOSC (European Commission 2017) or EUDAT (EUDAT 2018), offering basic generic services. With concentrated expertise both on infrastructural aspects and on actual research in the Digital Humanities, DARIAH can act as a broker and mediate between the needs of individual research projects and the large-scale technical solutions offered by e-Infrastructures. Several initiatives were started to lay the technical and organisational groundwork for such collaboration between DARIAH and related e-Infrastructures. For instance, the EGI DARIAH Competence Centre (Harmsen et al. 2015) helped with pilot projects like Storing and Accessing DARIAH contents on EGI (Wandl-Vogt et al. 2017), to analyse, distinguish and meet DARIAH requirements within the EGI infrastructure. The EOSC-hub initiative, which consolidates and integrates access mechanisms to e-Infrastructure resources, recently initiated its DARIAH Thematic Service (Dumouchel 2017) to strengthen the collaboration. Through institutions that are active in both CLARIN and DARIAH, there is cooperation with EUDAT, with particular regard to topics related to preservation and access to long-term storage resources.

3 National Flavours of DARIAH

In this Section, we give an overview over different approaches and national flavours of DARIAH that are working with and sharing a wide variety of data and services through software and tools as well as accompanying learning and teaching material. We present three different examples of DARIAH member countries that demonstrate how national activities contribute to the overall goals.

A crucial characteristic of the DARIAH research infrastructure is its distributed nature as a federated network where most of the services are not offered by a central instance, but through the contributions of individual partners. There are various ways in which DH research communities, their data, and their supporting infrastructures are embedded in the national research landscapes.

3.1 DARIAH in Austria

3.1.1 National consortium CLARIAH-AT

Right from the start, the national group of humanities research infrastructures in the humanities was set-up as one joint organisational structure comprising of both CLARIN and DARIAH (Ďurčo and Mörth 2014). This approach proved to be very efficient and successful. Interestingly enough, dynamics aiming at a higher degree of interaction and cooperation can also be seen in other countries. In the Netherlands, two infrastructures run one big national project; in Denmark and France, the coordination of both RIs is placed with the same person or institution; in Germany, talks on greater interaction are ongoing, and in other countries similar tendencies can be discerned. The Austrian Centre for Digital Humanities at the Austrian Academy of Sciences (ACDH-OeAW 2015) is the coordinating national institution for both research infrastructures. The centre was founded with the intention to foster the change towards digital paradigms in the humanities and pursues a dual agenda of conducting digitally enabled research and providing technical expertise and support to the research communities at the Academy and in the Austrian research landscape.

ACDH-OeAW is not the only player in Austria offering services for the digital humanities community. In CLARIAH-AT, the national group of institutions involved in the two European Research Infrastructure Consortia CLARIN and DARIAH, 14 partner institutions work together to provide a common framework to improve the situation with respect to efficiency of dealing with research data. In 2015, numerous partners of the consortium contributed to a national strategy for Digital Humanities in Austria (Alram et al. 2015). One of the central goals of this strategy, which was fleshed out at the request of the then Ministry for Science, Research and Economy, was the creation of infrastructures to guarantee long-term preservation of research data. One of the measures proposed in the strategy to achieve this goal was the establishment of a national repository federation to ensure long-term access to research data hosted by exchanging expertise, sharing technologies, and interlinking repository resources. The long-term goal is to reach an agreement between individual partners of the federation making sure that partners would step in with their repositories as fall-back options in case one of the participating repositories ceases to exist. Implementation of the measures is part of the agenda for the CLARIAH-AT consortium for the upcoming three-year period.

3.1.2 Data services – One-stop shop for DH projects

In the following, we highlight one specific institution, the ACDH-OeAW, to exemplify how local centres support their respective communities, contributing their share to the common cause. ACDH-OeAW strives to cover the whole research process: project planning, data modelling, data curation and processing, digitisation, application development, service hosting and especially long-term preservation of data. All of this is accompanied by personal consulting and support for individual research endeavours and knowledge transfer, as well as outreach activities promoting the use of digital methods in the various fields of the humanities.

Stable, reliable, long-term preservation of research data being an essential precondition for sharing of resources, the ACDH-OeAW is running a repository called ARCHE (A Resource Centre for the HumanitiEs) (ARCHE 2017) as one of its core services offering stable hosting of digital research data—in particular, for the Austrian humanities community. ARCHE welcomes data from all researchers in the Austrian Academy of Sciences, but also from other institutions in and outside the country. While its predecessor, *CLARIN Centre Vienna / Language Resources Portal*, was dedicated to digital language resources, ARCHE is open to a broader range of disciplines. ARCHE is mainly meant to preserve resources related to Austria, which would include resources that were collected or created in Austria, or involve a geographical area or historical period of interest to Austrian scholars. The collection policy details the types of data the repository is ready to accept and store. ARCHE has been awarded the CLARIN B centre status and certified under the Core Trust Seal (CoreTrustSeal 2018), formerly Data Seal Approval.

Secure and robust long-term preservation of data hinges on many factors. Next to the technical level (bitstream preservation), a host of data-related aspects (metadata, established formats), and the institutional setting are to be considered. ARCHE explicitly states which formats it recommends and accepts for depositing. The categories are 'preferred' and 'accepted'. Preferred formats are expected to be stable and usable also in the long-term. Accepted formats are considered less reliable for the long-term and are converted to one of the preferred formats during the ingest process, both formats being stored. The preservation plan, which is currently being developed, will describe the workflow for format monitoring and migration, so as to ensure that data is preserved if formats become obsolete.

ARCHE pursues the principles of Open Access and Open Data. It encourages data depositors to use open licences, like CC-BY and CC-BY-SA, adhere to rules for good scientific practice, and apply the FAIR Data Principles. The repository itself supports the FAIR principles in various ways. Not only does it make the data *findable* by offering search and browse functionalities, but it also makes it available for harvesting through third-party aggregators, such as CLARIN's metadata catalogue Virtual Language Observatory (VLO) (Van Uytvanck et al. 2010), by means of publishing metadata via OAI-PMH. It makes the data *accessible* by assigning persistent identifiers and *interoperable* by promoting the use of recommended formats and offering direct access to the data and metadata for both human and machine interaction. And, finally, all of these measures contribute to the *reuse* of the data.

In addition to ACDH-OeAW, two other participating institutions have been providing stable hosting and publishing solutions for research data: the Centre for Information Modelling, with the ACDH at the University of Graz running the repository GAMS (Stigler and Steiner 2014) and the University of Vienna, with the PHAIDRA repository

(Budroni and Höckner 2010). All three repositories build on Fedora Commons (Fedora 2018), GAMS being an integrated system which comes with a specialised ingest tool and a Text Encoding Initiative (TEI) based publication framework. The common technical framework is a good basis for establishing a repository federation, where data could be transferred to and hosted by one of the other partners in case one of the services would shut down.

Although sustainable preservation of data is an indispensable part of up-to-date data management in research, there are a number of other components required to cover the whole range of workflow steps in digitally working projects. We refer specifically to tools for automatic processing of data and also solutions supporting the manual collaborative creation and curation of born-digital data (commonly referred to as virtual research environments). Confronted with a multitude of projects with at times very individual needs, ACDH-OeAW adopted a pragmatic approach, trying to use what is there and to provide the missing pieces. In practice this means, e.g., that data encountered in projects encoded in MS Word or Excel files are converted to formats better suited to the long term, like TEI or Simple Knowledge Organisation System (SKOS). Yet, in other cases, we develop project-specific web-based applications with custom-tailored data models, which allow the project teams to create and curate data collaboratively. While this may seem inefficient, we increasingly witness consolidation tendencies and economies of scale, as the colleagues supporting the projects gain more experience in generic frameworks, which allows us to develop new applications with considerably less effort, and re-integrate new functionalities required by new projects back into the common code-base.

For ACDH-OeAW, knowledge transfer and outreach are central pillars of the DH strategy. The team organises numerous training activities, most notably the two event series ACDH Lectures and ACDH ToolGallery. The latter being a one-day format, in which various practical tools are presented in a combination with a theoretical introduction on a given topic and a hands-on session, giving participants a chance to try out a particular tool with the support of a qualified expert. ACDH-OeAW also runs the platform Digital Humanities Austria (DHA 2015), which is the main national dissemination channel for DH in Austria; it is used to announce events and features a comprehensive exhibition of DH projects and a DH bibliography, which serves as an entry point for humanities scholars to delve into DH. An essential part of the community-building efforts is the annual DHA conference, which was organised by ACDH-OeAW in the first three years, before starting to move to other Austrian cities: in 2017, the conference was organised by the Research Centre Digital Humanities at the University of Innsbruck.

Part of the institute's strong commitment to training & education is also the provision of two specialised services for the DH community: #dariahTeach (DARIAH-TEACH 2017), an e-learning platform for teaching material for DH, and the DH Course Registry (DH-registry 2017), an online catalogue providing an overview of DH-related curricula in Europe being collaboratively maintained by CLARIN and DARIAH.

3.2 DARIAH in Germany

3.2.1 National consortium – DARIAH-DE

DARIAH-DE is the German national contribution to DARIAH. It currently consists of a consortium of 19 partners, comprising universities, academies of sciences and independent research institutions, libraries, data centres, a non-governmental organization (NGO) and a commercial partner (DARIAH-DE 2018h). Now in its third project phase, DARIAH-DE receives funding from the German Federal Ministry of Education and Research. The project's current focus is the preparation of the operational phase in 2019, aimed at providing a permanent infrastructure for the arts and humanities in Germany, a process which DARIAH-DE and CLARIN-D are jointly advancing in close collaboration with the ministry, the academies of sciences and disciplinary stakeholders (Forschungsinfrastrukturen für die Geisteswissenschaften 2018).

The heterogeneous nature of the DARIAH-DE consortium enables the research project to address the multi-faceted challenges for research infrastructures. Two pillars of DARIAH-DE are its tight integration with research and teaching through its partners. Dedicated work packages focus on quantitative data analysis, visualisation and annotation with the two focal points addressed in each. Another work package researches the impact and reach of DH in the humanities community, while a strong collaboration with CLARIAH-AT under the umbrella of #dariahTeach focussed on curricular, educational and training materials on a wide variety of topics.

The third main aspect is the provision and operation of the technological infrastructure: from basic components such as servers, monitoring and user support through collaboration solutions and development toolchains to the layer of scholarly services. For these, DARIAH-DE's infrastructure partners, such as data and computing centres and libraries, provide existing and well-established components and services. This includes an authentication and authorisation infrastructure (AAI) that is part of the worldwide authentication network, built by the higher education and research institutions. Over the course of the DARIAH-DE project, the tight collaboration of the developers embedded in their fields and the service providers operating the services have been focused upon and sustainability solutions have been developed to ensure the basis for the long term operation of this infrastructure.

Finally, the pillar most relevant to the present article is dedicated to the processing and storing of research data, for which several tools and services are offered. Building on the TextGrid project, DARIAH-DE has continued the development of the TextGrid Repository, focussed on critical digital scholarly editions and optimised for XML-TEI encoded data, to build the DARIAH-DE Repository (cf. DARIAH-DE 2018g). The operation of the repository is institutionalised through the Humanities Data Centre (HDC), a joint venture of Gesellschaft für wissenschaftliche Datenverarbeitung mbH Göttingen (GWDG) and Göttingen State and University Library (SUB). Both institutions thus ensure the sustainability of all data stored in the repository. This repository is one component of the *Data Federation Architecture* (DFA, see (Gradl and Henrich 2016) for an overview of the underlying concepts and Fig. 1 for the underlying workflow) offered by DARIAH-DE to manage research data.

3.2.2 Data services – A federation architecture

The DFA consists of the DARIAH-DE Repository, the Collection Registry, the Generic Search and the Data Modeling Environment (DME). All components (services and applications) of the DFA are designed to interact with one another. They can be used all together or as standalone services depending on the individual needs of the researcher.

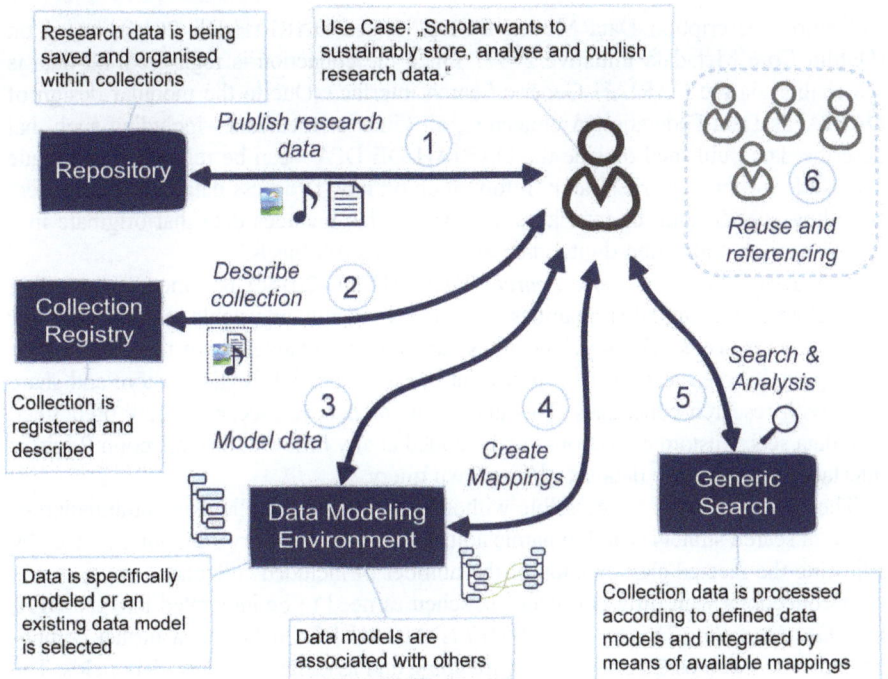

Fig. 1 DARIAH-DE Data Federation Architecture, Tobias Gradl (updated version from: Gradl et al., 2015, used with permission)

The *DARIAH-DE Repository* (DARIAH-DE 2018f) is a digital long-term archive for humanities and cultural scientific research data, enabling researchers to store and publish data in a secure and sustainable manner. At the entry point, the DARIAH-DE Publikator (DARIAH-DE 2018e) offers a user-friendly web interface for data management, description and ingest into the repository. The storage backend is divided into two areas: a restricted private storage area and a public area. All preparation for publication is done in the private storage area via the Publikator and involves three simple steps: First, a collection needs to be created; second, all associated data belonging to the collection has to be uploaded and, finally, all data has to be described by metadata. The repository uses the Dublin Core Simple (cf. Dublin Core Metadata Initiative 2013) metadata standard for description of data, only a few fields are mandatory, such as licence information. Furthermore, persistent identifiers for stable referencing are provided through the publication process – the collections as well as all associated objects get individual Digital Object Identifiers (DOIs). There is a dedicated PID-Service as part of the DFA for assigning unique identifiers and registering them at the DataCite DOI-network. Once published, all data is publicly available.

After publication, an optional but highly recommended possibility is the registration of the collection in the *Collection Registry* (DARIAH-DE 2018a). The Collection Registry enables researchers to make their published data even more visible and understandable and, therefore, more accessible. A draft entry with the metadata already mentioned is automatically created during the publication process and stored in the Collection Registry for further enrichment. For this, a dedicated metadata model for enhanced description of collections and associated data is provided: the DARIAH

Collection Description Data Model, DCDDM (see DARIAH-DE 2017), based on (Dublin Core Metadata Initiative 2007). Once the collection is registered, all data is searchable via the DARIAH Generic Search interface. Due to the modular design of DARIAH's Data Federation Architecture, all kinds of metadata—including such that describe data published outside the DARIAH-DE DFA—can be registered and made accessible for the Generic Search. Information on how to access data can be provided, including specification of interfaces and APIs. This includes data that originate in a digital form, but also non-digital data or collections of objects.

The design of the *Generic Search* (DARIAH-DE 2018c) is aimed at providing researchers in the Digital Humanities with an individually adjustable search facility for their research needs. The myCollections functionality enables them to compile their own query by preselecting the sources out of the Collection Registry, store and share them with research colleagues. This allows researchers to precisely query predefined metadata sets. Custom collections can be added at any time via the Collection Registry interface to enlarge the data set of their own query.

The Generic Search is accessible without registration and allows a combination of different search strategies and dynamic adjustment of the enquiry's granularity, e.g., by adjusting the faceted classification or the number of included collections.

If collections with different metadata schemes need to be integrated into the DFA, the *Data Modelling Environment (DME)* (DARIAH-DE 2018b), as a further component allows a web based user-friendly mapping and association of metadata fields. The web interface enables researchers to explicate their knowledge on the semantic description of their collections. This bottom-up approach allows for more flexibility when including additional external sources, without enforcing explicit standards. This is especially important for the arts and humanities disciplines with their variety of perspectives on collections, terminology and data models.

Besides the Data Federation Architecture, which is designed for research data management purposes of all disciplines within the arts and humanities, DARIAH-DE also offers tools and services that are used for specific project contexts or are related to specific research methods. There are general services for collaborative work and project management allowing collaboration across locations. Furthermore, tools for annotating, analysing and visualising data are provided. A prominent example is the *Geo-Browser* (DARIAH-DE 2018d), which allows the analysis of space-time relations of data and collections of source material, facilitating their representation and visualisation in a correlation of geographic spatial relations at corresponding points of time and sequences.

Additionally, a virtual research environment (VRE), especially designed for the creation of digital editions based on XML/TEI, offers open source tools and services to collaboratively edit and generate research data. The VRE TextGrid (TextGrid 2018) enables the editing, storing and publishing of data for scholars in the humanities in a protected environment.

DARIAH-DE is not only a digital research infrastructure, but also a social infrastructure. It fosters exchange of experiences and expertise and offers a variety of communication and training facilities, like user meetings, issue specific workshops with hands-on sessions, and regular events on the theme of Digital Humanities, spanning a broad range of topics. The information supply of DARIAH-DE is continuously being enhanced and provided through multiple channels and platforms, e.g. through a Digital Humanities blog (DHdBlog), a Twitter account with current news, a YouTube channel (DHd-Kanal) with tutorials, a "Doing Digital Humanities" bibliography as well as many publications and presentations which have been created during the seven years of project lifetime so far.

DARIAH-DE creates a network of digital humanities services, expertise and communities to support research and cooperation in the humanities and cultural sciences, and promotes open access sharing of digital resources.

3.3 DARIAH in France

3.3.1 National consortium – DARIAH-FR

The CNRS (Centre National de la Recherche Scientifique – National Centre for Scientific Research) is a public organisation under the responsibility of the French Ministry of Education and Research. The CNRS, in connection with universities, has implemented an ecosystem aiming to cover the entire lifecycle of the production of scientific data and publications in the Humanities and Social Sciences. This ecosystem is based on the following infrastructures: Open Editions (2018), CCSD (Centre pour la Communication Scientifique Directe 2018), PERSEE (Portail de diffusion de publications scientifiques) and TGIR Huma-Num (Très Grande Infrastructure de Recherche Huma-Num 2018).

Huma-Num coordinates the participation in DARIAH and CLARIN of the above-mentioned organisations, as well as other potential contributors, such as Huma-Num's national consortia (see below). It is also involved in other European and international projects like OPERAS (OPERAS 2018). Huma-Num is an infrastructure that aims to facilitate the digital turn in Humanities and Social Sciences and is part of the national ESFRI roadmap, which is in turn aligned with the European Union's ESFRI framework. This allows good perspectives for recurrent funding.

To perform these missions, Huma-Num's organisation is based on both human and technological layer. It funds "groups of people", called *consortia*, working on common areas of interest (e.g., similar scientific objects) and also provides a technological infrastructure, offering a variety of platforms and tools to process, preserve and disseminate digital research data.

The main idea of a consortium is to organise multidisciplinary collective dialogue within research communities by bringing together different types of actors (researchers, technical staff, etc.) coming from different institutions, with the aim of creating synergies. In return, a consortium is expected to provide technological (or scientific) good practices and produce corpora, new standards, and tools.

Furthermore, Huma-Num provides a technological infrastructure on national scale, based on a large network of partners. Technically, the infrastructure itself is hosted in a big data centre built by and for physicists. A long-term preservation facility from another data centre (CINES – Centre Informatique National de l'Enseignement Supérieur) is also utilised. In addition, a group of correspondents in the "Maison des Sciences de l'Homme" network (MSH Network 2018) all over France is in charge of relaying information about Huma-Num's services and tools.

3.3.2 Data services throughout the data lifecycle

Huma-Num provides tools and services for each step in the research data lifecycle. It coordinates the production of digital data, while offering a variety of platforms and tools to process, preserve and disseminate the data. It also provides research projects with a range of utilities to facilitate the interoperability of various types of digital raw data and metadata (see Fig. 2).

More specifically for digital collections, the aim is to foster the exchange and dissemination of metadata, and of the data itself, via standardised tools and lasting, open formats. These tools developed, by Huma-Num, are all based on semantic web technologies, mainly for their auto-descriptive features, and for the enrichment opportunities they enable. All our resources are, therefore, fully compatible with the Linked Open Data (LOD).

Three services have been designed and developed by Huma-Num to process, store and display research data, while preparing them for re-use and long-term preservation; to put it another way, the aim is to provide a chain of tools to make data FAIR. These complementary services embrace the research data lifecycle and are designed to meet the needs arising there from: constitute a coherent chain of research data tools. While they interact smoothly with one another, they are also open to external tools using the same technologies.

The scientific objective is to promote data sharing so that other researchers, communities, or disciplines, can reuse them, including from an interdisciplinary perspective and in different ways. A map, for example, may become a scientific object, which reflects both the point of view of a geographer and that of a historian. More generally, the principles and methods of the Semantic Web (RDF, SPARQL, SKOS, OWL), on which these services rely, enable data to be documented or re-documented for various uses without confining them to inaccessible silos. Another important point is to make the storage of data independent of the device used to disseminate the data. Another objective is to prevent the loss of data by preparing their long-term preservation. Documenting the use of appropriate formats, which are the basis of data interoperability, greatly facilitates the archiving process.

The workflow implemented by Huma-Num has been built on interoperability. The aim is to foster the exchange and dissemination of metadata, but also of the data themselves via standardised tools and lasting, open formats. Huma-Num uses different technologies for cold, warm and hot data. If the technology used for hot data was quite

SUPPORTING RESEARCH COMMUNITIES

CONSORTIA
Digitalisation
Good practices
Expertises

RESEARCH PROJECTS

TOOLS AND SERVICES
Store. Process. Disseminate
Share&Display. Tag&Push. Archive

INTERNATIONAL NETWORKS
Sharing. Expertise

Fig. 2 DARIAH-FR's Services for Data, Huma-Num

classical, for warm data, Huma-Num has established a mesh of distributed storage all over France (currently 9 nodes) using different storage technologies encapsulated. Thus, backup and versioning can be made on any node. Furthermore, the data center where Huma-Num's infrastructure is hosted provides a backup on tapes for cold data.

Huma-Num already provides a long-term preservation service based on the CINES (Centre Informatique National de l'Enseignement Supérieur, 2018) facility, a National Computer Center of Higher Education which is responsible for permanent archiving for scientific data in France. This is much more than the bit preservation done with the above-mentioned technologies. A long-term preservation project means that one needs to organise the data with a view to reuse by someone, who did not participate in its creation, that presupposes a lot of curation. In addition, the data should be expressed in a format accepted by the partner and additional information has to be provided to document the context of data production, metadata, etc. Huma-Num accompanies these projects by acting as go-between linking data producers, CINES, archivists and other actors.

After a detailed description of three national landscapes, we now shift our focus to the ongoing efforts towards a convergence on the European level in light of the heterogeneity of research data collections, of formats, tools and services.

4 Convergence of tools, methods and collections

It was always the vision of DARIAH to enable the DH research community to reuse and build on existing solutions, developed in and by the community. This includes both the social and the technical aspects of the convergence from individual solutions to a distributed infrastructure.

The social aspect builds around the idea of an Open Marketplace, which enables us to share and review existing services and solutions. From the technical side, DARIAH has identified the need to address the sustainability of the software, which provide some of the core parts of any digital infrastructure. In the following section, we describe how these are being addressed.

4.1 The open marketplace

The idea of developing DARIAH 'as a social marketplace for services' (Blanke et al. 2011) dates back as far as to the preparatory phase of the DARIAH initiative.

The long-term goal is to provide an Open Marketplace platform, which is planned as an easy-entry place where scholars can find solutions for the digital aspects of their daily research work, such as software, tools, (born-)digital data sets, repositories, services, learning and teaching material. The Marketplace targets all researchers from the broader SSH, not just those scholars who would regard themselves as *digital* humanists. Various approaches had been started in the past to provide collections and registries with similar goals. The most important difference between such approaches and the DARIAH Marketplace is that it will contextualise the tools and services offered, with user feedback, user stories, links to training material, showcases, contact addresses, ratings. It is going to be actively curated and sustained by the DARIAH community. The idea is not that these solutions would be produced by DARIAH itself, but that the Marketplace creates visibility for them to help researchers do their work (DARIAH 2017) (Fig. 3).

There have been previous attempts at providing an active, community-backed registry of digital tools and services. While most of them did not always live up to their expectations (for a prominent example cf. Dombrowski 2014), one can still learn from them and reuse their highly curated data. Such an attempt was undertaken within the framework of the H2020 project "Humanities at Scale" coordinated by the DARIAH-ERIC. Building on TERESAH, the "Tools E-Registry for E-Social science, Arts and Humanities" originally developed within the FP7 project "Digital Services Infrastructure for Social Sciences and Humanities" (DASISH) until 2014, a demonstrator for a central registry with distributed data sources was created (Engelhardt et al. 2017).

While the DARIAH Marketplace is still being formed, it is the declared goal not to just add another list-based overview of digital tools, but to assemble and highlight DH knowledge. The platform will create a place addressing and involving the entire research community and also, eventually, the public and industry (bearing in mind EOSC and EU access policy guidelines for research infrastructures).

4.2 Sustainability of tools and software

The social aspect of the marketplace is built on the idea of sharing and reviewing existing services and solutions. In the case of software, providing some of the core technical parts of any digital infrastructure, DARIAH has identified the need to address its sustainability problems (cf. Thiel 2017). In the current status-quo, the construction of sustainable infrastructures is done through grant-based research projects, which has a number of problems. Software built to address specific research questions is often developed in an ad-hoc manner. This is not helped by the fact that software is not yet generally accepted as creditable research output in and of itself. Without a recognition of

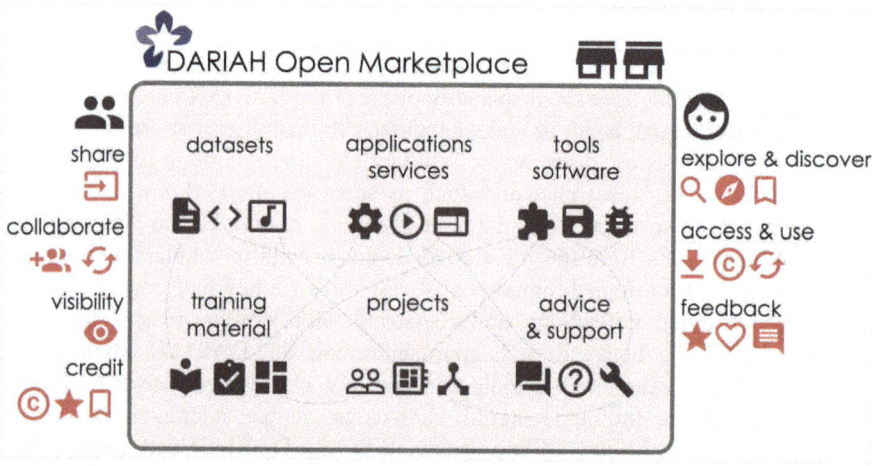

Fig. 3 Illustrative sketch of DARIAH Open Marketplace

the value of the software as a form of research, the individual researcher's willingness to invest additional time into improving the software in a way that does not directly impact the output will be minimal.

The requirement to provide data management plans as part of H2020 grants, which is implemented by national and other funders, sees source code as being identified as digital resources that need preservation. To address this, the UK's Software Sustainability Institute developed a solution to create a Software Management Plan through DMPonline (Software Sustainability Institute 2018) and GitHub and Zenodo have joined forces to add a simple possibility to publish GitHub releases in Zenodo, making software releases citable through DOIs (GitHub 2016). Archiving code is the first step in ensuring the availability for future re-use and reproducibility of research output generated with that software. The second step is making sure that the code can be processed and executed when needed, which goes beyond classical practices of data curation, (cf. Katz et al. 2016) for a discussion on the topic. In our context, two problems are most relevant. For reproducibility of results, access to the entire exact build environment is required and it must, therefore, be referenced in the archived software in a machine readable format. For re-use of the software, the adaptability to the constantly changing reality of information technology, such as changes to external libraries and dependencies, becomes relevant. As technology progresses, so do research questions and new applications not envisioned during the original development can emerge (cf. Harms, Grabowski 2011). For a future researcher to be able to actually adapt a given software product, sufficient documentation and code legibility must exist. While research thrives on innovative solutions with fast-paced development progress, the requirements for software maintainability for the long run are directly contrary (see Hettrick 2016, Chapter 3) for a more detailed discussion.

This is also a particular problem for infrastructures striving to sustain software developed within projects as services. To be able to do so, the infrastructure providers must make a judgement on the expected and unexpected cost that long-term software maintenance will incur. This can only be done if the software is of sufficiently good quality. To address this, infrastructures are developing guidelines and best practices for developers. At the same time, existing quality measures, such as ISO standards, can be one frame of reference (see e.g. Buddenbohm et al. 2017), while (Doorn et al. 2016) suggest establishing an independent certification, modelled on the Data Seal of Approval, now CoreTrustSeal (CoreTrustSeal 2018).

For an infrastructure to provide a valuable service to the scholarly community, the reliability and the trustworthiness of the services offered is a fundamental prerequisite. By improving the quality of the software and making this transparent to the end user of the technology through the Open Marketplace platform, DARIAH strives to address both. In particular, through DESIR work was started on a general Technical Reference (Moranville et al., 2018) as baseline for new development and the Marketplace will improve the findability and discoverability of research software. The combination of both supports and builds upon known recommendations for research software (Jiménez et al. 2017).

5 Conclusion

We have summarised ongoing developments and reflected current discussions within the research infrastructure DARIAH and within some of DARIAH's member states, which are creating and integrating solutions for challenges of heterogeneous research data, tools, services in the arts and humanities. We highlighted that the focus of DARIAH is not simply digitized analogue material of galleries, libraries, archives, and museums. As (digital) research produces born-digital materials (e.g. datasets, tools, softwares), which have to be managed, DARIAH's collection of data is much broader. The challenges, issues and factors of the heterogeneity of (born-)digital research data that DARIAH aims to address only become apparent in large international infrastructures willing to integrate heterogeneous research practices, data formats, tools and services from the wide range of DH disciplines. This article provided insights into this process, both on European and national levels, and reflected on discussions and solutions in the broader DARIAH network.

These discussions include the many factors and challenges that influence the sharing of resources in the arts and humanities. The DARIAH research infrastructure seeks to support the scholarly community to enable and foster the work with and sharing of digital resources in numerous ways. This includes the need to look at the activities on the European and national levels and is exemplified by the three examples from member countries, showcasing also the variety in the setups of the national consortia.

In order to support communities in reusing distributed existing resources in a coherent manner, a coordinated multi-faceted strategy is paramount. It has to involve technological provisions for robust services as well as sustainable software plans, work on policy level promoting use of standards and permissive licensing, all accompanied by training and outreach activities to raise awareness and convey practical skills on digital methods.

DARIAH also acknowledges its position in the general landscape of existing initiatives, infrastructures, as well as projects, and strives to promote exchange and leverage synergies with them. In addition to the collaborations with the initiatives of the SSH communities like CESSDA, CLARIN, EUROPEANA and OpenAIRE, the cooperations with e-Infrastructures like EGI, EOSC or EUDAT are intensified and expanded.

A central goal of this pan-European endeavour is to enable, promote, and simplify the discovery and access to the wealth of (born-)digital resources available in line with the FAIR principles. In order to achieve this, DARIAH has started developing a curated community-driven discovery platform, the DARIAH Open Marketplace. Once released, it will serve the researchers and broader audiences in finding data sets, tools and services that are applicable and reusable in their daily research. The key to success is to involve the communities, and in this regard, the Marketplace has a pivotal role for the future.

References

ACDH-OeAW (2015). *Austrian Centre for Digital Humanities at the Austrian Academy of Sciences.* Retrieved from https://www.oeaw.ac.at/acdh/. Accessed 26 Feb 2018.

Alram, M., Benda, Ch., Ďurčo, M., Mörth, K., Wentker, S., Wissik, T., Budin, G., et al. (2015). DHAUSTRIA-STRATEGIE. Sieben Leitlinien für die Zukunft der digitalen Geisteswissenschaften in Österreich. Wien. https://doi.org/10.1553/DH-AUSTRIA-STRATEGIE-2015.

ARCHE (2017). *A Resource Centre for the HumanitiEs*. Retrieved from https://arche.acdh.oeaw.ac.at/. Accessed 26 Feb 2018.

Blanke, T., Bryant, M., Hedges, M., Aschenbrenner, A. & Priddy, M. (2011). Preparing DARIAH. *IEEE 7th International Conference on E-Science*. IEE Digital Library: Stockholm (pp. 158–165). https://doi.org/10.1109/eScience.2011.30.

Buddenbohm, S., Matoni, M., Schmunk, S., & Thiel, C. (2017). Quality assessment for the sustainable provision of software components and digital research infrastructures for the arts and humanities. *Bibliothek Forschung und Praxis, 41*(2), 231–241. https://doi.org/10.1515/bfp-2017-0024.

Budroni, P., Höckner, M. (2010). Phaidra, a Repository Project of the University of Vienna; in: iPRES 2010, 7th International Conference on Preservation of Digital Objects, Vienna.

CCSD (Centre pour la Communication Scientifique Directe) (2018). *A center which offers a set of services for the management of open archives*. Retrieved from https://www.ccsd.cnrs.fr. Accessed 26 Feb 2018.

CESSDA (2018). *About CESSDA*. Retrieved from https://www.cessda.eu/About>. Accessed 26 Feb 2018.

CINES (Centre Informatique National de l'Enseignement Supérieur) (2018). *Digital archiving solutions for long term preservation*. Retrieved from https://www.cines.fr/en/long-term-preservation.

CLARIN (2018). *CLARIN in a Nutshell*. Retrieved from https://www.clarin.eu/content/clarin-in-a-nutshell. Accessed 26 Feb 2018.

CORDIS (2018). *DARIAH ERIC Sustainability Refined*. Retrieved from https://cordis.europa.eu/project/rcn/207190_en.html. Accessed 26 Feb 2018.

CoreTrustSeal (2018). *CoreTrustSeal Data Repository Certification*. Retrieved from https://www.coretrustseal.org/. Accessed 26 Feb 2018.

DARIAH (2017). *2020: 25 Key Actions for a Stronger DARIAH by 2020*. Retrieved from https://www.dariah.eu/wp-content/uploads/2017/02/DARIAH_STRAPL_v06112017.pdf. Accessed 26 Feb 2018.

DARIAH (2018). *Dariah in a Nutshell*. Retrieved from https://www.dariah.eu/about/dariah-in-nutshell/. Accessed 26 Feb 2018.

DARIAH-DE (2017). *DARIAH Collection Description Data Model DCDDM*. Retrieved from https://github.com/DARIAH-DE/DCDDM. Accessed 26 Feb 2018.

DARIAH-DE (2018a). *DARIAH-DE Collection Registry*. Retrieved from https://colreg.de.dariah.eu. Accessed 26 Feb 2018.

DARIAH-DE (2018b). *DARIAH-DE: Data Modelling Environment*. Retrieved from https://dme.de.dariah.eu/dme. Accessed 26 Feb 2018.

DARIAH-DE (2018c). *DARIAH-DE Generic Search*. Retrieved from https://search.de.dariah.eu/search/. Accessed 26 Feb 2018.

DARIAH-DE (2018d). *DARIAH-DE Geo-Browser*. Retrieved from https://geobrowser.de.dariah.eu/. Accessed 26 Feb 2018.

DARIAH-DE (2018e). *DARIAH-DE Publikator*. Retrieved from https://repository.de.dariah.eu/publikator. Accessed 26 Feb 2018.

DARIAH-DE (2018f). *DARIAH-DE Repository*. Retrieved from https://de.dariah.eu/repository. Accessed 26 Feb 2018.

DARIAH-DE (2018g). *Data Federation Architecture Technical Documentation*. Retrieved from https://repository.de.dariah.eu/doc/services/. Accessed 26 Feb 2018.

DARIAH-DE (2018h). *Der DARIAH-DE Forschungsverbund*. Retrieved from https://de.dariah.eu/der-forschungsverbund>. Accessed 26 Feb 2018.

DARIAH-TEACH (2017). *dariahTeach*. Retrieved from https://teach.dariah.eu/. Accessed 26 Feb 2018.

DHA (2015). *Digital Humanities Austria*. Retrieved from http://digital-humanities.at/. Accessed 26 Feb 2018.

DH-registry (2017). *DH Course Registry*. Retrieved from https://registries.clarin-dariah.eu/courses/. Accessed 26 Feb 2018.

Dombrowski, Q. (2014). What ever happened to project bamboo? *Literary and Linguistic Computing, 29*(3), 326–339. https://doi.org/10.1093/llc/fqu026.

Doorn, P., Aerts, P. and Lusher, S. (2016). Research software at the heart of discovery, DANS & NLeSC. Retrieved from https://www.esciencecenter.nl/pdf/Software_Sustainability_DANS_NLeSC_2016.pdf. Accessed 26 Feb 2018.

Dublin Core Metadata Initiative (2007). *Dublin Core Collection Description Application Profile*. Retrieved from http://dublincore.org/groups/collections/collection-application-profile/. Accessed 26 Feb 2018.

Dublin Core Metadata Initiative (2013) Dublin Core metadata element set, version 1.1: Reference description. Retrieved from http://www.dublincore.org/documents/dces/. Accessed 26 Feb 2018.

Dumouchel, S. (2017). *How the notion of access guides the organization of a European research infrastructure: the example of DARIAH*. Retrieved from https://dh2017.adho.org/abstracts/088/088.pdf> [Last accessed 17 May 2018].

Ďurčo, M. & Mörth, K. (2014). *CLARIN-DARIAH.AT – Weaving the network*, in: 9th Language Technologies Conference. Information Society – IS 2014, Ljubljana, Slovenia, pp. 14–18.

Edmond, J. (2018 Feb) Untangling Barriers: Director Jennifer Edmond on DARIAH's Commitment to Open Science. Retrieved from https://www.dariah.eu/?p=1997. Accessed 26 Feb 2018.

EGI (2018). *EGI: advanced computing for research. Retrieved from* https://www.egi.eu/about/. Accessed 26 Feb 2018.

Engelhardt, C., Leone, C., & Moranville, Y. (2017). Distributed Metadata Schema and Demonstrator for Open Humanities Methods. [Research Report] Göttingen State and University Library; DARIAH. 2017. Available at https://hal.archives-ouvertes.fr/hal-01637051v1.

EUDAT (2018). What is EUDAT? Retrieved from https://www.eudat.eu/what-eudat. Accessed 26 Feb 2018.

European Commission (2017). *EOSC Declaration. Retrieved from* https://ec.europa.eu/research/openscience/pdf/eosc_declaration.pdf. Accessed 26 Feb 2018.

European Commission (2018). *Commission Recommendation of 25.4.2018 on access to and preservation of scientific information*.Retrieved from http://ec.europa.eu/newsroom/dae/document.cfm?doc_id=51636. Accessed 26 Feb 2018.

European Roadmap for Research Infrastructures. (2006). Report 2006. Luxembourg: Office for Official Publications of the European Communities. Retrieved from https://ec.europa.eu/research/infrastructures/pdf/esfri/esfri_roadmap/roadmap_2006/esfri_roadmap_2006_en.pdf. Accessed 26 Feb 2018.

Fedora (2018). Fedora Repository. Retrieved from http://fedorarepository.org/. Accessed 26 Feb 2018.

Forschungsinfrastrukturen für die Geisteswissenschaften (2018). *Wissenschaftsgeleitete Forschungsinfrastrukturen für die Geistes- und Kulturwissenschaften in Deutschland*. Retrieved from https://www.forschungsinfrastrukturen.de/. Accessed 26 Feb 2018.

GitHub (2016). *Making Your Code Citable. Retrieved from* https://guides.github.com/activities/citable-code/. Accessed 26 Feb 2018.

Gradl, T., & Henrich, A. (2016). Die DARIAH-DE-Föderationsarchitektur – Datenintegration im Spannungsfeld forschungsspezifischer und domänenübergreifender Anforderungen. *Bibliothek Forschung und Praxis, 40*(2), 222–228. https://doi.org/10.1515/bfp-2016-0027.

Gradl, T., Henrich, A., & Plutte, C. (2015). Heterogene Daten in den Digital Humanities: Eine Architektur zur forschungsorientierten Föderation von Kollektionen. In Baum, C. & Stäcker, T.(eds.) *Grenzen und Möglichkeiten der Digital Humanities. Zeitschrift für digitale Geisteswissenschaften*, 1. DOI: https://doi.org/10.17175/sb001_020.

Harms, P., & Grabowski, J. (2011). Usability of Generic Software in e-Research Infrastructures. *Journal of the Chicago Col loquium on Digital Humanities and Computer Science, 1*(3) 1–18. http://resolver.sub.uni-goettingen.de/purl?gs-1/9238.

Harmsen, H., Kalman, T. & Wandl-Vogt, E. (2015). DARIAH meets EGI. *Inspired newsletter – Issue 19*. Retrieved from https://www.egi.eu/news-and-media/newsletters/Inspired_Issue_19/dariah.html. Accessed 26 Feb 2018.

Hettrick, S. (2016). *Research Software Sustainability: Report on a Knowledge Exchange Workshop*. Retrieved from https://www.esciencecenter.nl/pdf/Research_Software_Sustainability_Report_on_KE_Workshop_Feb_2016_FINAL.PDF>. Accessed 26 Feb 2018.

Jiménez R.C., Kuzak M., Alhamdoosh M., et al. (2017). *Four simple recommendations to encourage best practices in research software* [version 1]. *F1000Research*, 6:876. https://doi.org/10.12688/f1000research.11407.1.

Kalman, T., Thiel, C., Van Uytvanck, D., Moranville, Y. (2018). Sustainable Research Software – Managing a Common Problem of SSH Infrastructures. Digital Infrastructures for Research 2018, Lisbon, Portugal Retrieved from https://indico.egi.eu/indico/event/3973/session/22/contribution/111

Katz, D. S., Niemeyer, K. E., Smith, A. M., Anderson, W. L., Boettiger, C., Hinsen, K., & Hooft, R. (2016). Software vs. Data in the Context of Citation. *PeerJ Preprints, 4*. https://doi.org/10.7287/peerj.preprints.2630v1.

Moranville, Y., Rodzis, M. & Thiel, C. (2018). *DARIAH Technical Reference*. Retrieved from <https://dariah-eric.github.io/technical-reference/. Accessed 26 Feb 2018.

MSH Network (2018). *Réseau National des Maisons des Sciences de l'Homme*. Retrieved from http://www.msh-reseau.fr. Accessed 26 Feb 2018.

Open Editions (2018). O*pen access to comprehensive services in journal publications, books, scientific blogs and scientific events*. Retrieved from https://www.openedition.org/. Accessed 26 Feb 2018.

OPERAS (2018). *An European research infrastructure for the development of open scholarly communication, particularly in the social sciences and humanities.* Retrieved from http://operas.hypotheses.org. Accessed 26 Feb 2018.

Software Sustainability Institute (2018). *Software Management Plans.* Retrieved from https://www.software.ac.uk/software-management-plans. Accessed 26 Feb 2018.

Stigler, J. & Steiner, E. (2014). GAMS and Cirilo client. Policies, documentation and tutorial. Retrieved from http://gams.uni-graz.at/. Accessed 26 Feb 2018.

TextGrid (2018). *Virtual Research Environment for the Humanities.* Retrieved from https://textgrid.de/en/. Accessed 26 Feb 2018.

TGIR Huma-Num (2018). *An infrastructure for humanities which offers a range of services dedicated to the production and reuse of data.* Retrieved from https://huma-num.fr/. Accessed 26 Feb 2018.

Thiel, C. (2017). Workshop: Software sustainability: Quality and re-usability. DHd-Blog. Retrieved from http://dhd-blog.org/?p=8685. Accessed 26 Feb 2018.

Van Uytvanck, D., Zinn, C., Broeder, D., Wittenburg, P. & Gardelleni, M. (2010). *Virtual language observatory: The portal to the language resources and technology universe.* In *Seventh conference on International Language Resources and Evaluation [LREC 2010]* (pp. 900-903). Tübingen: European language resources association (ELRA).

Wandl-Vogt, E., Barbera, R., La Rocca, G., Calanducci, A. & Kalman, T., (2017). Brid[g]ing the GAP: 100 Jahre Dialektlexikographie als Cloud Service. Der SADE Use Case im DARIAH Competence Centre. Elisabeth Burr. DHd 2016. Modellierung – Vernetzung – Visualisierung. Die Digital Humanities als fächerübergreifendes Forschungsparadigma. Konferenzabstracts. 2. überarbeitete und erweiterte Ausgabe. Universität Leipzig, 7. bis 12. März 2016. Duisburg.

Wilkinson, M. D., et al. (2016). The FAIR guiding principles for scientific data management and stewardship. *Sci. Data, 3*, 160018. https://doi.org/10.1038/sdata.2016.18.

Affiliations

Tibor Kálmán[1] · Matej Ďurčo[2] · Frank Fischer[3] · Nicolas Larrousse[4] · Claudio Leone[5] · Karlheinz Mörth[2] · Carsten Thiel[5]

Matej Ďurčo
Matej.Durco@oeaw.ac.at

Frank Fischer
ffischer@hse.ru

Nicolas Larrousse
nicolas.larrousse@huma-num.fr

Claudio Leone
leone@sub.uni-goettingen.de

Karlheinz Mörth
Karlheinz.Moerth@oeaw.ac.at

[1] Gesellschaft für wissenschaftliche Datenverarbeitung mbh Göttingen (GWDG), Göttingen, Germany

[2] Austrian Academy of Sciences, Vienna, Austria

[3] National Research University Higher School of Economics, Moscow, Russian Federation

[4] CNRS, Paris, France

[5] Göttingen State and University Library, Göttingen, Germany

International Journal of Digital Humanities (2019) 1:133–136
https://doi.org/10.1007/s42803-019-00010-y

BOOK REVIEW

Web 25. Histories from the first 25 years of the world wide web

Niels Brügger (editor), Peter Lang. New York, Bern, Berlin, Brussels,
Frankfurt am Main, Oxford, Vienna, 2017. XXVI, 258 pp., num. Ill.,
ISBN: 978–1–4331-4065-5, https://doi.org/10.3726/b114925. Series:
Digital formations. Recommended retail Price: €44.20

Peter Mechant[1]

Published online: 25 February 2019
© Springer Nature Switzerland AG 2019

Web 25. Histories from the first 25 years of the world wide web, edited by Niels Brügger, is part of the Digital Formations series. Brügger's collection takes the challenge of placing the (hi)story of the World Wide Web in a critical perspective seriously. The volume seeks to foster those working in web archiving, internet studies or web historiography to undertake innovative, cross-disciplinary research. The editor has brought together authors who collectively have contributed to a book that is a valuable addition to the emerging scholarship surrounding the study of the web and the web's history. The book, divided in four sections, comprises 'a number of probes into the vast and multifaceted past of the web' (xi). However, the volume is neither designed to be exhaustive, nor comprehensive. It is broad in scope in relation to a number of aspects: (i) its variety of topics, (ii) its combination of case studies and methodological reflections and (iii) the compilation of chapters focusing on national as well as international WWW phenomena.

The first section of the book, aptly entitled 'The early web', includes four chapters that focus on the history leading up to the emergence of the World Wide Web, including how the web was narrated and understood in the early years. Brügger's own contribution provides a brief history of the hyperlink. It argues that the hyperlink is part of the latest phase in the history of how segments of text are deliberately and explicitly connected to each other by the use of specific textual and media features. The second chapter by Natale & Gory focuses on 'the particular imaginary hidden behind the story of the emergence and development of the World Wide Web' (30). Drawing on sources such as Tim Berners-Lee's autobiography and other web histories, the authors show how the story of the web follows the pattern of Campbell's monomyth, with the hero in

---

Chapter 9 was originally published as Mechant, P. International Journal of Digital Humanities (2019) 1: 133–136.
https://doi.org/10.1007/s42803-019-00010-y.

✉ Peter Mechant
     Peter.Mechant@UGent.be

[1] imec-mict-Ghent University, Ghent, Belgium

different stages (departure, initiation, return and reintegration of the hero). Natale & Gory show how narratives about the 'birth' of the world wide web played an important role in shaping the public's imagination towards elements such as plurality, openness and creativity, while demonstrating that these 'biographies' of the web function as fields through which understandings of the web are constructed, reproduced and communicated. Next, Deken, describes the first years of the Stanford Linear Accelerator Center website, the first www site outside of Europe. The section ends with a descriptive discourse analysis by Barry deconstructing the language around the early web and examining how the web entered general public discourse.

The second section of the book contains three chapters each of which tells the story of a cultural phenomenon on the web in three different national settings; China, Italy and Australia. Hockx-Yu shows that the Western characterization of the web in China as nothing but censorship and repression does not do justice to the rich social and cultural significance that the web has there today. Next, Locatelli discusses the technological, economic, institutional and cultural dimension of early Italian blogs and identifies three phases in their history: 1999/2000–2003 (early bloggers with the first blogs); 2003–2006 (the success of Splinder, the first Italian blogging platform); 2006–2008 (when Google redesigned Blogger, and the blogosphere went mainstream). The third and last national setting is Australia; here, Nolan explores the creation of the Age Online, the first major newspaper website in Australia launched in February 1995. Drawing from his own experience working as a journalist on the newspaper (not the website) and from interviews with five key actors in the creation of the Age's website, he notes that in 1995, forward-looking newspaper executives could already see the threat that internet advertising posed to the press and that, at first, online advertisements were described on the website as a free service to readers.

While the first two sections of Web 25 focus on web history and bring detailed accounts of specific historical examples, the discussion of various methods of web historiography in the third section titled 'Methodological reflections' may be more valuable to digital scholars. First, Weber sets out to consider key research problems that researchers had in the past. His chapter highlights three specific research challenges for working with web data today: (i) size and time dimensions of research, (ii) reliability and validity of web data, and (iii) ethical research questions. In the next chapter, Helmond takes a historical perspective on the changing composition of a website, considering the website as an ecosystem, through which we can analyse the larger techno-commercial configurations that it is embedded in. In her fascinating contribution, she develops a novel methodological approach by repurposing the browser add-on Ghostery to detect trackers in archived websites and to reconstruct the historical tracking ecologies the New York Times (NYT) website has been embedded in. Finally, Chakraborty & Nanni use websites as primary sources to trace and examine activities of scientific institutions through the years. Somewhat surprisingly they conclude that these institutions' websites, traditionally viewed as authoritative and top down, have become key in interactive, multidirectional communication channels between museums and their visitors.

The book's fourth and final section discusses 'Web archives as [a] historical source' and discusses the impact of web preservation on web historiography. Webster takes a closer look at the cultural history of the web archiving movement, investigating why, by whom and on whose behalf web archiving is done. This is important. It '[…] serves to orient users as to some of the questions they should be asking of [about] their sources, and of the institutions that provide them' (176) as web archiving constitutes an interplay between the interests of 3 key stakeholders: libraries, owners of content (in particular established media companies) and end users. The section continues with Koerbin presenting short case studies of web artefacts from the National Library of Australia's PANDORA archive, reflecting upon research issues related to early web content. He uses the framework of taphonomy, the branch of palaeontology that studies decaying organisms and their processes of fossilization, and argues that 'web archives present artefactual evidence for the digital archaeologist that also comes with biases resulting from the processes that led to the objects being removed from the "living" web to be held in the digital archaeological locus of the web archive' (205). In 'Looking back, looking forward. 10 years of development to collect, preserve, and access the Danish web', Laursen & Moldrup-Dalum do just this from three perspectives: legal, technical and curatorial. In line with Koerbin, they contend that a web archive's history is pertinent to all users of the archive, in particular, it is relevant in order to evaluate it as a source. They also stress the importance of data mining skills and supporting systems when looking at, or working with web archives. They extensively describe their multiple-method approach. As such, they demonstrate that the so-called 'computational turn' in humanities and social science – the increased incorporation of advanced computational research methods and large datasets into disciplines which have traditionally dealt with considerably more limited collections of evidence – indeed requires new skills and new software. The final chapter of Web 25, written by Paloque-Berges, deals nicely with records of computer-mediated communications (CMC) and, in particular, with the Usenet archives, which have not, as yet, become the focus of institutions' appraisal process of web archiving, despite the fact that this aspect of the web can function as a critical environment for building and studying the heritage value of CMC.

Web 25 has several important merits. Firstly, it emphasizes how a set of fundamental web features such as http, html and the hyperlink have transcended time and still function as the 'nuts and bolts' of the web. The book also shows that the discourse on the history of the web follows the recurring pattern of heroic narratives. Secondly, it demonstrates that web culture is not necessarily by definition a uniform, globalizing phenomenon, but that it can have surprisingly local characteristics. It shows that there is no one single and fixed history of the web, but rather, there are multiple local, regional and national webs and a variety of ways that the world wide web has been imagined, used, shaped and regulated. Thirdly, by providing methodological reflections on web archiving, the book emphasizes that all web archives, to a greater or lesser degree, can only attempt comprehensiveness, and that the processes involved in harvesting and preserving content from the live web involves biases resulting from technical, resource and curatorial constraints. In this way, it offers an important point of departure for further critical examination of the web and its history. Finally, the book offers valuable and realistic starting points for further methodological development. Not only does it point to some novel and out-of-the box methods, such as repurposing the browser add-on Ghostery to detect trackers in archived websites, or utilizing the framework of taphonomy to consider how certain web archives came about, but it also illustrates how various methodological approaches can be applied.

Springer

If Web 25 has any shortcomings, it is that, in a few instances, the book leaves the reader in the dark about the overall context. I would have welcomed a timeline or an infographic, showing an overview of important events or websites in the history of the web in order to contextualize the issues discussed in the various chapters better. Secondly, sometimes the book might have needed a more developed methodology: for example, archiving social media content is hardly discussed. However, this is quite problematic as the methods for preserving digital artefacts are currently not up to the challenge of preserving what happens on social networks. Hence, archivists and memory organizations will need to develop new methodologies in order to probe and document social networks, such as Twitter or Facebook, in order to accurately capture what it is like to live online today and to understand these algorithmic systems. Thirdly, to conclude, the book could have benefited from some more editing and proofreading work, especially in terms of internal cross-referencing. Although this is a shortcoming seen in many edited books, it is a shame that not more effort was made to textually link the individual chapters and, as a result, creating less of a mix of various probes into the vast and multifaceted past of the web, which this book ultimately presents.

Web 25 provides a critical and thoroughly documented guide to understanding the first 25 years of the web and is a noteworthy contribution to the field of web historiography. It is a well-written and accessible contribution to an expanding field. Throughout the book, I found a clear analysis of the history of specific websites and methodological reflection, founded on well-selected sources. This makes it a must-read both for web historians, academics and cultural heritage professionals, involved in web archiving and for a wider audience with an interest in Web history.

Correction to: Born-Digital Archives

Thorsten Ries and Gábor Palko

Correction to:
Thorsten Ries and Gábor Palko (eds.), *Born-Digital Archives, Volume 1,*
issue 1, April 2019, **https://doi.org/10.1007/978-3-031-19941-7**

The original version of this book has been revised as the author "Thorsten Ries" affiliation has been updated. The book has been updated with the changes.

The updated version of the book can be found at
https://doi.org/10.1007/978-3-031-19941-7
https://doi.org/10.1007/978-3-031-19941-7_1

Milton Keynes UK
Ingram Content Group UK Ltd.
UKHW020616161023
430687UK00001B/2